Pack of Thieves

Richard Z. Chesnoff

Pack
OF
Thieves

How Hitler and Europe
Plundered the Jews
and Committed
the Greatest Theft
in History

Doubleday   New York   London   Toronto   Sydney   Auckland

PUBLISHED BY DOUBLEDAY
a division of Random House, Inc.
1540 Broadway, New York, New York 10036

DOUBLEDAY and the portrayal of an anchor with a dolphin are trademarks of Doubleday, a division of Random House, Inc.

Library of Congress Cataloging-in-Publication Data

Chesnoff, Richard Z., 1937–
Pack of thieves: how Hitler and Europe plundered the Jews and committed the greatest theft in history / by Richard Z. Chesnoff.
p.   cm.
Includes index.
1. Holocaust, Jewish (1939–1945) 2. Jewish property—Europe—History–20th century. 3. World War, 1939–1945—Confiscations and contributions—Europe. I. Title.
D804.3.C446   1999
940.53'18—dc21   99-33257
CIP

ISBN 0-385-48763-0
Printed in the United States of America
November 1999
First Edition
10   9   8   7   6   5   4   3   2   1

For my son Adam,
his children and his children's children

Contents

Contents

If there is no justice, there is no peace.
  —BAHYA BEN ASHER, thirteenth-century kabbalist,
  Kad Hakemach

Both are thieves, the receiver as
well as the stealer.
—PHOCYLIDES, sixth-century B.C.E. poet, *Moral Epigrams*

Introduction

This is a book about justice for victims. This is also a book about the evils of hatred and greed, about the maelstrom of deceit and injustice that swallows people who allow their basic human compassion and decency to be overwhelmed by an all too willing embrace of avarice and noncaring.

For ideological Nazis and devoted anti-Semites, stealing from the Jews of Europe was a vital step in the historic crusade to "Aryanize" the world. It was a totally normal stage in what they perceived as a totally reasonable "Final Solution." "In the Nazi mind," says Yale University's Daniel Goldhagen, author of *Hitler's Willing Executioners,* "depriving Jews of anything and everything they had worked for, then further pauperizing them by denying them a means of livelihood was part of the punishment the Jews 'deserved.' "

Yet not all those who joined the pack of thieves that howled through Europe were pure ideological Nazis. For many, running alongside the raucous bandwagon of Hitler's National Socialist crusade was simply a means of enriching themselves at the expense of the Jews—from the wealthiest Warburgs and Rothschilds to the poorest of the shtetl and urban Jews who made up the predominant number of Holocaust victims. Certainly not all the predators were Germans or Austrians. There were Frenchmen and Dutchmen, Norwegians and Czechs, Belgians and Slovaks, Lithuanians, Poles, Estonians, Hungarians, Romanians, Croats, and Bosnians.

[1]

In every nation of Europe where the genocidal Nazi machine dragged Jews away to their death, there were upstanding local citizens waiting to loot what was left behind—art dealers in Paris, hotelkeepers in Budapest, stockbrokers in Amsterdam, grocers in Lyons, department-store owners in Brussels, manufacturers in Oslo, peasant farmers and housewives from Latvia to Transylvania, and everywhere bankers, lawyers, and financiers—all barely able to contain themselves at the prospect of picking at the bones of their Jewish neighbors.

The evil continued well beyond the destruction of the Third Reich and the end of Europe's World War II. Newly liberated nations like France and the Netherlands conveniently absorbed into their own governmental coffers much of what remained from Nazi loot. Few made any intense effort—or any effort at all—to find the heirs of victims.

Nor was it only the conquering and conquered who took advantage of the slaughter years that decimated European Jewry. A lofty policy of neutrality enabled the national and private financiers of Switzerland, Sweden, Portugal, Spain, Argentina, and other noncombatants to trade with both Axis and Allies and reap enormous profits in the process—not the least of them from the laundering of the tons of gold the Nazis had looted from the vaults of the nations they conquered or torn from the ring fingers and teeth of the victims they slaughtered.

The Allies were also far less than faultless. In the wake of the war, and in an eagerness to win and keep postwar power, they turned a blind eye to justice not only for the victims who died but for those who survived to live under stifling clouds of anguished memory and physical suffering.

This book is not intended to be an encyclopedic record of what was arguably the greatest theft in history. Indeed, not every nation guilty of sins of omission and commission is detailed here; I have focused only on those whose actions make them major players in this sad drama. Nor is this book a definitive record of what was stolen and what was withheld—or even of the unpaid earnings of the hundreds of thousands who slaved in forced labor. The attempt to track all those billions in total loot continues and may never be completed because so much evidence has already been destroyed, so many witnesses have died or are dying.

Nor is this book intended to be a purely academic work. I would like to think that my five years of work on it reflect whatever reporting talents I have developed in three and a half decades as a working journalist. But while I believe that this book is authoritative and accurate, in the end it is a journalist's report—an attempt to provide as wide an audience as possible with some sense of the massive injustice that was spawned by the worst single crime of this century: the Holocaust.

Why has justice been so long in coming? Why has it taken half a century to raise what now seem like such obvious questions: What happened to the billions stolen from Europe's Jews? What was the complicity in the plunder by the nations occupied by or collaborating with the Nazis? How truly neutral were the neutrals? Did the West do enough to seek redress for the survivors?

As with most reconsiderations of history, there is no single reason behind the urge for total recall that has captured world headlines in recent years. The enormity of the Nazis' crimes makes it impossible ever to truly close this savage chapter of history. And the Holocaust will always haunt our memories—as well it should. But the passage of time, as well as political changes, has recently opened troves of long-hidden or long-ignored documents in both America and Europe.

The paper trail has led to as many new and embarrassing questions as it has to answers to old ones—not only about how Jewish property was disposed of but also about how the neutrals played financial footsie with the Nazis, trading gold and diamonds for cash and supplies that helped keep the Nazi war machine rolling for as much as two years longer than it might have. The new transparency has sparked an unprecedented soul-searching even among the hitherto self-righteous. Switzerland is still in the throes of no fewer than three investigative commissions, and the United States, Canada, Sweden, Norway, the Netherlands, France, Belgium, Spain, Portugal, Argentina, and Hungary—not to name all—have launched individual investigations into their own dealings with the Nazis and their handling of stolen or unclaimed Jewish assets.

In great measure, says scholar Saul Friedlander, author of *Nazi Germany and the Jews,* "the continuing thirst for the truth about the Nazi horrors is a reaction to the silence on the subject that reigned during the first two postwar decades. For years the subject was almost taboo. No one was interested."

Indeed, scholars such as Raul Hilberg and Nobel laureate Elie Wiesel had difficulty finding publishers for their earliest works. The world, caught up in a Cold War battle against communism, had little time to dwell on battles seemingly won and feared losing new allies. Ghetto and concentration-camp survivors, still terrorized by the horrors they had witnessed and often feeling guilty that they had survived, had little appetite for anything but a desperate, usually futile search for other survivors. Many, like the father of Dutch economics professor Victor Halberstadt, hidden during the war by Christians, returned to their prewar home to find gentile families living in their place, using their household goods. "My father simply turned his back and walked away to rebuild his life," he says.

Others feared that merely asking for what had been theirs would trigger new anti-Semitism. The fear was not ungrounded. Only 10 percent of Poland's prewar Jewish population of 3.3 million survived, but those who dared return to their kindred worlds were sometimes greeted with anger, hatred, and even violence. In the two years after the Nazis were chased from Poland, 2,500 Jews died at the hands of Poles.

Those who did seek to recover lost property found themselves rebuffed by officials who claimed no knowledge or by robotic bank clerks who asked for unproducible evidence such as death certificates from Auschwitz. Some bureaucrats systematically hid the facts and records. "The Swiss stonewalled for more than fifty years," says World Jewish Congress secretary general Israel Singer, himself the son of Holocaust escapees. But Switzerland's banks were not alone.

American Jews were no more eager to rock the postwar boat. Activists were concerned with rehabilitating displaced persons, with the birth and securing of Israel, with freeing Soviet Jews; others were concerned simply with "fitting in." There was little time or inclination to push for comprehensive restitution from the rebuilding nations of Europe.

All that has changed over the past five years. A more secure generation of Jews has finally demanded a historic reckoning. For the estimated 600,000 aging Holocaust survivors in the world—including some 60,000 in Eastern Europe who have never received restitution payments from anyone—it is a last opportunity to seek some justice, to write the final chapter and live out their lives in some degree of dignity. And the spirit of reexamining the past encompasses a new generation of non-Jews as well, Europeans and Americans who are seeking to come to terms with the actions and inaction of their elders. It was a young non-Jewish Norwegian journalist whose reporting launched a parliamentary investigation into his country's ignoble failure after the war to return most of what the Quisling regime had stolen from Norway's tiny Jewish community. It was a duo of non-Jewish Dutch historians who traced the cloaking of Nazi assets by Swedish banks. And while it was international pressure that finally forced Switzerland to face up to its shameful World War II game, it is young Swiss who have asked what their grandparents and parents did while Switzerland enriched itself laundering Nazi loot and turned away more than 30,000 Jews, most of whom ended up in Nazi death camps.

On a personal note, I am of that fortunate generation of American Jews who grew up surrounded by shadows of the Holocaust but not directly affected by it. My family left Europe long ago; Henry Zeltner, my maternal great-grandfather, arrived in New York on the eve of the Civil War. Until recently, when I serendipitously discovered a Viennese-born branch of my family, I knew of no relative who perished in Auschwitz, no blood relative uprooted and disenfranchised by the haters and the avaricious. But the Holocaust and its victims have been etched in my consciousness since childhood. This is my attempt to add a voice to the cry for some justice for them.

In French-Jewish writer Marek Halter's prizewinning film *Tzedek* ("The Righteous") a Bosnian-Muslim woman who risked Nazi death by hiding two Jewish families during the war says that "compassion knows no fear." So it is with facing up to history—no matter how ugly, no matter how soul-searing. Facing up to history is what this book is all about.

1

Germany

The Plunder Plot

I would not want to be a Jew in Germany.
—Reichsmarschall HERMANN GÖRING

Berlin's main boulevard was not the best place for a young Jewish boy to be on the morning of November 10, 1938. But to the crowds that quietly packed the Kurfürstendamm the day after Kristallnacht, the thirteen-year-old, blond-haired, blue-eyed youth in short pants and knee socks seemed the perfect "Aryan." Six decades later, Michael Blumenthal still remembers every detail of the Nazis' infamous orgy of anti-Semitic destruction and looting. "I have never forgotten the sight," says the Holocaust survivor who went on to become an American Secretary of the Treasury. "Every Jewish store had been wrecked, glass from shop windows littered the sidewalks, . . . and from the direction of the major synagogue on the Fasanstrasse I could see rising clouds of smoke. . . . No one helped. People just stared. There was a kind of strange silence."

For Adolf Hitler and his most willing executioners, Jews were a cancer on society, a malignancy that had to be surgically but brutally excised with no anesthesia: The Jews of the world, declared Hitler, are "vermin."

But for the Führer and the clique of officers and technicians who helped him mastermind the mechanics of the Holocaust, Jews—particularly Europe's Jews—represented much more: They were also a golden cow to be milked dry and eventually melted down for the greater glory and profit not only of the Reich but of those who fanatically supported it.

This state plunder was part and parcel of a coalescent ideology of exclusions, expropriation, and finally extermination. And in that wicked process of exclude and annihilate, the Reich managed to amass many of the multimillions needed to finance the brutal war it launched in 1939 and fought to defeat in May of 1945.

Germany's program of economic exclusion of the Jews, and individual Nazi profiting from that exclusion, developed in overlapping stages. In early 1933, during the first days of the Hitler regime, it was Germany's Communists—not necessarily its Jews—who became prime targets of Hitler's goon squads. In the aftermath of the February 27 Reichstag Fire, almost 10,000 German Communist Party members were rounded up and shipped to the newly opened concentration camps. Only after the Nazis had consolidated their power did they launch the first steps in what was to be their systematic dehumanization and isolation of the country's half million Jews.

The process was called *Arisierung*—Aryanization—the elimination of Jews from all aspects of German life. Though cloaked in racist ideology, its fulcrum was pragmatic: the systematic transfer of Jewish-owned businesses, factories, shops, and any other economic enterprise from the hands of the Jews who had built them to Aryan-German ownership. Marked by extortion and outright plunder, it would be a hallmark of Nazi rule in Germany and in the nations the Reich occupied during the six dark years it held sway over Europe.

"It was a way to dehumanize, to isolate and destroy," says Nobel Prize–winning scholar and author Elie Wiesel. "It appealed to one of man's basest desires: greed."

Indeed, by early March 1933, swastika-armbanded squads of storm troopers had already begun a series of organized attacks mainly on East European Jews living in Germany. By March 13, they had begun forcibly closing Jewish shops—promoting first boycotts, then looting. Though initially limited to smaller provincial communities, the violence soon spread to cities. In the eastern town of Breslau (now Wroclaw, Poland), Jewish lawyers and even judges were attacked in the local courthouse and brutally beaten. In Munich, bands of S.A. *(Sturmabteilung*—"storm troopers") men tore the beards off the faces of Orthodox Jews.

Larry Orbach of New Jersey, then five years old and called Lothar, recalls how, as the Nazis rose to power, his father was forced to sell their general store in the tiny Pomeranian village of Falkenberg. "The same people who had once shared tables in the local pub with my father were now swaggering around in brown shirts. Our store was boycotted, our windows smashed. And there was no one to complain to."

Compelled to liquidate at a fraction of the shop's value, the Orbachs abandoned Falkenberg, where the family had lived for three centuries, and moved to Berlin, where they sought refuge with relatives. Orbach's father, Arnold—a bemedaled World War I veteran—found work as a salesman for a textile company; the young Orbach began school. But the respite would be short-lived.

By the spring, cemeteries were desecrated and synagogues were torched in provincial towns. Elsewhere in Europe, as well as in America, Nazi "hooliganism" began to provoke public protests. And it was these protests that became the pretext Hitler needed for his national boycott of all Jewish businesses and shops. The first, scheduled for April 1, 1933, was personally planned by Hitler and coordinated by his most notorious Jew baiter—propagandist and SA general Julius Streicher.

Streicher posted squads of Nazi bullies in front of Jewish businesses, covering shop windows with anti-Semitic slogans and bullying clients who dared to enter. Jews unlucky enough to be caught on the street were often severely beaten.

Yet ugly as this first Nazi boycott was, the public responded to it with a degree of indifference. In fact, the boycott had only middling success and support—not out of any moral outrage but because most Germans simply needed their Jewish businesses and found it inconvenient to have to pass by shops and firms with which they had done business for generations. Besides, as historian Saul Friedlander points out in his monumental *Nazi Germany and the Jews,* "it became increasingly clear to Hitler himself that Jewish economic life was not to be openly interfered with, at least as long as the German economy was still in a precarious situation."

As a result, while the Reich quickly placed boycott pressures on smaller Jewish-owned firms and shops like the Orbachs', large Jewish businesses—such as Hamburg's Warburg Bank and other major banking firms—were left alone. At the highest levels of the German economy, notes Friedlander, "the attitude toward extortion of the Jews [was] still negative because the enterprises involved had higher international visibility. The Nazis decided, therefore, to avoid any head-on clash."

The Jewish-owned Tietz department-store chain, with thousands of employees, even received a government loan, a loan personally approved by the Führer himself. The powerful Dresdener Bank still had five Jewish directors as late as 1938. And for the first two years of Hitler's *judenrein* policies, three Jews remained on the German Central Bank's eight-member board. Ironically, when Reichsbank president Hjalmar Schacht was named Hitler's Minister of the Economy, Jews were among those who signed the proclamation appointing Hans Luther to replace him. This selective

Aryanization extended to several large companies. IG Farben, the chemical-industrial giant one of whose companies would later produce the Zyklon-B gas used to kill millions of Jews, retained key Jewish executives throughout most of the thirties—albeit many of them conveniently transferred to assignments outside Germany.

This strange calm was brief. The total exclusion of Jews from German society—especially their segregation from its economic life—was simply too central to Nazi policy to be indefinitely postponed. By 1934, Schacht began insisting that all German bank boards dismiss their Jewish directors.

The process of economic ostracism eventually touched German Jewry's "aristocrats." Like several other of his prominent "coreligionists," Max Warburg, the high-profile banker and respected communal leader, at first suggested considerable economic accommodation with the Nazis. To no avail. Warburg, scion of what was arguably Germany's most prominent Jewish family and once eagerly sought after by other German economic barons, now found himself forced from one board after another. At 1936 ceremonies marking his departure from the executive board of the Hamburg-Amerika Line, most of Warburg's Aryan colleagues remained loudly silent. None among them wished to be seen offering him a toast, a gesture that would have been viewed as more than politically incorrect by the Gestapo. So the crusty Warburg sarcastically delivered his own corporate eulogy: "And now I would like to wish you, dear Herr Warburg, a calm old age, good luck and many blessings to your family."[1]

Thus commenced the systematic exclusion of Jews from Germany's economic life—the prelude to the theft of the fruits of their labors, begun in earnest in 1935 after the promulgation of the Nuremberg Laws—themselves reflections of medieval Catholic canon law. Universities were closed to Jewish students. Jewish pro-

---

[1] Warburg, who found refuge in America, later served in the United States Army and was one of Hermann Göring's interrogators at the war's end.

fessors and teachers were dismissed from all but Jewish schools. The small number of Jews serving in the German civil service— about 5,000, or less than .5 percent of the total government personnel—were summarily fired. And while 70 percent of the 4,585 Jewish lawyers practicing in Germany were allowed to continue working with Jewish clients, they were ejected from the National Association of Lawyers and treated as pariahs by most of their gentile colleagues. As attorney Fritz Feuchtwanger, who emigrated to Palestine in 1937 recalled, "We worked under a boycott of fear."

Eventually all German-Jewish lawyers were disbarred by the Reich. Anti-Semitic restrictions stretched into every facet of life. Jews were forbidden from working the land or owning farms. Jewish musicians were dismissed by their orchestras, actors and directors by film studios and theaters. Jewish boxers were expelled from the National Boxing Association and forbidden to fight non-Jews. Shops were regularly surrounded by Gestapo thugs who threatened and dissuaded Aryan customers from entering by shouting, *"Deutsche, kauft nicht bei Juden!"*—"Germans, don't buy from Jews!" All Aryans—first women, then men—were warned not to see Jewish doctors. Medical billings by Jewish physicians were reimbursed by insurance companies only if the patients were Jews. In time, Jewish doctors were barred from any practice. It was a concerted, inexorable campaign of exclusion.

Few voices were raised in protest. With a handful of notable exceptions, Germany's church leaders, Catholic and Protestant, said or did nothing. Some even preached support for the economic and cultural ethnic cleansing. These laws, wrote the official Catholic *Klerusblatt,* are "indisputable safeguards for the qualitative make-up of the German people." The measures against the Jews, declared Bishop Otto Dibelius, general superintendent of the Evangelical Church, "were perfectly justified." And in a proclamation issued by the Evangelical Church, thanked "the Lord God" for having given the German people "a pious and trusty overlord."

Amazingly, Nazi anti-Semitism provoked little panic among German Jews. In 1933, fewer than 38,000 of Germany's 525,000 Jews chose to read the writing on the wall and leave Germany voluntarily. In the four years that followed, fewer than 100,000 more chose exile—tragic testimony to an overwhelmingly delusional German-Jewish conviction that Hitler and Nazism were merely a "passing madness."

"Those were my father's precise words", recalls eighty-year-old Maria Bamberger, now a New Yorker but then a young Berlin Zionist. "My sister Eva and I tried to convince him that we should all leave for Palestine." But Dr. Walter Weinberg, who would later flee to London, insisted, "Girls, this is passing madness; the German people will never put up with it."

"They could not grasp it," explains Saul Friedlander. "Most expected to weather the storm."

Still others who might have considered departing were frightened away by the enormous economic cost of emigration—not to mention the scarcity of visas from countries to go to. Jewish-owned property could be sold only at increasingly lower prices. And while the Reich maintained that it was eager to be rid of its Jews, transferring whatever was left of their funds overseas became more and more expensive. The emigration tax on "capital flight," already high, had been raised by the Nazis. And waiting did not make it less expensive. With each month of the Nazi regime, prices dropped on Jewish property—both personal and communal, and especially in rural areas. In December 1935, the Austrian *Reichspost* gleefully reported from Germany that an "Aryan" farmer in Franconia was able to purchase an abandoned synagogue for 700 marks and convert it to grain storage. By the same year, in certain areas of central Germany, 40 to 50 percent of all Jewish businesses had been liquidated.

As if that were not bad enough, exchange rates offered for the purchase of foreign currency became progressively lower. Until

1935, emigrating Jews were entitled to exchange their Reichsmark at 50 percent of their face value. It then dropped to 30 and finally, on the eve of the war, to 4 percent.

Those who dared to smuggle funds out of the country welcomed Switzerland's new banking laws. Promulgated in 1934 largely to attract German-Jewish capital, they ensured total secrecy through numbered accounts. More than half a century later, the fate of many of those accounts would provide Switzerland with a staggering historical and ethical dilemma.

The onslaught of economic restrictions on Jews also produced one of the more bizarre—if one of the few effective—negotiations between the Jews and their worst enemies. Eager to crush what promised to be a worldwide Jewish boycott of Germany, and to encourage Jewish emigration from the Reich, the Nazis enthusiastically agreed to an exchange deal that became known as the *Haavara* (Hebrew for transfer) Agreement. Signed in August 1933 between representatives of the German Ministry of the Economy and Zionist organizations from Germany and Palestine, Haavara quite simply facilitated the export to Palestine of goods and products produced in Nazi Germany against the assets of German-Jewish emigrants. All told, at least 100 million Reichsmark were transferred to Palestine under the system. They provided seed money for the 60,000 German Jews who settled in the British-controlled mandate between 1933 and 1939.

Haavara was controversial, to say the least. Some Jewish leaders in Europe and America, eager to pariahize the Nazi regime, vehemently objected to any cooperation with Hitler's Germany. Haavara, declared New York's Rabbi Stephen Wise, was "an aberration." But the Zionists and the Jewish community of Palestine, anxious to attract the well educated and often well-to-do Jews of Germany to the embryonic Jewish homeland, argued that dancing with the devil was better than allowing Hitler to rob German Jews of everything that they had worked for. Besides, they argued with some justification, the chances of an effective boycott of Germany were slim at best.

The symbiotic accord between Zionists and Nazis was oft-times surreal. Zionist leaders like Socialist Moshe Beilinson and the German-born Arthur Ruppin paid semiofficial visits to the Reich. Ruppin was even received by the Nazi theoretician Hans Günther, who patronizingly told him that "the Jews were not inferior to the Aryans, merely different." In fact, while the Nazis feared that the creation of a Jewish state would strengthen Jewish world power, some Nazi theoreticians voiced a grudging approval of Zionism as an expression of the need to segregate Jews from the rest of society.

For their part, the Germans sent their own strange delegations to the Jewish homeland. In early 1933, Baron Leopold von Mildenstein, who would later become chief of the Jewish sections of Reinhard Heydrich's SS intelligence operation, Sicherheitsdienst (SD), toured Palestine in the company of Kurt Tuchler, a leader of the Berlin Jewish community. According to Israeli author Tom Segev, the Germans even cast a special medallion to mark the occasion—a medallion with both a swastika and a Star of David. Most sinister was the one-day visit to Palestine in the fall of 1937 by two other leading figures from the SD's Jewish sector—Herbert Hagen and his devoted deputy, Adolf Eichmann. Eichmann's conclusion: The establishment of a Jewish state in Palestine was not in the interests of the Third Reich.

Nonetheless, the Haavara Agreement remained in place until a few months before war was declared in 1939.

Nazi propaganda played on populist anti-Semitism. Non-Jews were constantly reminded that the well-educated, motivated Jews of Germany, who formed just under 1 percent of the national population, were "abnormally" represented by much greater percentages in many professions, as well as in commerce. Five percent of all German writers, theatrical personalities, and journalists were believed to be Jews. At least 10 percent of doctors and dentists were Jews, as were 16 percent of all practicing lawyers. Among bankers, the figure was as high as 17 percent in 1929. Moreover, 25 percent of the nation's retail stores—and 79 percent of its department stores—belonged to Jews.

In fact, most of Germany's Jews were neither as overwhelmingly influential or as wealthy as the Nazi propaganda machine painted them. According to communal records, one in three Jewish taxpayers in 1933 had an annual income of less than RM 2,400 ($600 at 1933 rates), and 31,000 Jews living in Berlin—one out of every four—were on the receiving end of communal charity.

Yet it was the poor and middle-class Jewish families like the Orbachs who were subject to increasing exclusion and deprivation. Fired from his salesman's job, Arnold Orbach was reduced to renting space in his Berlin apartment to a Jewish welfare society, which used it to house mentally handicapped patients.

Hitler's campaign of terror against the Jews reached a devastating new high on November 9, 1938. Using the assassination in Paris of German diplomat Ernst vom Rath[2] as his excuse, Hitler authorized the state's first mass pogrom: Kristallnacht, a nightmarish nationwide attack on Jews, their homes, their synagogues, and their businesses. "From our veranda overlooking the Greifswalderstrasse," says Lothar Orbach, now seventy-six, "I could see a caravan of open military trucks filled with brown-shirted troopers, yelling at the top of their lungs, *'Jude verrecke, Juden raus'*—'Jews should rot, out with the Jews.'

But while Aryans were discouraged from buying from Jews, they were certainly not discouraged from wholesale looting. With the police standing by to direct traffic (or to arrest Jews "for their own protection"), frenzied mobs plundered and destroyed Jewish homes and shops. Many Germans watched in silent shock. Most

---

[2] The diplomat, Third Secretary Ernst vom Rath, had been shot by Jewish student Herschel Grynszpan, distraught over the deportation of his parents from their home in Hannover.

onlookers appeared cruelly apathetic. And some saw it all as a grand spectacle to be enjoyed. "Racial hatred and hysteria seem to have taken complete hold of otherwise decent people," reported the *London Daily Telegraph*'s Hugh Carleton Green. "I saw fashionably dressed women clapping their hands and screaming with glee, while respectable, middle-class mothers held up their babies to see the fun."

Many years later, one survivor vividly remembered witnessing SS men toss a grand piano from an apartment balcony. "Well," he heard a bystander sniff, "I suppose a piano can't help who it belongs to."

Göring was at first worried that the pogrom would destroy too much property that the Nazis could otherwise seize. "We must agree on a clear action that shall be profitable to the Reich," he warned. But most of the party leadership was thrilled. A witness reported that "Hitler squealed with delight and slapped his thigh in his enthusiasm" when he heard of the plan.

"At long last," Goebbels later noted in his diaries, "Berlin's man in the street had an opportunity to fill himself up again. Fur coats, carpets, valuable textiles were to be had for nothing. The people were enraptured."

"It was Kristallnacht," says Holocaust authority Avraham Barkai, "that marked the transition to open and undisguised robbery of Jewish property in Germany by official institutions of the Nazi regime." This was followed by a new series of regulations that completely forbade any independent economic activity by German Jews. It was the beginning of the Final Solution.

But the atrocities of Kristallnacht also brought the Reich a potential financial hangover. Göring already worried about foreign retribution, still angrily bemoaned the loss of property that might have fallen into the Reich's—and his—hands. "I wish you had killed two hundred Jews instead of destroying such valuables!" he shouted at SD chief Reinhard Heydrich. But the biggest problem was paying for the damage. According to Friedlander, "a representative of German insurance companies, Eduard Hilgard, estimated it in the multimillions. Just the windows destroyed in Jewish shops were insured for about $6 million. And because the glass was Belgian, at least half of this amount would have to be paid in foreign currency"—still in short supply. It represented half the Belgian glass industry's total yearly production.

Faced with that prospect, the Nazis dreamed up a solution that almost matched the evil of the Kristallnacht pogrom: The Jews themselves were ordered to bear the costs of repair, while the Reich would confiscate German insurance payments of more than 250 million Reichsmark. As if that were not odious enough, a special decree was promulgated ordering German Jews to "contribute" a one-billion-mark *Sühneleistung,* or "atonement payment." It would consist of 20 percent of the declared capital of every German Jew owning more than 5,000 Reichsmark. Germany's Jews were even ordered to repair their own damaged synagogues, lest they prove a "public danger."

The same order,[3] issued by Göring at Hitler's behest, commanded the cessation of all Jewish business activity as of January 1, 1939. Jews would have to "sell" their enterprises as well as any land, stocks, jewels and artworks. *Treuhänder*—Reich-appointed fiduciaries—would help them complete the transactions within the allotted period.

To drive the point home, the order also forbade Jews to drive or have cars, to ride in trains, to go to theaters or cinemas. They were banned from city districts containing government offices—unless summoned there. Special measures were reserved for Berlin's Jews, who were officially banned from all concert and conference halls, museums, fairs, exhibit halls, and sports facilities—especially public swimming pools. A November 29 order from Heydrich's office even prohibited them from owning carrier pigeons.

---

[3] The Decree of Eliminating Jews from German Economic Life, November 12, 1938.

As Avraham Barkai points out in his landmark study of the Reich, Nazi economic policy had two stages: The first dates from 1933 to 1938, when Jews, facing a rising tide of exclusion and discrimination, "voluntarily" sold or disposed of their businesses—usually at greatly discounted prices. The second period, which followed Kristallnacht, lacked even the pretense of volunteer sale. Under direct order of Hitler via Göring, Germany entered the final phases of the *Entjuden der deutschen Wirtschaft*—the dejudaization of the Germany economy. It was among the central points Göring announced on November 12, 1938, in his program "to exclude the Jews from the economic life of Germany." Much had already been swallowed up by the voracious economic masters of the Reich—and both Austria and the Sudetenland had proved rich plunder fields (see Chapters Two and Three). Now it remained, says Barkai, "to liquidate the little that was left in a single stroke and within the space of a few weeks."

The November laws also triggered the organized confiscation of any Jewish-owned property. Directors of state collections were ordered to undertake "the safekeeping of works of art belonging to Jews." In exchange, the owners were issued meaningless receipts. A Reich Legal Notice of January 16, 1939, designated municipal pawnshops as the Öffentliche Ankaufstellen—the Public Acquisition Offices—where Jews were to hand over art objects and jewelry. A follow-up February memo from the Reich's Economic Minister required all Jews to deliver "any objects in their ownership made of gold, platinum or silver, as well as precious stones and pearls." That included scrap precious metals, and even fillings, the memo notes. "A refusal of the offer by Jews can no longer be considered." Even holy objects were prey. In Frankfurt, the Nazi-sponsored Research Institute on the Jewish Question became a repository for priceless plundered Judaica, much of it centuries old.

Jewish businesses that still existed were placed under the control of a government-appointed *Treuhand,* who earned sizable fees and commissions for Aryanizing an enterprise. In some cases, huge industrial plants, such as the Simson armaments factory in Suhl, had already been confiscated without any compensation. Other firms were now grabbed by high-ranking members of the party—or by hitherto loyal employees who had fortuitous connections to senior and not so senior Nazis. "Our senior saleswoman was the girlfriend of an SS officer," says Stefanie Blumenthal-Dreyfuss, whose parents owned Wally's, a chic Berlin woman's-wear shop. "After Kristallnacht she became very ugly. My parents had no choice; she 'bought' the shop from them for practically nothing. My mother wept—not so much out of the loss, but out a sense of the unfairness of it, that someone we'd trained could turn on us, could get something we had worked so hard for, for nothing."

Adds her brother, Michael Blumenthal, "Some Christians might sympathize with the Jewish plight, but no one really complained. When all was said and done, taking over a Jew's business for a song was an opportunity many did not want to miss."

The Nazis weren't finished with the Blumenthals. In late 1938, two plainclothes Gestapo men came to their apartment on Berlin's fashionable Kurfürstendamm and carted Stefanie's father off to Sachsenhausen concentration camp. Like many other German Jews, Ewald Blumenthal was released only after he could prove that the family would leave Germany—and had a place to go to. With visas to the United States and even South America unavailable to them, the Blumenthals took the only option open: In April of 1939, a scant four months before the outbreak of the war, the Blumenthals left the remainder of their possessions behind and headed for Shanghai, China. There they spent the war years in Shanghai's Japanese-run ghetto, Ewald working as a sausage salesman, their mother, Valerie, as a seamstress, seventeen-year-old Stefanie as a governess for a British family. Her thirteen-year-old brother, Michael, did odd jobs. At the war's end, the entire family finally managed to receive their long-awaited visas for America. Michael went on to become Secretary of the Treasury in the Carter administration.

Though the Nazis often used Aryanization as a way to reward party stalwarts, Hitler became increasingly anxious to exercise his own perogatives. By December 10, 1938, Göring moved to ensure that most if not all the illicit profits from "dejudaization" flowed directly into Hitler's coffers—to finance the regime and its rapidly growing war machine. "[Jewish] assets have to flow into the hands of the Reich," Göring told a closed-door meeting of his inner circle, "not serve as a source of riches for incompetent party members."

Just how much was stolen? The value of Jewish property—liquid and real—in Germany, Austria, and the Sudetenland was estimated in 1933 to be anywhere between 10 and 12 billion Reichsmark ($2.5 and $3 billion). Most of the property of the 140,000 Jews who were still able to emigrate from Germany between 1938 and 1941 went directly into official Nazi coffers in the form of what Barkai calls "legal" levies, such as the notorious Reichsfluchtsteuer, the "escape tax." The balance was deposited into blocked accounts that the holders never saw again. Experts such as Barkai estimate that only "a small fraction" of the RM 8 billion ($2 billion) in assets declared by the Jews of Germany and Austria in April 1938 ever left Germany with them. The approximately 170,000 Jews who remained behind had their funds taken from them in early 1939. German emissaries had already begun to transfer funds to Switzerland and Sweden—special slush funds of plundered Jewish wealth.

Once the war began, funds began to accumulate in a special government-controlled account belonging to the Reichsvereinigung der Juden in Deutschland—the Nazi-controlled Council of Jews remaining in Germany. These consisted of the profits from the sale of liquidated communities and "donations" from emigrating Jews. Parts of these monies were used to finance those Jewish welfare institutions that the Nazis still allowed to subsist. When the full-scale deportations of Germany's remaining Jews to Theresienstadt Camp in occupied Czechoslovakia began in 1941, the Reich forced all deportees to sign over their homes and insurance policies to the

Reichsvereinigung. In exchange for these "home purchase agreements" and the deposit of a minimum of 1,000 RM to the Reichsvereinigung, the German government cynically undertook to take care of the deportees "for the rest of their lives." Most would have little time left.

The same was true for the majority of those who remained in Germany. In May 1942, Arnold Orbach was suddenly taken away for "routine questioning." Two months later, a package from Sachsenhausen arrived at the Orbach apartment with a COD bill of 144 marks. It contained Arnold Orbach's ashes. Shortly thereafter, his widow and his son, Lothar, acquired false papers and disappeared, spending the rest of the war as *Taucher*—"divers," those estimated 1,400 fugitive Berlin Jews who survived the Holocaust hiding or posing as Aryans.

By 1943, when the deportations to the extermination camps were virtually complete, the special blocked accounts all had been confiscated by the Gestapo through the Reich's Treasury. By direct order from Himmler, the funds were to be used to finance the Final Solution. The Jews would pay for their own murders.

2

Austria

Last Year at Mauerbach

The Austrians are neither as brutish nor as barbaric as the Germans.
—SIGMUND FREUD, a year before he was forced to flee Vienna

Franz Klepner and his classmates from Vienna's prestigious Akademisches Gymnasium were on their annual winter ski trip in the mountains near Salzburg when the news came crackling over the radio: Austrian Chancellor Kurt von Schuschnigg had been bullied into signing an accord with his German counterpart, Adolf Hitler. It was only a matter of time before the Nazi leader would declare his pan-Germanic Anschluss and the Republic of Austria would become an integral part of the Nazi Reich. "We Jewish boys looked very glum. But almost all our gentile classmates cheered loudly," says Klepner, now a seventy-six-year-old retired jeweler living near Melbourne, Australia. "I knew immediately that terrible things were going to happen."

They did. On March 12, less than a month later, German troops crossed the Austrian border. More than 70,000 Austrian Jews would die in Nazi ghettos and death camps, and at least 90,000 would be forced to flee into exile. Out of the 190,000 Jews living in Austria before the Anschluss, fewer than 10,000 returned home after the war. Yet for more than half a century, Austria has lived a lie. Desperate to be part of the prosperous postwar West, Austrian leaders have clouded historic reality and—with no mean amount of Anglo-American and Soviet complicity—methodically perpetuated the myth that Hitler's 1938 swallowing of neighboring Austria was brute aggression. "We Austrians were Hitler's first victims in Europe" goes the postwar Vienna waltz. Accordingly, goes the tune, Austria has no responsibility for Nazi crimes and owes no compensation to anyone, least of all Austrian Jews.[1]

"Austria as a country did not do anything," insists Austrian diplomat Ulf Pacher. "Austria as a country was wiped out on March 12, 1938."

The logic is skewed. For as witnesses to the events and records of the time confirm, the vast majority of Austrians welcomed the Anschluss with unbridled enthusiasm. Though it took Hitler weeks of bluster and threats to cow Austria's leadership into submission, in the end he gobbled up his eastern neighbor with scant public protest, let alone military resistance. Austrian Nazis, like Arthur Seyss-Inquart, quickly seized power. For Austrian-born Adolf Hitler, the poor boy from Linz who once swore he'd return in glory to the Vienna that had rejected his unimpressive artistic talents, it was a crowning moment.

The Nazi conquest of Austria was more of a successful seduction than a rape and was quickly accepted by all but a handful of

---

[1] Although the postwar Austrian government has refused to pay restitution or reparations to Austrian Jews, it has provided some increased pension and social-security benefits for Austrian Holocaust survivors—a legal fine point that Jewish organizations such as the Claims Conference were prepared to accept and that till now has effectively let the Austrians off the hook.

stalwart Austrian patriots. For most Austrians, Hitler's invasion was not the destruction of a pluralistic, democratic, and proudly independent nation but a golden opportunity for Austria and its Aryan folk to share in the benefits of a brave new Reich, among them ridding Austria of its troublesome Jews while holding on to their assets.

Indeed, within minutes of the Anschluss announcement by a choked government official, swastika banners sprouted all throughout Austria and anti-Semitic gangs took to the streets. In Vienna, buildings, walls, and even churches were quickly draped with Reich flags and crowds flowed onto the boulevards and town squares. Workers in some offices began the first day of the New Order singing *"Deutschland über Alles."* As column after column of Nazi troops paraded through the city, hundreds of thousands of buoyant Viennese lined the streets, crowded balconies, or climbed lampposts to cheer and roar their support.

The demonstrations were more than matched several days later when the Führer himself arrived in the once proud capital of Emperor Franz Josef. There, the man whom postwar Austria would try to disown as "an invader" was heartily greeted by official welcoming committees, including one led by the beaming Primate of Austria, Cardinal Theodor Innitzer. Throngs jammed the streets outside Hitler's suite at the Imperial Hotel, chanting his name over and over until he finally appeared at the window to acknowledge them. Next day, with the victorious Führer smiling broadly, 200,000 jubilant Austrians jammed Heldenplatz ("Heroes' Square") to hail their new Nazi leader. That afternoon, Cardinal Innitzer, who once prided himself on warm relations with Austria's Jews, arrived at the Imperial, gave the Hitler salute to the crowd in the lobby, and then went upstairs for a private meeting in which he pledged his loyalty and that of the church to the Reich and its Führer. His fervor shocked the Vatican.

Hitler and his entourage were delirious. *"Ich bin verrückt* ["I am crazy"]", wrote Hitler's mistress, Eva Braun, to her sister, Ilse, in an attempt to describe the moment's excitement.

Austria's Jews were less enthusiastic. Anti-Semitism was hardly new to largely Catholic Austria—it wasn't till 1994 that the Austrian Bishops' Conference finally got around to banning the cult of Little Andrew of Rinn, a toddler whom canardous legend says was ritually murdered by Jews for his blood. Yet Jews had flourished there in spite of the malevolence shown them. Granted the right to organize as a community in 1849, they had achieved legal equality by 1867. If anything, Vienna under the Habsburgs had become a center of Jewish culture and a "cradle of Zionism" (its founder, the Budapest-born journalist Theodor Herzl, had been a star reporter for Vienna's *Neue Freie Presse*). By the turn of the century, Jews began to play a major role in Austrian economic and cultural life, producing writers like Franz Werfel, musicians like Bruno Walter, and great thinkers like Sigmund Freud. Lured by opportunity, thousands of Jews from the eastern and southern stretches of the Habsburg Empire flocked to Vienna in the years just before and following World War I. By 1933, almost 91 percent of Austria's more than 190,000 Jews lived in Vienna. By the end of 1943, there would be fewer than 800 still alive in the city.

The 1938 Anschluss was quickly followed by widespread anti-Semitic rioting. Jews were publicly attacked and beaten by pro-Nazi gangs. Elderly men were forced to strip naked and crawl about on all fours, Orthodox women to dance on desecrated Torah scrolls. One young Austrian Jew, Leah Sachs, reported seeing storm troopers urinating in a Jew's face before they savagely beat him. Others were seized by Nazi troops, forced to their hands and knees and ordered to wash the city streets, to the delight of jeering crowds of otherwise proper Viennese. Among those Jews so humiliated was Konrad Singer, a Viennese salesman, who later escaped with his wife, Anna, to Portugal and then the United States. It was Singer's American-born son, Israel, who would eventually help spearhead the battle for Jewish restitution as secretary general of the World Jewish Congress.

By mid-March of 1938, Nazi troops had occupied the Great Synagogue of Vienna and launched a wholesale looting of Jewish property. Art, carpets, books, furniture—anything of value that Austria's energetic Nazis could find was quickly stolen. The famous Rothschild art collection was a primary target, with the best items designated for Reichsmarschall Göring. Baron Louis himself was seized when he tried to board a plane at Vienna airport. His passport was torn up and he himself imprisoned at the Gestapo's Métropole Hotel headquarters until his family paid ransom.

Many other works of art were shipped to Hitler's boyhood hometown of Linz, where the Führer planned on building a major art museum. The balance was divided up institutionally. "Almost every major museum in Austria helped itself to Rothschild's artworks," says Viennese investigative author Hubertus Czernin.

Baron Alphonse de Rothschild, whose art holdings were internationally renowned, was stripped of 3,444 important artworks and objets d'art taken from his *Hohe Warte* property in Vienna as well as from his country palace. His older brother, Baron Louis de Rothschild, lost 919 artworks to the Nazi plunderers. Amazingly, all the stolen items, as well as confiscated artworks from other important Jewish-owned collections, were carefully inventoried by the Nazis.[2] The lists were then published in limited edition by the wartime Austrian government press in Vienna.

Other Jewish collectors began to try to preempt the looting by selling off their best paintings—usually for a pittance. Gentile-owned Austrian galleries and collectors benefited. But thousands of these "Aryanized" paintings and sculptures also found their way into government collections both before and after the war. At least 10 percent of the thousand paintings acquired by Vienna's august

---

[2] A long-lost copy of the actual inventory was discovered in March 1998 by Alphonse de Rothschild's seventy-four-year-old daughter, Bettina Looram.

Österreichische Galerie Belvedere between 1938 and 1950 came originally from Jewish owners, either stolen or sold by panic-stricken collectors at bargain prices. Among them was *Harlequin and Columbine,* the marvelous Degas pastel of a ballerina and her clown, considered among the Belvedere's most popular works. The deal, which took place at the late date of 1942, was prompted by a letter from a Nazi official recently discovered in the National Archives in Washington. "In the possession of Mrs. von Mendelssohn," says the note, "there is a Degas available which is of great interest. . . . The price . . . is not expensive. Heil Hitler!"

Even more shocking is the Österreichische Galerie's inventory catalog listing for two paintings by the nineteenth-century Austrian painter Rudolf von Alt: "1961 accepted from the National Monument Museum Office at Salzburg—previously owned by Martin Bormann." Bormann, who was hardly a well-known prewar art collector, was Hitler's personal assistant, one of the most powerful men in the Third Reich, and among those who helped organize the Holocaust.

"The Germans confronted their past. The Austrians unconsciously put it behind them," admitted the Belvedere's Michael Krapf in 1998. "No one ever thought to look at how these paintings got here."

The Nazis also moved to destroy the fabric of Jewish communal life. Within a month of the Anschluss, all 635 Jewish organizations in Austria had been dissolved and most of their officers jailed. Among the SS men leading the campaign, Adolf Eichmann, like many of the other architects of the Holocaust, himself an Austrian. At least 110 of the most important Jewish communal personalities were shipped to Dachau. Other arrested Jews were set to work building concentration camps such as Mauthausen. All the while, the looting continued under the aegis of Aryanization.

Franz Klepner, then a boy of fifteen, remembers being home alone with his brother Robert in their family apartment on the comfortable Untere Weisgerberstrasse. "Two men in SA uniforms burst into the apartment. A neighbor had tipped them off that our father, Ignace, who was a successful jeweler, kept a safe at home."

While one of the Nazis held the Klepner boys at gunpoint, the other broke into the safe and ransacked it. "Our father considered it lucky that we had not been shot."

Not even the home of Sigmund Freud was inviolable. A somewhat drunken gang of storm troopers invaded his famous apartment at Berggasse 19 and stole about $12,000 in cash that the father of psychoanalysis kept on hand for emergencies. A week later, Freud's daughter Anna was taken away by the Gestapo for several hours of questioning.

The Nazis moved swiftly on every front. Within six months, all Austrian Jews had been fired from civil-service jobs. Nazi propaganda made it eminently clear that loyal Aryan businessmen and professionals would begin to dismiss them from commercial and other private firms as well. Jews were forbidden to use parks and other public places. Shops began to advertise that they would no longer sell to Jews.[3] All across Austria, Jews were summarily arrested. Many were held in prison until they agreed to sign statements "voluntarily" forfeiting their property to the Reich. Those in Vienna who would not quickly agree were often sent to a synagogue that had been converted into a Gestapo torture center. The number of suicides among Vienna's Jews jumped radically—from 4 in February of 1938 to 311 just two months later.

So too did the murder and terror rate. "A few days after Anschluss, SA men took Franz Rothenberg, chairman of Austria's leading bank, the Creditanstalt, for a car ride and threw him out of

---

[3] Some Jews even found ways to protest. A young blond member of the community entered a large, well-known department store, and after spending more than an hour trying on suits, hats, and jackets, waited till the cashier had carefully wrapped everything before announcing, "I'm sorry, I forgot you don't sell to Jews." The young man, named Teddy Kollek, then left—and departed for Palestine some weeks later, where after the establishment of the state of Israel he became the mayor of Jerusalem.

the moving vehicle, killing him." This, reports Saul Friedlander, was followed a few weeks later by an attack on Isidor Pollack, director general of the chemical works Pulverfabrik, who was so badly beaten during the SA "search" of his home that he died shortly thereafter. The Deutsche Bank subsequently confiscated the Rothschild-controlled Creditanstalt, while Pulverfabrik, a subsidiary of the bank, was absorbed by the giant IG Farben.

Orderly as ever, the Nazis were eager to see that their program of Aryanization did not become a helter-skelter operation. Gauleiter Josef Burkel, charged with the unification of Austria and Germany, was given strict instructions to personally set up the special office in Vienna that coordinated the seizure of Jewish property. He in turn appointed Walter Raffelsberger to run it, and commanded him to introduce strict order into the ongoing plunder.

Major businesses like the Shiffman Brothers department stores were quickly grabbed. And while most of the 26,236 Jewish-owned businesses that existed in March 1938 were "modest" enterprises," according to historian Isaac Gutman, even they "did not escape the furious Aryanization" drive that marked the first few weeks of the Anschluss. Within days of the arrival of Hitler's troops, Ignace Klepner's Taborstrasse jewelry shop, which had been founded in 1889 by his parents—Samuel and his wife, the former Fanny Zeltner—fell under the jurisdiction of a Kommissarischer Leiter. "The first commissar was fairly decent," says Franz Klepner (who's now known as Frank). "But he was soon replaced by a series of Nazi-appointed bureaucrats, each of whom was tougher and more abusive."

Eventually, leaving all their belongings behind, the Klepners fled Austria, arriving first in Hungary. Then, after a time, thanks to visas secured by a wealthy Australian relative named Myer Zeltner, made their way to a new life in Melbourne.

Others found themselves displaced more than once. Gabrielle Törsch, the daughter of one of Austria's most established Jewish families, and her husband, Arthur Goldschmidt, moved to Moravia, where Goldschmidt, who had a Czech passport, ran the family's oil refinery, the Privozer Mineralölraffinerie.

After the Törsch family's Vienna bank, Törsch & Söhne, was confiscated by the Nazis, the Goldschmidts lost access to all funds there. When the Nazis moved on Czechoslovakia, their Moravian refinery, home, and belongings were also seized. Unlike many others, the Goldschmidts were able to flee, first to Belgium and ultimately to Canada.

By the summer of 1939, more than 40,000 Austrian Jews had been dismissed from private-sector jobs and 18,800 Jewish enterprises had been closed down or confiscated, among them more than 606 factories. Even when the Nazis "purchased" property from Jews, they basically stole it. German and Austrian records estimate that Austria's Jews were paid RM 35 billion less than the actual value of their property. Some of the swindles were particularly outrageous. One Jewish-owned business documented by Gutman was valued at 500,000 Reichsmark with liabilities of 50,000. When the Jewish owner was unable to come up with the full balance needed to cover the debt, he was arrested on a charge of "negligence."

The emigration process was as brutal as it was thoroughly devastating. George Berkley describes it in his book *Vienna and Its Jews:* A Jew would enter the emigration center in the morning and "after being processed as if on a conveyor belt, would leave in the afternoon stripped of everything he owned, including his dignity, but equipped with a short-term passport and instructions to use it as soon as possible if he wished to escape the concentration camp. It was also customary to leave him with a 10-mark note, worth $2.50."

Others simply lost venerable businesses with the flick of an Aryanization order. In the Burgenland town of Grosspetersdorf, not far from the Hungarian border, Eugen Lowy was ordered to vacate the general store his family had owned and operated for three generations and turn it over to a representative of the Reich.

"Ever since Hitler took power in Germany, friends had warned my father to start sending money to Switzerland," says his daughter, Henny Lowy King, now of Dundee, Scotland. "But my father would only laugh and say, 'It will never happen here.' "

Lowy says her father took whatever cash was left after the confiscation of his business and gave it to a man who promised to help the family arrange safe passage to Argentina. The fixer disappeared with the money. Eventually the Lowys—Eugen; his wife, Maria; Henny; and son, Frederick—escaped to Portugal with funds provided by a relative. (From there the family eventually made it to Canada, where Frederick, a renowned psychiatrist, is today principal of Montreal's Concordia University.)

Unlike many German Jews, Austrian Jews like the Lowys were not granted the right of orderly exodus to Palestine under the Haavara Agreement. The only exception: the Jews in the area of Hitler's hometown, Styria, which Eichmann and others in his entourage were eager to see *Judenrein*—"Jewless"—in time for Hitler's birthday on April 20, 1939.

Despite stringent restrictions against it, Jews who could tried desperately to transfer personal belongings and cash out of the country. Veteran London *Guardian* journalist Hella Pick, only seven years old at the time of the Anschluss, remembers her own mother, Johanna Marie Pick, meeting a courier who said he was willing to smuggle family savings out of the Reich. "There was no shortage of such people in Vienna. But she made contact with a Swiss named Allenstech, and she and my grandmother gave him a substantial amount of stocks, bonds, and valuables—including cash. He promised he would get it to Switzerland—for a fee, of course."

But Allenstech disappeared. In March 1939, Mrs. Pick managed to get Hella aboard a *Kindertransport* of Jewish children that reached London; she herself escaped three months later, and the Picks spent the remainder of the war years in London, with little money to support themselves. "When it was all over," recounts Hella Pick, "my mother tried tracking Allenstech down through her London solicitor."

The lawyer contacted a Swiss colleague named Dr. A. Billinger in Winterthur. Finally, in November of 1947, says Pick, "a letter arrived in London from Allenstech. It was postmarked Zurich, but without a return address." In it Allenstech denied ever having received any monies or papers for transfer to Switzerland. Instead, he insisted, he'd merely been given them for "safekeeping." Unfortunately, he claimed, they had all been taken from him when he himself was picked up by the Gestapo. Indeed, he hinted that Frau Pick had been responsible for his arrest, claiming she had "provoked the Gestapo by her own behaviour." If anything, wrote Allenstech, "she had every reason to be thankful" that her financial papers were found on him, not on her.

As in Germany, the Aryanization process was relentless. Within months of the Anschluss, says historian Saul Friedlander, 26 percent of the industry, 82 percent of the economic services, and 50 percent of the individual businesses owned by Jews had been taken over by Austrian Nazi authorities or their agents. "Of 86 Jewish-owned banks in Austria, only 8 remained after the first sweep"—and those were used primarily as funnels for the Reich's confiscations. By 1939, the pauperization of Austria's Jews was almost complete.

To give some legal fiction to its theft of Jewish property, the Nazis had promulgated a "Law for the Compensation of Damages Caused to the German Reich by Jews." Under the tenets of this twisted piece of legislation, a portion of the monies from the Austrian confiscations and expropriations were earmarked to "compensate losses suffered by fighters of the Nazi party" during their pre-Anschluss struggle in "Jewish-Socialist Vienna." Another part of the funds went to support the growing lists of Jewish poor, who, unable to emigrate or to work, were reduced to welfare lists. But the bulk of the stolen booty went directly into the Reich's war chest or to the coffers of individual Austrian Nazi functionaries.

By mid-August 1939, Walter Raffelsberger, the head of the Vermögensverkehrsstelle (Property Transfer Office), could announce to Himmler that within less than a year and a half his agency "had practically completed the task of de-Judaizing the Ostmark[4] economy." In Vienna, all Jewish-owned businesses had disappeared. So had most Jewish housing; by the end of 1938, some 44,000 of the approximately 70,000 apartments owned by Jews had been Aryanized. The balance would soon follow. By May 1939, more than 100,000 Jews—over 50 percent of the pre-Anschluss Austrian-Jewish population—had been forced to emigrate.

Among the very last to depart: Sigmund Freud, who before being given permission to leave Vienna for refuge in London was forced to leave most of his possessions behind (some of Freud's books and invaluable records were smuggled out by friendly diplomats or passed on to institutions for safekeeping). Before boarding the train in Vienna on June 4, 1939, the by then cancer-ridden Freud was made to sign a Gestapo document saying that Nazi authorities had treated him "with all the respect" due the great scientist. Later he would remark that he regretted not having added an ironic sentence: "I can heartily recommend the Gestapo to anyone."

Three months later, Freud was dead of cancer. Four of his five sisters had refused to leave Vienna. The approximately 160,000 Austrian Schilling (about $375,000 in today's dollars) that Freud left behind for their maintenance were apparently confiscated. They themselves all perished in the Holocaust.

The exodus of those Austrian Jews who managed to escape provided Nazi racial-law enforcers with an unexpected bonus. Under the rules, those wishing to emigrate had to attach three passport photos to their application forms. Ever-alert officials in

---

[4] The new name Hitler gave to Austria.

Vienna soon drew the attention of the Nazi Party's Racial Policy Office to the existence of "an outstanding collection of Jewish faces."

Though Aryanization had been launched in Germany, it was clearly in Austria that the Nazis decided to refine their "rational" policy regarding the Jews. Between 1938 and 1940, says Friedlander, the Austrian economic model would dictate all the Germans' "initiatives in this domain." The main thrust would be a radical restructuring of local economies, whose premier tenet was the absorption of any and all Jewish-controlled businesses that lived up to profitability assessments prepared by the Reich Board for Economic Management (Reichskuratorium für Wirtschaftlichkeit). Those enterprises deemed without benefit to the Reich's avaricious plans would not be Aryanized but simply liquidated.

The pauperization that resulted from the Nazis' economic plundering and isolation of Austria's Jews helped the Austrian and German authorities with their subagenda: disposing of the newly created Jewish proletariat through accelerated emigration. Under the Nazi master plan then in effect, a portion of the assets stolen from wealthy Jews would be earmarked for the *Zentralstelle für jüdische Auswanderung*—to help finance the emigration of already destitute parts of the "non-Aryan" population. In addition—and for those who couldn't leave for lack of visas—the Reich's Aryanization blueprint would establish labor camps where the upkeep of the Jews would be maintained at a minimum and, in fact, financed by the labor of the Jews themselves.

"In essence," says Friedlander, "those in charge of the Jewish question in annexed Austria were supposedly motivated by economic logic and not by any Nazi anti-Semitic ideology."

Some believe that the argument is bolstered by the fact that the entire Aryanization process in Austria was masterminded by the pragmatic administrators of Göring's Four Year Economic Plan. They also point to the fact that it was the technocrats of Aryanization who were initially given the task of solving the problem of what to do with the impoverished Jewish masses that resulted from Aryanization.

It is true, as Friedlander insists, that the liquidation of Jewish economic life in Nazi Germany had started at an accelerated pace in 1936. By late 1937, with the elimination of all conservative influences on Hitler, enforced Aryanization had become the main thrust of the Reich's anti-Jewish policies—policies that were even harsher in post-Anschluss Austria.

But the argument that these policies were largely if not entirely motivated by economics hold little water. For by clearly singling out the Jews for economic persecution, the Nazis—and later their Austrian supporters—were not only submitting to avarice but energetically fulfilling one of the anti-Semitic prerequisites of Hitler's racist philosophies: the isolation of Jews from Aryan society. Even the initial stages of this supposedly benign economic policy included forced-labor concentration camps, the precursors of the ghettos and eventually of the network of extermination camps that was to come all too quickly a few years later.

As Friedlander puts it, "the link between economic expropriation and expulsion of Jews from Germany and German-controlled territories did characterize *that stage* of Nazi policies until the outbreak of the war. Then, after an interim of almost two years, another 'logic' appeared, one hardly dependent on economic rationality."

That new logic—otherwise known as the Final Solution—all but destroyed an already decimated Austrian Jewry.

With the crushing of the Reich in 1945, barely 1,000 Jews—mostly partners of mixed marriages—were left in Vienna. More than 65,000 had died in ghettos and concentration camps. Of those who survived, only 1,747 chose to return to live in their former homeland. Austria itself was in ruins—and defeat had not excised its penchant for anti-Semitism. Vienna's universities remained hotbeds of anti-Semitic agitation. And a few scant months after the war, Leopold Kunschak, head of the Christian People's Party, felt free to declare proudly that he had "always been an anti-Semite." That incendiary statement did not prevent him from being elected president of the new postwar Austrian parliament.

Under a four-way occupation by the United States, the Soviet Union, France, and Great Britain, Austria began to rebuild—with the Western powers vying to outdo the Soviets in aid and support. Strategically located between the free world and the growing Communist bloc, Austria received more per capita dollars under the European-recovery program, the Marshall Plan, than any other European nation.

Compensating the losses of its Jews was low on the new Austria's list of priorities. In the immediate aftermath of the war, Austria did return most Jewish communal property to the remnant community, even paying some compensation for synagogues and other buildings destroyed under Nazi rule. In theory, survivors and their heirs could also reclaim private real estate—though according to a report of the World Jewish Congress, those who did were also required to refund any sums they might have received via Aryanization transactions.

But Austrian Jews who'd been forced out of rental properties had no recourse—nor was anything done to provide restitution for the unclaimed property of owners and heirs who had died in the war. According to scholar Thomas Albrich, "recovery under Austrian restitution law was secured only to the extent of approximately $250–280 million, meaning that at least $720 million worth of property and several hundred million dollars' worth of non-property damages remain unrecovered."

Austria was equally hard-nosed when it came to individual reparations. Though Wehrmacht and SS veterans received and continue to receive postwar pensions, victims of Nazism received little or no special compensations for their suffering. The government Fund for the Aid of Victims (created in 1956) soon ran out of cash. And even when monies were available for Holocaust survivors—through increased social-security benefits, for example—Austrian officials carefully referred to any payments to victims of their homegrown Nazism as "assistance" rather than "reparations" or "compensation."

Few issues remained more shocking than the fate of the hundreds of thousands of art and other cultural treasures looted from Austria and other European Jews by the Nazis and their allies. (It is estimated that by 1945, the Nazis had stolen a total of 3 million pieces of other people's art—about one-fifth of the world's entire art.)

Vienna, with its passion for culture and its affluent population, provided a particularly rich picking field for Nazi loot. By the time the war had ended, thousands of paintings plundered from Jews by the Nazis had been transferred to Austrian museums or sold to individual collectors. Many more were stored away in the network of salt mines and other controlled-temperature locations in Germany and Austria that the Nazis used to safely warehouse huge quantities of stolen art.

Liberation did not entirely liberate the stolen artworks. Between 1948 and 1952, Allied authorities returned to the postwar authorities numerous shipments of art believed to be Austrian in origin. The returns had been conditioned on Austria's making every effort to find the original owners or their heirs. American prodding resulted in the return of some 10,000 objets d'art—paintings, sculptures, and porcelains. But in a confidential 1950 memorandum, U.S. State Department official Ardelia R. Hall accused Austria's leading public auction house, Dorotheum, not only of having served as one of the major wartime "fences" for Nazi plundered art but of still playing that role. During a visit to Vienna in March 1950, Hall reported, she had discovered thousands of "suspect" paintings stored in the basement of Dorotheum's Vienna headquarters, paintings that she indicates in her memo were undoubtedly subject to restitution claims from their original owners and heirs.

Despite continued urgings from Washington, there was little

change. Another State Department report, this one dated December 1, 1952, charges that the "Austrian government has made no progress in the matter of restitution or indemnification . . . and, in fact, has endeavored to make effective legislation which would compensate former Nazis ahead of victims of Nazi persecution."

Austria earnestly promised to mend its ways when it signed the 1955 Treaty of Vienna, reestablishing its independence. The largely U.S.-sponsored agreement charged the new Austria with the "duty" to return stolen property to its rightful owners—and in cases where no claims were made, to search for those who might not be aware that they were heirs. "Yet for fourteen years after independence," says art historian Gilda Van Dunshim, "the Austrians never made a single serious attempt to find any Holocaust survivors who had fled Austria and might own the art."

To the contrary. For twenty-four years, no list of unclaimed art items was ever published and released by the Austrian authorities. Instead, a law was passed declaring a claims period scheduled to end in 1957. After that, a government-established agency called the Sammelstelle was authorized to offer for sale property that could be proven heirless—including that of Holocaust victims. Some $220,000 worth of items (about ten times that value in today's dollars) was thus sold. The money was absorbed by the Austrian state treasury.

Some of the better "heirless" artworks had already been distributed among Austrian museums and diplomatic missions. The balance of the unclaimed art—some 8,422 objects, including paintings, sculptures, and furniture—was quietly shipped to a fourteenth-century monastery in the tiny village of Mauerbach, on the edge of the Vienna Woods, just fifteen miles west of the city. There it was hidden away in five of the monastery's largest rooms—with some objects occasionally distributed to "needy" Austrian museums.

Nor were paintings and sculptures the only cultural treasures that the Austrian government snatched when the postwar world wasn't looking. According to documents discovered by the World Jewish Congress in the U.S. National Archives in Washington, Austrian authorities expropriated more than a quarter of a million precious books, most of them stolen from Holocaust victims. The cache of literary loot, most of it plundered by the Nazis from the libraries of Austrian and Dutch Jews, had been discovered in the immediate aftermath of the war and then hidden again by Austrian officials in the basement of a former Habsburg palace in Vienna. No attempt was ever made by the Austrian government to find the lawful owners or their heirs. Instead, in 1955, Austrian officials quietly began distributing more than 186,000 of the looted books to their own governmental network of libraries—among them the official library of the Austrian Chancellor.

World Jewish Congress executive director Elan Steinberg insists that Austria was obliged under international law to seek the heirs of the original owners of any stolen goods. "Books are especially important to Jews—to all people. In the end," says Steinberg, "to us books are more precious than gold."

Even owners who claimed their paintings found themselves facing mammoth bureaucracy—and in some cases were directly prevented from taking possession. A seventeenth-century Frans Hals painting of a woman, one of the mainstays of Vienna's Kunsthistorisches Museum, has always been officially identified by the museum as "a gift" from Baroness Clarisse de Rothschild. In fact, it was "given" to the museum in 1947 as the baroness's payment for a deal that allowed her to remove two other family-owned paintings from Austria. All the paintings in question had originally been confiscated from the Rothschilds by Austria's Nazi regime. (Until 1985, Austrian law forbade the export of native artworks.)

Clarisse was not the only Rothschild forced to make postwar deals with the Austrian government. In all, the Rothschilds found it necessary to "donate" 170 artworks—5 percent of the massive collection that had once belonged to barons Alphonse and Louis de

Rothschild—to Austrian museums in return for permission to export other paintings.[5]

Less notable claimants have had less luck. In one case, reports British journalist Peter Watson, the Austrians argued that since a specific painting had been in the "control" of the Germans on May 15, 1945, "it had legally passed into the possession of the Austrian state at the end of the war, and therefore did not belong to the claimant from whom it had admittedly been taken." Others had the documentation of ownership they submitted summarily rejected by the Austrians as "insufficient." Still others have complained that after describing their family paintings in detail, they were refused permission to view the paintings in storage—and had to rely instead on the word of Austrian authorities, who usually said they "could not find" them.

In 1969, after repeated appeals from Jewish leaders, including the World Jewish Congress and Vienna-based Nazi hunter Simon Wiesenthal, the Austrian government agreed to publish a comprehensive list of looted and unclaimed art objects in its possession. Their choice for the man to oversee its preparation was callous at best: Walter Frodl, head of the Monuments Office, which regulates "ownerless property," had been among those who had assisted Nazi authorities in choosing what was worth stealing in the early 1940s.

A seventeen-page list of 8,422 Mauerbach treasures was finally published in 1969, albeit with limited circulation. It immediately gave the lie to constant Austrian claims that the Mauerbach items were of little value—"baubles and kitsch," as one Austrian official once put it. In fact, the 657 paintings, 250 drawings, 84 watercolors, 365 pieces of silver, 114 books, 35 pieces of furniture, and other items included works by some of Europe's greatest artists, among them Bruegel, Archipenko, Teniers, and even works attributed to Botticelli and Leonardo da Vinci.

---

[5] The Austrian authorities reversed their position in 1999.

It also indicated the degree to which Austrian officials had been prepared to deceive applicants. An Austrian-born Holocaust survivor living in New Zealand had written to Vienna in the 1950s and early '60s claiming that her family had lost a painting by Frans Hals. She had been officially advised, she later said, that there was no painting at Mauerbach by Hals. When the list of Mauerbach paintings was finally published in 1969, the Hals painting was there. The woman had already died.

In the end, it is estimated that only 3.2 percent of the Mauerbach treasures were ever returned to their rightful owners. And many of those who did receive their family's possessions were charged exorbitant "storage fees" before they could collect their long-lost objects.

In 1994, after years of pressure and an investigative article about Mauerbach that appeared in the prestigious American magazine *Art News*—not to mention the flood of embarrassing revelations about the Nazi past of Austria's President Kurt Waldheim—Austrian authorities finally agreed to turn over the balance of the stolen paintings and other Mauerbach art objects to Austrian-Jewish communal organizations. On October 30, 1996, the Mauerbach artworks were sold for charity at a pro bono auction run by Christie's and co-chaired by World Jewish Congress president Edgar Bronfman and cosmetics heir Ronald Lauder, a former U.S. ambassador to Austria. The crowd of a thousand that packed Vienna's Museum of Applied Arts placed bids that raised $14.4 million—seven times the estimated results of the sale. The Austrian-Jewish community pledged to give it all to funds aiding Holocaust survivors (some 12 percent of the proceeds were earmarked for non-Jewish victims' organizations). Among the "baubles" that sold: a floral still life of peonies, roses, tulips, and poppies by the seventeenth-century French painter Abraham Mignon, which yielded $1.35 million.

Austrian Chancellor Franz Vranitzky was quick to warn his countrymen "not to be too proud of something that should have happened much earlier." But other officials were just as quick to crow that Austria had "lived up to its obligations."

In fact, they hadn't. The emotionally charged Mauerbach auction, which attracted international attention, did not close this ignoble chapter in Austrian history. "The truth is that Austrian museums still possess hundreds if not thousands of art objects stolen by the Nazis from 1938 on," insists Hubertus Czernin. "Many are worth more than the objects auctioned off in 1996."

Nor can the Austrians successfully run away from this past. The 1997 exhibit at New York's Museum of Modern Art of a collection of paintings by prewar expressionist Egon Schiele "owned" by the Austrian Leopold Foundation turned into an international art incident when it was discovered that two of the borrowed paintings—*Portrait of Wally* and *Dead City*—had been confiscated from Viennese Jews during the 1930s. When the rightful owners' American heirs demanded the paintings back and blocked their return to Austria, a Supreme Court legal battle was launched that pitted Robert Morgenthau, New York City's no-nonsense district attorney, against the influential MOMA and its board chairman, Ronald Lauder. It would trigger new questions about many of the masterpieces in Austria's museums—and send the global museum community into a panic over the possibility that, like their Viennese colleagues', their walls too may be decorated with Nazi loot. The waltz goes on.

3

Czechoslovakia

PART ONE
Czech Republic:
The Ganef of Prague

The warders mentioned certain depots where the property of prisoners is kept. I should like to see these depots where the hard-earned property of arrested men is left to rot, or at least what remains of it after thieving officials have helped themselves.
—FRANZ KAFKA, *The Trial*, 1925

If Austrians became Hitler's willing allies, then Czechs were among his most unwilling victims—at least those of them who believed in their young, multiethnic nation. Tomás Masaryk's twenty-year-old democracy was a fragile mix of Czechs, Slovaks, Germans, Jews, Gypsies, and Hungarians, a concept that Nazism could hardly tolerate. The Austrian Anschluss was a signal for the 3-million-strong German-speaking population of Czechoslovakia's Sudetenland to clamor for union with the Reich. Czech leaders resisted. But when Western allies betrayed them during the Munich Conference of

1938, the Czechs were forced to knuckle under to Hitler. The Sudetenland was ceded to Germany.

Six months later, on March 15, 1939, Nazi troops rolled across the Sudeten border, occupying the rest of the now shattered country. Bohemia and Moravia became German "protectorates," Slovakia a Nazi puppet state. Eastern Ruthenia was ceded to Fascist Hungary. In the capital, Prague, signs with Czech names were quickly painted over and replaced with German ones. "Czechoslovakia has ceased to exist," Hitler gloated.

The six long years of harsh occupation that followed were predictably disastrous for the 357,000 Jews of Czechoslovakia. They constituted one of Europe's oldest and most productive communities. Records of Jewish life in Prague go back to the ninth century; Jewish presence in Slovakia could be traced to Roman times. And while there had been ups and many anti-Semitic downs over the centuries, the Jews in Czechoslovakia had flourished as scholars and goldsmiths, physicians and farmers, carpenters and philosophers—producing visionaries from the sixteenth-century mystic Rabbi Judah Low, the hero of the golem legend, to twentieth-century author Franz Kafka.

Under Masaryk's democracy, Czech Jews who wished to could even register as Jews—not under anti-Semitic regulations but in recognition of their unique ethnic community, which in 1938 numbered 118,000 in Bohemia, Moravia, and Silesia alone.

Massive arrests began almost instantly—first of anti-Nazi German émigrés, then of Czech public figures, and of course, of Czech Jews. Synagogues were burned in Vsetin and Jihlava. And in cities like Brno, local Nazi thugs rounded up Jews on the street or in cafés and beat them.

Within two months, Adolf Eichmann himself had arrived in Prague to set up a *Zentralstelle für jüdische Auswanderung*—a central office for emigration of Czech Jews. Those who could afford it—and could obtain precious visas—were allowed to leave the

"Reichsprotektorat." Until exits were banned in 1941, a total of 26,629 Jews eventually fled. Among them were more than 2,500 who took advantage of a special Haavara Agreement and managed to reach Palestine. (Czech Jews in Palestine later formed a special Free Czech unit that fought at Dunkirk. Another Free Czech unit, formed in the Soviet Union, was 70 percent Jewish.)

Still other Czech Jews emigrated to England, France, the United States, and South America. The temporarily lucky made short-lived escapes to Poland.

But while Eichmann still allowed Jews to leave Czechoslovakia, his major job at that stage of the Nazi occupation was to strip Czech Jews of their assets and properties and deliver them to the Reich's treasury *before* they could escape. By 1940, all Czech Jews had been ordered to declare any property they owned worth more than 10,000 crowns (about $300 today). It was then confiscated against orderly receipts and stored in some sixty depositories in and around Prague.

Eichmann also ordered Jews to register and sell precious metals and jewelry they owned to the Czech government's Hadega public purchasing agency. Stocks, bonds, and securities were to be handed over to a special foreign-currency bank. The major cash flow was activated by imposing rules that drained Jewish accounts in Czech banks. Threats of violence and imprisonment helped speed the entire process. In Czechoslovakia alone, this ultimately brought the Reich an estimated half billion dollars in new assets.

The plundered amounts were staggering by the standards of that period. According to recently uncovered Czech bank records, in just one three-week period of 1941, more than 30 million crowns (about $1 million) were stolen from Jewish clients of the Boëmische Bank, the Gewer Bank, the Landesbank, and the Prague Credit Bank. Like the rest of the billions of crowns thus stolen, these plundered assets were transferred into the Reichsprotektor's account #870 at the Kreditanstalt der Deutschen in Prague.

With cash and other liquid assets safely flowing into Nazi

hands, the Germans moved to take over Jewish-owned commercial enterprises and shops. Many had already been "cleansed" of their goods by the invading German Army. Others, large and small, now found themselves subject to "visits" from Czech officials charged by the Nazis with overseeing Aryanization.

Detailing the experience in Prague of Franci Rabinek, her own mother, American writer Helen Epstein[1] writes, "One month after the invasion, a tall blond man appeared at the door of [my family's dress shop] Salon Weigert, identified himself as a commissar appointed to 'Aryanize' businesses owned by Jews, and asked politely for a tour of the premises. My mother reciprocated his politeness. She led him through the workroom and salon, estimated the annual number of customers, income and expenses, and answered his questions in her excellent German. The young commissar concluded that he would be unlikely to benefit from 'Aryanizing' the salon. But in confidence, he told my mother that she would have to sell Salon Weigert to a non-Jew or sell pro forma to one of her seamstresses and stay on, ostensibly as an employee. He allowed that his wife could use some new clothes and left."

A longtime Rabinek employee, a seamstress, did agree to become the "pro forma" owner. A contract, drawn up by a non-Jewish Czech lawyer and signed by both sides, was surreptitiously buried in a garden to be retrieved "after the war."

The entire fabric of life had changed. By August of 1939, the "wholesale exclusion of Jews from Czech public life" had begun. All Jews in Bohemia and Moravia were ordered to abandon their homes and relocate to assigned quarters in Prague. Jews were barred from cafés, restaurants, museums, theaters, swimming pools, and hospitals. JEWS NOT WANTED signs were posted everywhere. From time to time, the Gestapo would make a sweep of public places demanding papers and "inspecting noses."

---

[1] *Where She Came From—A Daughter's Search for Her Mother's History.* Little, Brown, 1997.

Some Jews, like nineteen-year-old Franci Rabinek, sought out plastic surgeons in a frantic attempt to conceal their identity—hiding themselves during the postoperative healing. "I imagine that [my grandmother] tended her daughter sadly, understanding the futility of straightening a nose when it was the whole world that was askew," writes Helen Epstein.

Franci Rabinek continued as her shop's "employee" until just before September 1942, when she and her parents, like tens of thousands of other Czech Jews, were notified that they must report to Nazi collection centers for "transport."

Franci herself was taken off the train at Terezin. Her parents were ordered to stay aboard and were shipped directly to the gas chambers at Auschwitz. On May 18, 1944, Franci, still dressed in a coat from her shop's 1939 collection, was herself shipped to "the East."

By July 1940, after the fall of Belgium and France, anti-Semitic restrictions were increased. Jewish children were barred from schools everywhere in the German-occupied Czech lands. In January, Czech Jews had their phones disconnected and were even ordered to turn in any stamp collections. Daily life became a battle against starvation. In a market already short of commodities, Jews were forbidden to buy fruit, nuts, cheese, candles, meat, poultry, onions, or garlic. By the midsummer they were excluded from Prague's parks and wooded areas, in September from libraries—and ordered to wear the yellow *Judenstern* (Jew star).

Like many well-integrated Czech Jews, Lisa Lichtenstern Mikova lived a life of comfort, blanketed, she recalls, "in a sense of belonging and safety. We weren't religious, which means one ate everything, but on holy days my mother and I went to the synagogue. We knew we were Jews, but we were Czechs. My father came from pure Czech country, and that's what we spoke. But my mother, who spoke perfect Czech, preferred German and also taught me French."

Her father, she says, was an importer of oils for "everyone

from chemists to painters—and he had a baking business as well. . . . We were well-to-do—with a huge apartment not far from Prague's National Theater with four big rooms and a terrace."

The Lichtensterns traveled a great deal, vacationing in Italy, Yugoslavia, and Switzerland—which is where they were in the summer of 1938, just after the Anschluss in neighboring Austria. "We met some interesting people, including a man who I think was related to Sigmund Freud. And everyone said to us, 'You can't be going back to Czechoslovakia! That's mad. You will see, within a year the same thing will happen to you as happened to us.'

"But my parents said, 'Never, never! Not in Czechoslovakia.' Still, it cast a pall over the holiday, and finally my parents wanted me to stay in Lugano. But I refused, so we all returned."

In early 1939, Lisa left for England at her father's insistence. "They would all join me, he said. But I was homesick, and I came back. And my father said, 'Now you spoiled everything'—and he was right."

When the Nazis descended on Prague on March 15, 1939, "everything changed. A German came to my father's office and announced he was taking it over but that my father would remain to work for him as a *wirtschaftswichtiger Jude.*[2] If father tried to object, he warned, 'You go straight to the concentration camp.'

"For a while," says Lisa, "we had an advantage—we stayed in our flat while others had to move from our section of the city. Then they began to deport the very rich to Lodz in Poland, which was really the beginning of the *Endlösung*—the Final Solution—because most of those who survived the horrors in Lodz ended up in Auschwitz anyway."

Then came the transports to Terezin—or Theresienstadt, as the Germans called it—an impregnable garrison town fifty miles north of Prague whose star-shaped prison had once housed the Bosnian

---

[2] Literally "the Jew of economic importance"—in other words, a Jew without whom the business could not run.

Serb who murdered Archduke Franz Ferdinand in 1914 and triggered World War I.

The Nazis emptied Terezin of its local population. Originally the site of an eighteenth-century fortress and prison, it had been now designated by the Nazis as the site for what they told the Red Cross and the rest of the world would become Hitler's "model Jewish town." In effect, the entire town of Theresienstadt was nothing more than a brutal, overcrowded, disease-ridden holding camp for Auschwitz. Between November 24, 1941, and March 16, 1945, 122 trains with 73,608 Czech Jews aboard made the short, tragic trip to Theresienstadt. Among them: Arnost and Olga Korbel and Anna Spieglova, the paternal grandparents and maternal grandmother of the little girl who would eventually become U.S. Secretary of State, Madeleine Korbel Albright.

In January 1942, it became the Lichtensterns' turn to make the one way journey. "Nobody asked, nobody explained anything. All they said was, 'You are going to Terezin. You can take fifty pounds of belongings.' We had to leave everything behind—at least everything that was left. They'd already taken our fur coats. Then our radios. As a Jew you could not have a pet, a cat or a dog. Then your jewelry. When we left, some friends said they'd keep some things for my dowry. But everything else—our furniture, our paintings—it all remained behind, and we never saw it again."

The abandoned possessions—textiles, furniture, dishes, glassware, bedding—were stored in fifty-four *Treuhandstellen* (trustee office) warehouses, eleven of them confiscated Prague synagogues.

The Jews were given just three days to prepare themselves and ordered to carefully list all their possessions, then officially sign them over to facilitate orderly "pickup" once they'd left. The process was touchingly recorded by then twelve-year-old Hella Weissova-Hoskova. "I did a drawing of my father seated at the table, writing down everything—even handkerchiefs—while my mother is going through the wardrobes. A very few things we did not list—a picture or a watch and a rug my grandfather had handwoven.

These we secretly gave to some Czech friends to hide—and some we even got back at the war's end. But everything else was left behind. We just closed the door and handed over our keys to the Nazis."

Weissova-Hoskova, today one of Prague's recognized artists, hid the drawing together with dozens of others she later managed to make in Theresienstadt. Several of those wartime works now hang in New York's Museum of Jewish Heritage. "But I have always kept the one of my parents making their lists. It was a terrible moment."

Far worse was the first sight of the gloom and foreboding of Theresienstadt. Lisa Lichtenstern Mikova arrived there on January 31, 1942. "It was a shock, this dreary place. There was no train station, so we had to walk four or five kilometers through the snow. It was my twentieth birthday."

The Jews were housed in basement barracks in large empty rooms of twenty to twenty-five people each whose only furnishings at first were mats on the floor. "The food was horrible, and we were so upset we couldn't eat," recalls Lisa Lichtenstern Mikova. People who'd been there longer than we cried, 'Give it to me, give it to me.' And then they told us, 'You will soon eat it.' And they were right. A month later, we ate anything there was to eat—and with pleasure."

Assigned to do technical drawings, she met Frantisek Mautner (later Mika), an engineer eight years her senior. Eventually they wed, and the camp commandant allowed her to take his name—something that meant they could stay together if one of them was deported eastward.

When her husband was finally ordered eastward in September 1944, he told Lisa to stay behind. "At least Theresienstadt is in Bohemia,' he told me. 'It's not a foreign country.'"

But Lisa chose to leave on the same transport anyway. "Of course, neither I nor any of the other wives who volunteered to go ever saw our husbands there. Never! And when we came to the train, we found a small note hidden in the toilet corner of our cattle car. *ACHTUNG GAS!*—but none of us understood what it meant until we arrived at Auschwitz."

Mikova describes the horrendous scene in bursts of words. "It was midnight. Flashlights everywhere. We saw barracks and high chimneys and a lot of SS. There on the spot other prisoners took our watches and wedding rings. 'Give it to me. If you don't give it to me, they will take it from you anyway.'

"Then they began to separate us: children here, mothers there. It was awful, awful! Beatings and screaming and crying. Then they shaved our heads. We had no hair. And I asked an older Czech prisoner who was shaving me about the transport that had taken our parents. And he looked at me and said, '*Himmelfahrt*'—journey to heaven, the camp term for gas-chamber victims. And then he told me, 'You are in Auschwitz now. Never ask anything. You will see everything, but never ask.' "

Mikova, like almost every survivor of that hell camp, says nothing could have prepared her for "Planet Auschwitz." "We slept ten people on one wooden bunk. When someone moved, we all had to move. Our covers were rags, dirty with lice and fleas. Together we would receive one pot with soup, and nobody was interested whether you could eat or you couldn't. It was a nightmare, really a nightmare."

A lesser nightmare saved her. "One day some armament-factory people came looking for slave workers—like in *Schindler's List*. They were big and arrogant, with leather coats. We had to parade before them, and they would say, 'This one, this one, not that one. How old are you? Show me your teeth.' We were like animals. But I was chosen, and they gave us clothes. I received a fashionable silk dress—it seemed silly. We were shipped to an aircraft factory in a town near Dresden, and the whole winter, from the end of October 1944 till the end of the war in May, 1945, I lived in that silk dress. No underwear, no coat, no jacket—but a silk dress and some dress shoes.

"They would march us from the barracks to the factory and back through the town, and German people looked and said terrible things to us or threw stones. . . . There were no angels. . . . Then in April, with the Allies advancing, they suddenly closed the factory, and we were ordered to leave."

For fifteen days, Lisa and her companions were ferried in circles in lorries and cattle cars. At one point, most of the men among the prisoners were taken away and shot. When she and others who survived finally arrived at Mauthausen concentration camp in Upper Austria on April 28, Czech prisoners there told them "the Germans had already lost the war." Best of all, in a desperate attempt to cover their murderous tracks, the Nazis had already dismantled the gas chambers at Mauthausen. " 'The Americans are only thirty or so kilometers away. Nothing more can happen to you,' they told us.

"When the Americans finally came, some of the German guards stole our clothing and tried to make believe they were prisoners. But we knew them and pointed them out. There was great joy—but there was also sorrow. Hundreds died because they suddenly had food to eat that was too rich for their system. We were all so weak—I weighed just forty-one kilos."

Sent "home" by train, Mikova arrived in Prague on May 14, 1945. Return was devastating. "Sometimes I hear people say, 'Why are the Jews receiving something now and not we others? We were all prisoners.' But they came home and knew where to go. We came home and stood there at the station with nowhere to go. Even in the case of political prisoners where they sometimes took a whole family, there were usually grandparents left. But we came back and there was nobody waiting for us. . . . There was no family. No keys for an apartment. There was nobody."

Eventually Mikova made her way to the home of an aunt who'd married a German gentile and had survived thanks to him. "I stood outside and shouted, 'Auntie, it's me Lisa.' She couldn't believe it. Then she told me the radio had announced my husband was among the list of survivors. It was at that moment," recalls Lisa Lichtenstern Mikova, "I fainted."

Three days later, she was reunited with her husband, their joy dampened by the news that her brother-in-law, imprisoned since 1939, had been executed four days before the war ended.

Thus began the painful procedure of trying to return to a semblance of normality. It included attempts to find her family possessions. "Some things we'd given to trusted friends were returned: some china, some glass, a ring, a watch. And there was my dowry of linens that my mother had given our family cook to hold, and it was returned to me neatly ironed and cleaned.

"But there was also a wealthy Czech, a business associate of my father's to whom my father had given a sizable amount of money to hold—some 300,000 crowns. For me it was a fortune. But when I went to this man, he said there was nothing. 'Besides,' he said, 'anyone can come and claim something.' So I said, 'I know I am telling the truth, and you know.' And I turned and left."

Six months later, Mikova received a phone call from the man's lawyer. " 'Well, he is dying,' he told me, 'and he wants to know how to give you the money he owes you.' Perhaps in that moment he was afraid of God."

Mikova had less success trying to reclaim her father's business. "The Czech who'd been the right hand of the German who'd taken it over was still there. Workers told me he'd helped the German loot the place before he fled back to Germany. 'Who are you and what do you want?' the Czech demanded.

" 'I am the daughter of the owner, and I want my father's business back.'

"He looked at me like I was an insect and said, 'Well, it belongs to me now' and shut the door in my face."

Thus began a Kafkaesque traipse from authority to authority. "First the government told me I had to prove my father was dead. Then they wanted me to prove that I could manage the company.

But then for this I needed a special document that I could only get if I proved I owned a business. It was horrible."

Other newly liberated Czech Jews found they could not even collect on family insurance policies. Adolf Stern, who lost his father, mother, wife and eleven-month-old son to the gas chambers, tried to make a claim on a large prewar policy his father had maintained with the Czech office of the Italian insurance company Assicurazioni Generali. "They asked me for the death certificate," recalls Stern, now eighty-two and living in Florida. "But I said, 'Hitler didn't give death certificates.' . . . I was crying because they treated me like dirt. When they saw that I didn't want to go, they kicked me out."

The crush of constant frustration bore down heavily on already frail survivors like Stern and Mikova. "One day my husband finally said, 'Now enough! Stop it!'" says Mikova. "Next day he got a job in a technical high school, and we tried to find a place to live. The German family that had taken my parents' apartment emptied it of all its beautiful handmade furniture—and in any case, I could not bring myself to step into it, let alone live in it. Every corner had a memory."

Like many other Holocaust survivors, Lisa soon sank into a postwar depression. "Everyone was gone, and somehow I lost my will. The whole time of the war and the camps I was quite all right—and now at the end I could only sit and stare and cry."

Then, eight months or so later, Mikova noticed a man standing in front of her apartment building. "Do you remember me?" he asked. It was the man who had thrown her out of her father's office. "'I brought you a photo that your father had on his writing table,' he said. 'It's when you were a little girl, and I wanted to give it you, and I think we should have a talk.'

"'I have nothing to say to you,' I told him and started to close the door. But he put his foot in and told me, 'Don't be stupid. We'll reach an agreement. You know, I'm rather rich now.'

"I was furious, and I said, 'Don't speak to me and go away. I won't speak with people of your kind. It's finished for me, and I won't hear any more of it.' It was stupid of me perhaps, but that's how I felt."

The man's change of heart had been inspired by charges that he had collaborated with the Nazis. "Eventually," says Mikova, "he went to jail. Then, in 1989, after the anti-Communist Velvet Revolution, I took a lawyer and tried to regain something. But the company had been liquidated, and I never saw a crown. Not anything at all."

The same was true of property in Germany that Mikova had inherited from her father. "It was a large apartment building he had bought during the Depression. My husband joked with me after the war that I had inherited a pile of stones—we were sure the building had been destroyed in the air raids. But in fact it still stood in the American sector of West Berlin, a corner building with thirty-five apartments, a shop, and a restaurant—quite valuable.

By now the Communists had taken control of Czechoslovakia, and they advised Mikova that the income from the building would have to be forwarded to a government office in Prague. "We would receive a small part of it in the form of foreign-currency vouchers; the balance went into 'a special account,' they said. Which meant the Czechoslovak state collected it. Then they began to pressure me to sell the building for DM300,000 which was maybe 10 percent of its value. 'The state needs the foreign currency,' they said. They took our passports away and said we could have them back if we sold. Then, one day in March of 1968, just before the wonderful Prague Spring, they called me to the Ministry of Finance with my husband. There were also people there from Czech security, and they said, 'Do you want to go to prison because of your house? Here is a contract—sign it.'

"I asked to see my lawyer, but they said, 'Your lawyer is here, but he has no right to tell you anything. . . . Either you sign or you are arrested.' So I signed. My husband would have lost his job.

My son was twenty years old. If I refused, it would have ruined the family—either prison or exile to some village in East Slovakia. But I never saw any money, just some useless paper bonds."

As the years passed, Mikova thought less and less of what had been taken from her. "I had other troubles—life was difficult under the Communists, then my husband's health failed. After I recovered from his death in 1993, I went to another lawyer and told him my story. And he said, 'Why did you not tell me this in 1990 [after the Velvet Revolution threw out the Communists] when there was still time to do something? You have passed the deadline for applying for restitution. Now you can't get anything.'

"Now they tell us that perhaps next year something will come from the Swiss. Those of us who wait laugh; we can only laugh. We are the last of the living. Each week when I go to visit the cemetery, I see new announcements of death. So when they say next year, it's ridiculous—it's really an offense."

The offenses have come steadily since the end of the war. Barely 50,000 Czechoslovak Jews survived the Holocaust—about one-seventh of the prewar population of 357,000. More than half were in Slovakia. Many left immediately after the German defeat and before the Communist coup of February 1948. Another 25,000 emigrated to Israel and the West between mid-1948 and 1950. Then, except for brief, sporadic periods, the gates were closed for emigration, especially of Jews. Many Czech Jews who remained fervently believed that socialism would solve all their nation's problems—including anti-Semitism. As with the rest of the Communist covenant, they were sorely disappointed.

Czech Jewry's lowest postwar point came in 1952, when Communist Party secretary general Rudolf Slansky and ten other leading Jews in the party and Communist government were arrested and charged as "Zionists," "bourgeois liberals," and "Western spies." After a stridently anti-Semitic show trial, Slansky and seven of the others were hanged. In the years that followed, the community was cast into the shadows: The teaching of Hebrew was banned, Czech Jews were forced to sever ties to international organizations like the World Jewish Congress, synagogues were closed, and what Jewish communal life did remain in Czechoslovakia was all but stifled under a government-sanctioned leadership network of party toadies and communal spies. For most Czech and Slovak Jews, Jewish roots were to be hidden—certainly by those who continued to be active in the party, and even among that proportionately large number of Jews who helped found the fledgling democracy movement that would eventually topple the Communists.

When forty-one years of Marxist rule crumbled in 1989 together with the Berlin Wall, the registered Czech-Jewish community had shrunk to fewer than 900. But the election of democratic President Václav Havel, who quickly voiced support for Israel and Jews, helped trigger new optimism. There was a flow of people suddenly discovering—or admitting—their Jewish roots, people who packed synagogues and Jewish cultural events. "We will never be what we were," says Tomás Kraus, the erudite director of the Czech Republic's Federation of Jewish Communities, whose offices are in Prague's seventeenth-century Jewish Town Hall, "but now at least we have a future."

With that future in mind, Kraus and other communal leaders soon began pressing demands for the return of communal property—everything from tiny ruined synagogues in now *judenrein* Moravian villages to the world-famed Jewish Museum in Prague.[3]

In March 1994, the Czech government declared that some 30 communal Jewish properties—including the Jewish Museum—would be returned. But the government of Prime Minister Václav Klaus gave no sign of plans to return the 202 other communal properties the Jews requested. And since its pledge to restitute

---

[3] Hitler had planned a macabre museum of the "vanished Jewish race" in Prague and ordered that many of the Judaic artifacts confiscated from destroyed synagogues and individual Jews be centralized in warehouses at Prague's Jewish Museum.

property had been formulated by the government as a "unilateral commitment" (as opposed to a law), it became impossible for the Jews to seek legal redress. Worse yet, some state-owned former Jewish communal property had already been sold as part of the Czech privatization program *after* the government declaration in what appeared to many observers as a clear violation of the general legislation governing restitution of property.

Indeed, 40 of the 202 pieces of real estate still claimed by the Czech republic's nine Jewish communities had been already irreversibly privatized and sold. Nor could the Jews even seek governmental compensation; a law providing for it had been blocked in Parliament by then Prime Minister Václav Klaus's Civic Democratic Party.

A still more disagreeable problem involved Jewish communal property that the Communist government had "given" to Czech towns during Marxist rule. Though the Klaus government "appealed" to towns to restore Jewish communal property, most local councils refused even to discuss the matter. "We got back a few dilapidated former synagogues and some overgrown cemeteries," says Kraus. But for the most part, any Jewish communal real estate of value had already been either rented out for town income or used as collateral for loans.

In the town of Kolin, a short ride from Prague, a beautiful seventeenth-century synagogue with a pink marble columned Torah ark and polychrome walls of charming folk designs has now become the town's cultural center. There are no more Jews in Kolin. But the town is eager to cash in on the tourist trade. A small hotel in the former ghetto street calls itself U Rabina—"At the Rabbi's." Its menus and delivery truck bear the same Star of David symbol that the town's 2,200 Jews were forced to wear when they were marched off to Auschwitz in 1942. Kolin's tiny town museum proudly displays several items of local Judaica, including a richly embroidered mauve *parokhet*—Torah cover cloth—that bears the year 1763. But there is little inclination to return the items or the synagogue to Jews. "I must admit that to some extent they are right," declared Deputy Mayor Jaromir Cabela. "But we were given the building in the 1970s, and we have invested 12 million crowns in trying to restore it." If the board of Czech Jews reimburse the town, he suggests, then "the Jews can rent the building to Kolin as a meeting hall."

Even government bodies defied the restitution declaration. In one particularly outrageous case, reported the London-based newsletter, *Eastern Europe,* Prime Minister Klaus's office, which held title to the luxurious Villa Lauretta in the spa town of Karlovy Vary (Carlsbad), "continued to use the villa for its officials' recreation and apparently tried to stall the transfer of the title to the Jewish community (whose claim is indisputable) by making a transfer contingent on economically unrealistic conditions." Contingencies included asking the tiny remnant community in Karlovy Vary to assume costs for running a private facility for the handicapped that the government alleged was long scheduled to be installed at the villa. In mid-1995, a compromise contract for title transfer was finally signed.

Similar demands to assume financial burdens were slapped on other properties returned to the Czech-Jewish community. Even, says Kraus, after the government buckled to international pressures and agreed in May of 1995 to return another 100 of the 202 properties the community claimed. The net result, says Jiri Danicek, chairman of the Czech Federation of Jewish Communities, is that many restituted properties are not generating enough income to finance either their restoration or their maintenance.

Laws supposedly intended to help individual Jewish owners whose properties were confiscated by the Nazis and not recovered under the Communists have proven no less anomalous. Claimants were given a scant five months in which to procure all the complicated documentation needed to file claims. More discriminatory yet, unlike the laws regulating claims for Communist-confiscated property, this "Jewish law" disallowed any claim for the return of property whose title had been acquired by a third non-state party after October 1, 1991—or on properties the government had simply decided to privatize (though the claimants would be eligible for some financial compensation).

It also excluded from restitution and/or compensation any agricultural land and property confiscated from Jews by the Nazis and then taken over by the Communist Czech state after 1948.

No less typical is the case of the American family of Otto Witrofsky, which has been struggling unsuccessfully for three generations for the restoration of property owned in Brno. A wealthy Czechoslovak industrialist with a lavishly furnished villa in Vienna, Witrofsky had been the sole owner since 1905 of a major fruit-juice and spirits manufacturing complex with a large factory in the Czech city of Brno as well as a branch in the Hungarian capital of Budapest.

The Anschluss convinced Witrofsky there was little future for Jews in Central Europe. Packing what he could, he and his family fled to Switzerland, leaving most of their possessions behind, including his factories and Viennese home at 33 Pyrkergasse. Eventually he made his way to California and became a U.S. citizen. His ex-wife and his son, Franz (later Francis Witt), settled in New York.

Witrofsky, like many wealthy Europeans, maintained Swiss bank accounts. But unlike many other European Jews, he still had access to them, a fact that allowed him to live out his life comfortably albeit modestly. He also kept track of his factories' fate and after the war spent the balance of his life trying to reclaim them. In a letter to the U.S. embassy in Prague in 1949, Witrofsky details what happened after their expropriation: "In [November] 1939 the Nazis seized the firm as Jewish property and appointed a Dr. Edgar von Payersfeld as trustee with unlimited administrative power."

Von Payersfeld, an ethnic German and Nazi sympathizer, was the official representative of the Reichsprotektorate for Bohemia and Moravia. As such, he sold the firm's real estate to a Brno machinery company "at bargain prices," probably pocketing a hefty commission-cum-bribe in the process. The company's other assets—including its distilling equipment—were sold to a local Czech.

With the defeat of the Nazis, the firm was seized by the postwar Czech government. Yet all of Witrofsky's attempts to regain control of his property came to naught, and in fact led only to the same frustration that Mikova and others faced. A Brno lawyer he'd hired managed to negotiate a cash settlement for the property with the postwar Czech government. But the deal stumbled when Witrofsky asked for at least part of his payment in U.S. dollars. "All this took place a few weeks before the [Communist] overthrow of the Czech government in 1948," Witrofsky wrote in his 1949 memo to the U.S. embassy in Prague. A renewed plea for restitution of the factory was dismissed by the Communist-controlled Czech Supreme Court on the grounds that the "firm of Horowitz and Witrofsky no longer legally exists." Moreover, the postwar Czech government argued that Witrofsky the Jew, who had had an Austrian passport before the Nazi Anschluss forced him out of Europe, was "an enemy alien with allegiance to the German nation" and therefore deserved no restitution.

After his death in 1953, Witrofsky's property and the struggle to regain it was passed on to his son Francis, a U.S. Army veteran who'd changed his name to Witt. In letters to the Department of State, Witt laid claim to the Brno factory, valuing it at "a minimum of $500,000," and to the Budapest branch of Horowitz & Witrofsky, which had been bombed and destroyed in 1944 and which Witt valued at "about $100,000." An additional claim of $100,000 for the family home in Vienna, which had been destroyed in a bombing raid on the night of September 12, 1944, had been filed with both the U.S. Treasury and the Austrian government. The contents of the home—including Witrofsky's art collection—had been "removed" by the Nazi government after he fled.

The response from the State Department, which Witt's son

Peter, Otto Witrofsky's grandson, has carefully preserved, is a chilling exercise in the bureaucratic runaround that Holocaust survivors endured in the postwar years. In effect, writes Francis E. Flaherty, the State Department's assistant director of Special Consular Services, the U.S. government can do nothing on behalf of the Witts. Instead, it advises them to submit separate claims to Austria, Hungary, and Czechoslovakia.

"That's what my father did and continued to do to no avail," says Peter Van Witt, who's added the Van to his father's version of the family name and now lives in Westport, Connecticut. "It was a constantly frustrating, draining procedure. It added to my father's own sense of failure, and I am convinced it led to his premature death [by suicide] in 1954."

In 1990, Van Witt and his mother, Hilda, traveled to Czechoslovakia and visited the site of the family factory in Brno, now a branch of Fruta, a Czech state company. "The place was in a shambles. I couldn't even bring myself to go in. It was a wrenching experience." But Van Witt did decide to pick up the battle where his father had left off. Hiring a local attorney, he hoped to gain some compensation for the family's losses and was ready to bring suit to do so. Otto Witrofsky's family still waits. "It's not something you give up on," says Peter Van Witt, now forty-seven. "It's like turning your back on your heritage, on what my grandfather built and my father fought for. It's ours."

Offensive too is the fact that the details of the theft of the Witrofsky family property have probably been available to the Czech government since 1945—as have been the histories of some 130,000 other Czech Jews whose assets were stolen. The records are still there—carefully hidden inside the imposing walls of the former Strahov Monastery, a twin-towered building that stands beside Prague's much heralded Hradcany Castle, where Havel holds court and Kafka was imprisoned. The grim white monastery structure, not far from the fifteenth-century Charles Bridge, was the central archive where the Nazis recorded, as British writer

Adrian Levy puts it, "the bureaucracy of death—the nuts and bolts of genocide and, most painfully, the shame of Czech complicity, betrayal and theft."

As Levy reported in *The Times* of London, "Warrants for the transportation of Jews are filed next to receipts for their confiscated property: the Jew Adolf Korn's green onyx fireplace, the Jew Zdenka Fantylova's grand piano, the Jew Hans Adler's pewter tea service and the Jew Frank Stransky's gold fob watch."

Other ledgers detail the eviction from their homes of thousands of families. Worse yet, and one of the reasons it has been so hidden from view, it is a clear paper trail that, says Levy, shows "how a network of Czech banks and institutions conspired to steal more than UK pounds 1.2 billion [in property, paintings, goods, and cash] from Jews and how the people of Prague betrayed their neighbors and former business partners."

In many postwar cases, goods belonging to Jews and recouped from the Nazis after their defeat were simply redistributed among approved Czech Communist Party cadres. Needless to say, during the Communist era, the Czech government made certain that these and other records of Germany's wartime plunder and murder were completely off-limits to everyone but a tiny number of government officials. Those denied access to the records included the one out of six Czech Jews who survived the Holocaust. Even now, ten years after the fall of communism that brought democracy to the Czech Republic, the Strahov Monastery files shamefully remain all but sealed from view: "Four million or so typed and handwritten documents, stamped with swastikas, bundled and crammed into rotting cartons and piled on sagging metal shelves," concludes Levy.

Gaining access to the files has become a major issue for the Czech-Jewish community. "These files are both our history and our future," says Tomás Kraus.

"While there has never been an outright halt to restitution of Jewish property in the Czech Republic," wrote the *Eastern Europe*

Newsletter, in May of 1995, "there has been deliberate obstruction and procrastination."

Freddy Liebrich is one of the select few who have had access to the files. A German-born retired technical manager at Mercedes-Benz in London, he had wangled his way into the archives in 1997 by making a deal: He would give the Czechs a rare collection of news photos of their 1968 Spring Revolution in exchange for access to the Strahov archives. His goal: to discover what had happened to a cache of gold bars belonging to his father-in-law, Alfred Borger, who fled Prague for England in 1939.

In April of 1997, Liebrich, who as a young volunteer helped found Israel's navy in 1948, was given a week in which to peruse selected files. Accompanied by his wife, Kitty, he discovered "the archives in a total mess." Worse yet, several staff members confided there were plans to shred most of the papers. Then, four days later, after barely beginning their research, the Liebrichs were abruptly told they had to leave because "the archives are closed."

"This was part of the legal battle for restitution, and I wasn't about to give up," says Freddy Liebrich. After tracking down more historic Czech news photos in London, Liebrich negotiated another brief stint at Strahov Monastery. This time he sent two "relatives" in his place, Adrian Levy and Cathy Scott-Clark of the London *Times.*

Their work was stringently controlled, and after five days the pair was told that "the law had changed and nobody, no organization or individual can look at any files." They were then ordered to leave. But not before the two journalists took with them several "bags heavy with furtively copied files."

Among their finds were some of the most glaring examples of the greed, cruelty, and betrayal that pervaded the plundering of the Jews. Consider the letters of Johanna Nalezna of Prague. Writing to a local Nazi inspector named Massalsky in February of 1941, Nalezna complains about an apartment block at 25 Langegasse in the center of Prague: "So many jews [sic] live in this house, and yet my family (my son is in the Hitler Youth and is only 12 years old) live in a tiny flat in Prague VII. I would like a two bedroom flat at the above address so my son could go to school nearby. Heil Hitler!"

One month later, according to the documents, Mrs. Nalezna was allocated the apartment of Adolf Korn, a Jew who was eventually deported. But even that didn't satisfy Nalezna. Writing to the Reichsprotektor on December 3, 1941, she says, "Thank you for my new flat, but it is too small for my family. There is another jew [sic] still refusing to leave one of the flats in this building because he is afraid he will be sent to prison by the Gestapo. He lives in such a big room and I live in such a small room with my son who is in the Hitler Youth. The jew's [sic] name is Reichner. I am sorry to trouble you, but can I have his flat?"

She received it; the "jew Reichner" went to Auschwitz.

Herr Oberinspektor Massalsky was less understanding when it came to Jewish supplicants. According to another document quoted by Levy and Scott-Clark, Mrs. Elsa Gruenbaum, who together with her two small children had been evicted from her apartment in central Prague, sent the following plea in November 1943: "Please," she wrote, "could I return to my home to retrieve some winter clothing and maybe a small heater?" Her request was denied. The family was deported to Terezin and from there to Auschwitz one month later.

Similar records, including individual cards registering a mass of expropriated objects that included everything from bank accounts to pianos to sets of china, are also believed hidden in the lofts and cellars of scores of Czech government buildings. They have not been released, apparently by order of the new post-Communist Czech government. But a handful of conscience-ridden administrators and scholars have made private, highly unauthorized efforts to rectify that injustice. One of them, Dr. Helena Krejcova, a research fellow at the semigovernmental Institute of Contemporary History in Prague and a specialist in Holocaust-period studies, personally discovered thousands of property-seizure cards stashed in the attic of a ward building in Prague's Seventh district. "My sister worked there—she found them—and after hours I went there and very quietly copied them, then turned the originals over to the authorities."

Krejcova's find included records for thousands of missing objects. Working out of a garretlike office in a shabby section of Prague, Krejcova says the lists of Nazi loot include details of paintings—and from whom they were stolen. "They prove who were the original owners. Not everything went to Germany or stayed there. With such lists," she insists, "auction houses, museums, and galleries could help trace their heirs."

Nothing could be further from the minds of Czech museum and government officials, not to mention international auction-house owners. Indeed, in some cases, even proof of ownership has not been enough to retrieve stolen property. While some Czech institutions have been pressured into returning objects to rightful owners, others have simply refused.

Such has been the case of Peter Glaser. The son of a well-to-do wire-rope manufacturer in Bohemia, Glaser was the grandnephew of renowned geographer and explorer Eduard Glaser, a prodigy from the Bohemian town of Rohovec who became the nineteenth century's premier explorer of the mysterious southern Arabian peninsula. Adventurous and gregarious, Glaser was especially drawn to Yemen, even suggesting at one point that it rather than Palestine become the Jewish homeland. This Jewish Indiana Jones later befriended the local pasha, became an honorary member of a bedouin tribe and in 1880 received permission to excavate at the fabled palace of the Queen of Saba (Sheba). There, surrounded by the expanse of desert that he loved, Glaser uncovered both the secrets of ancient Saba's wealth—including its unique irrigation system—and many archaeological treasures, some of which experts maintain are still unmatched in their quality and uniqueness.

Most of Glaser's artifacts found their way back to museums in Vienna, whose imperial court had financed his expeditions, as well as to Berlin and London. Others went to Prague, where he'd studied. But Glaser, who never married, also gave a sizable collection of his findings to his only brother, Alois. When the brother died in Bohemia in 1937, his will left the forty-piece collection to his eldest grandson, Peter. "It had a very special place in our home, in specially constructed display cases," says Glaser, who still has photographs of the collection taken in the large home of the then prosperous Glaser family.

When the Nazis took over, the Glasers quickly fled, first to Italy and eventually to England. Their home, the family factory, and all their belongings were taken by the Nazis—or stolen by neighbors. The only exceptions: a few items the family's loyal chauffeur hid at his own home. Eduard Glaser's archaeological artifacts were taken to a local museum.

In England, Glaser, then nineteen, joined the Free Czech Forces. Two years later, he returned to Bohemia with the liberating troops of the U.S. Third Army and reclaimed his family home. The family factory, nationalized by the postwar Communist regime, remained inaccessible. But when Glaser appeared at the local museum in his British Army uniform, the curator quickly, if unhappily, returned the Glaser artifacts.

When the Stalinist net tightened, Glaser was warned to flee. "Anyone who'd served in the Free Czech Army," his former commanding officer told him, "would probably be arrested as a Western agent and subject to horrors."

Leaving his collection for safekeeping with the Jewish Museum in Prague, from which he received a very specific receipt, Glaser and his family left for America. There he won his doctorate at Columbia University, and eventually became a rocket engineer for Arthur D. Little, Inc., in Cambridge, Massachusetts, where he worked on NASA moon-exploration projects.

Glaser later discovered that Communist authorities had confiscated his antiquities collection and incorporated it into their own. After 1991, he journeyed to Prague to ask for their return. "They don't deny they are mine—and are even ready to officially acknowledge my ownership," says Glaser, "but only on condition I agree to turn official ownership of them over to the Czech state."

So far Glaser has refused. "If there's anyone I want to give them to, it's the Smithsonian Institution. America gave me new life. Czechoslovakia turned its back on me."

Why has the Czech government been so recalcitrant about releasing belongings like Glaser's or providing access to documents—or about making amends for the sixty years during which first the Nazis and then the Communists stole and absconded with the property of Czechoslovakia's Jewish citizens? Why has the Czech government chosen 1948 as the cutoff date for restitution claims?

Some officials of the new Czech Republic, such as former Czech ambassador to the United States Michael Zantovsky, claim, "It is simply unfair to expect that all problems can be solved overnight" and attempt to take refuge in the relatively short period that's elapsed since Czechoslovakia's Communist walls were torn down. Yet the inability to pass legislation and establish restitution mechanisms cannot be explained away as simply a question of not enough time.

At least part of the true answer comes in private conversations with Czech officials such as Zantovsky. Speaking in his seventeenth-century offices at the Czech Senate, where he is chairman of the Foreign Relations Committee, the media-savvy Zantovsky, who served as Czech President Václav Havel's press secretary during the 1989 Velvet Revolution, offers a two-word explanation: "Sudeten Germans."

The reference, of course, is to the more than 3 million ethnic Germans whom the Czechs evicted from their territory in 1947. It was the Sudeten Germans' overwhelming support for Hitler that gave the Nazis the excuse they needed to grab the Sudeten territory in 1938 and to begin the process that dismembered the tender

Czechoslovak Republic. As punishment, Prague's postwar leaders ordered them sent to Germany—and confiscated their properties in the process. Says the energetic Zantovsky, himself the son of a Czech Jew, "People are concerned that a full return of properties to Czech Jews will simply open a floodgate of demands from Germany for restitution for the Sudeten Germans. We have sympathy for Jewish claims, but the sensitive Sudeten question is not one we can afford to deal with."

How much more so as the Czech Republic tries to tighten its ties to its wealthy neighbor to the north, Germany. Nor do the Czechs feel they can ignore the ripple effect restitution to Jews might have on the Catholic Church and other property claims.

But Zantovsky (who during the repressive Communist era was best known as Czechoslovakia's expert on Woody Allen), as do many other Czech government officials, fails to forcefully acknowledge that there is still a vast moral difference between the racial persecution of Czechoslovakia's Jews and the expulsion of the Sudeten Germans. The former were innocent victims. The expulsion of the latter might have involved excesses and affected some innocent people. Yet the fact remains that it was in direct retribution for the treason of a majority.

Not all Czech officials agree with the ostrich-in-the-sand view of Havel's court. Viktor Doubal, a former member of the Czech Parliament and Deputy Prime Minister, has been a lonely fighter for justice. "Part of the problem," he says, "is that many of the rules that were promulgated after the war were contradictory. Under Hitler it was a crime to be a Jew . . . and under the Communists it was enough to accuse someone of being a social enemy of the people. So many people just never received what was due them. The laws were complicated, perhaps purposely so."

Doubal raises a basic question that is the ethical crux of the restitution issue. "There are many people who claim that you cannot right an injustice with a new injustice," he says, "that if someone now lives in a house that was stolen from someone a very long time ago, they are not at fault.

"But some principles are very basic. If I steal your car and sell it to a third person and you then find the car, it is still your car. The justice is to return it to you. And there must be restitution made by the stealer—or by the state. No one should be able to steal property by force. It's basic human decency."

Doubal has been trying to amend the Czech law that says that claims can be made only for property that was confiscated after 1948—a date that means most Czech Jews have no opportunity to reclaim property stolen by the Nazis. "I know the law is based on a practical reason—not to return property to Sudeten Germans, and to correct the crimes of the Communists. But there were two kinds of Communist crime. Their direct crime was to steal people's property. But their second crime was not to fulfill the restitution process that began in 1946."

In 1991, Doubal presented a law to Parliament that would have overridden the 1948 cutoff dates to enable Czechs, particularly Jews—and especially those who'd survived the death camps—to seek restitution. The law did not win a majority, and did not pass.

The net result has been a painful and continuing cycle of injustice and suffering for aging Czech Holocaust survivors. No worse example exists than that of Eliska Fishman Fabry, whose family owned a forty-seven-hectare farm in a Moravian village some eight kilometers from the town of Jihlava. "My grandfather had bought it, and my father inherited it in 1905. There was a dairy farm, a small château, and a pond, woods and fields, a starch factory, a small distillery and woodworks. There were also many [ethnic] Germans in the area, and when Hitler came to power, they began to act terribly."

In 1939, the Nazis imposed "Aryan caretakers" on all the Jewish farms, and the Fishmans were forced to move. Her father was arrested by the Gestapo in 1941, and in February 1942 the family was officially informed that he had died. "Later we found out it was in Auschwitz."

Fabry herself was sent to Theresienstadt in August of 1942, and in the autumn of 1944, at the age of twenty-eight, deported to Auschwitz with her mother and sister-in-law. It was the next-to-last transport to leave for the East. At the war's end, only Fabry and her brother had survived. Weak and sick, she returned to Prague, her shaven head hidden under a scarf. Her brother, who'd been shot by an SS officer just before the liberation of Auschwitz, survived thanks to a group of Red Army soldiers who found him wounded.

"My brother was like a skeleton, but as soon as he had recovered he had to put on a uniform and join the [Czech] army." Passing through the family village of Jihlava with his unit, he met a childhood friend. "You'd better go to the town hall. They've posted a paper saying your farm was confiscated because it belonged to Germans."

There then followed a truly Kafkaesque procedure of trying to prove that while the Fishman family, like many other prewar Jewish families in Czechoslovakia, had been German-speaking, they hardly qualified as Nazi sympathizers. In fact, the Fishmans, who had Zionist sympathies, had declared themselves in 1930 to be of Jewish nationality—a status that the Masaryk government's ethnicity laws allowed.

All of this was to no avail. "We fought in the courts till 1951. But the officials who dealt with the case and the people who'd grabbed our property behaved like wild dogs. The acreage, the farm, the château, even the little forest—it was all divided among eighty-three people who stole it from us, and we received nothing.

The Communist years were hard for the family. Their prewar Prague property was never returned, and while they managed to find another apartment and to get work, as Jews they remained "suspect."

"The revolution in 1989 made us hopeful for many things," says Eliska Fabry. Initial restitution rules made 1948 the earliest confiscation date for clear claims. But a subsequent rule, which concerned restitution for ethnic Germans who had resisted the Nazis, seemed to offer an opening. Fabry and her ninety-year-old husband, a Czech Army veteran, traveled to Jihlava in 1990 to visit the property. "The mayor was quite nice to us," she recalls. But word of their visit spread quickly among the village population. When they reached the local bus stop to return to Prague, they discovered that someone had scribbled *"Juden raus!"*—"Jews Out!"—on the walls.

"After two years, the courts finally said we didn't qualify because Father was a Czech citizen and died as one. This law was for Czechs, like Sudeten Germans, who'd lost citizenship and then regained it. Also, because we'd been in concentration camps, we obviously hadn't been able to register our property claims when my father died in Auschwitz. We appealed to the courts in Prague, and we lost on a technicality—the documents had been a day late."

In despair, Fabry who'd been a fervent supporter of the new Czechoslavakia, wrote to both Czech President Havel and then Premier Klaus. Havel never replied. ("I don't think he ever saw it," Fabry insists in his defense.) But in May of 1994, Klaus personally responded to the eighty-six-year-old Eliska Fishman Fabry, pompously noting that he'd "read between the lines your indignation at the imperfection of our restitution laws." Then Klaus, whose chief of staff, Igor Nemec, once shamelessly compared an American congressional debate on the restitution of Jewish property in Eastern Europe to the image of the Czech Parliament discussing the return of American Indian tribal lands, continued to declare that the aim of Czechoslovakia's restitution law was "not to trace all the nuances and rectification of all the wrongs. The fact is that the Communist regime committed so many crimes that a total amendment of all the wrongs will never be possible."

He then asks her to accept the idea that her fifty-year-old

claim is completely invalid because of a minor technicality and that as a good Czech she should roll over and accept it. "I would like you to accept [my view] as one that reflects the laws of this country. . . . It can certainly happen that an individual citizen's wish will not be granted and they will take it merely as another injustice from their subjective point of view. But this is a regular phenomenon that cannot be eliminated in any society."

In late 1997, Klaus was forced out of office after he was accused of maintaining secret political and personal slush funds, including several in Switzerland. He remains a powerful political figure. Eliska Fishman Fabry, now ninety, still awaits justice.

PART TWO

Slovakia:
The Shops on Main Street

For the good of the Slovak nation and to free it of its pests.
　—FATHER JOZEF TISO, explaining the deportation of his country's
　Jews and the confiscation of their property, August 1942

When Adolf Hitler strutted into Prague Castle on March 18, 1939, world attention was riveted on Czechoslovakia's sad fate. Almost lost in the headlines was other news: the founding only four days before of a Nazi puppet state in the country's eastern half.

Most Slovaks had never asked to join multiethnic Czechoslovakia to begin with. If anything, local nationalists bridled at the idea of Prague's "colonialism," especially when the 1918 founding of the new nation brought droves of wealthier, more educated Czechs to the poorer Slovak regions, where they set up schools, hospitals, and a civil service and controlled the army.

But as Prague-based American journalist Peter S. Green puts

it, "Slovak nationalists had little national identity to work with. Even their language was a recent innovation—the work of a nineteenth-century linguist who unified a dozen disparate dialects."

Thus Hitler's decision to establish an "independent" state in Slovakia was warmly welcomed by Slovak nationalists. With Berlin's approval, a totalitarian regime took immediate control in Bratislava: the Slovak People's Party of Hlinka (known commonly as the Ludaks). Its leader, the radical priest Jozef Tiso, promoted a social order he claimed was based on Catholicism and espoused an ideology of nationalism, anti-communism, and anti-Semitism. His prime minister, Dr. Vojtech Tuka, was even more of an extremist.

Slovakia's Jewish population had shrunk from 135,000 to 89,000 when Ruthenia, with its large Orthodox Jewish community, was ceded to Hungary. Those Jews who remained under Tiso's rule soon found themselves subject to his variations of Hitler's racist rules: the Slovak Codex Judaicus. They were also the special domain of Dieter Wisliceny, an emissary of Adolf Eichmann's, who arrived in Slovakia to act as "adviser for Jewish affairs."

Eager to curry favor with Berlin—and to make profit for his puppet state—Tiso authorized the Ustredny Hospodarsky Urad (Central Economic Office), the UHU, and linked it to his prime ministerial office. Its task was to oust Jews from the Slovak economy and oversee the Aryanization of Jewish property, some of it little more than small shops and farms, but a great deal of it extensive commercial and industrial enterprises.

According to historians Yeshayahu Jelinek and Robert Rozett, "Jewish assets were estimated to be worth more than 3 billion Slovak crowns (approximately $120 million), of which 44 percent was real estate, 23 percent business enterprises, and 33 percent capital. The 'Aryanization' process was accomplished by the UHU within one year; 10,025 Jewish businesses were liquidated and 2,223 transferred to 'Aryan' owners." As in the poignant novel (and later classic film), by Slovak-Jewish author Ladislav Grosman, *The Shop on Main Street,* local "patriots" vied for the right to take over Jewish enterprises.

In addition, house-to-house confiscations of personal property—jewelry, silver, antiques, etc.—were also carried out by Slovak forces, netting millions more. The loot was all carefully registered in the records of the Slovak National Bank.

At first, the Slovak government failed to formally confiscate community property. And as secular-Jewish students were expelled from state schools, the number of Jewish schools actually increased. "We can only guess that they thought once they'd got rid of the Jews, the state would inherit the property," says Fero Alexander, today's leader of Slovakia's Central Union of Jewish Religious Communities.

In 1941, when Slovak troops officially joined the Nazi war effort, the pace of anti-Jewish legislation soared accordingly. Young Jews had already been drafted into forced labor. Now all Jews were banned from many public places, forbidden to congregate, and forced to wear yellow Star of David armbands.

Though it would later claim that it had no idea that the Nazis planned to annihilate Slovak Jews, the Tiso government actively supported the idea of deporting them. At the secret 1942 Wannsee Conference in Berlin, where plans for the Final Solution were approved, participants were told that "Slovak cooperation . . . seemed assured."

But when the Nazis asked for twenty thousand young Jews "to build new Jewish settlements,"[4] the Slovak government panicked, not because it worried about the fate of its Jews, but because it feared being left with only the old and sick. Tiso demanded that the entire Slovak Jewish community be deported—and not return.

The Nazis, sensing a good deal, agreed on condition the

---

[4] One shipment of a thousand Slovak-Jewish women was used by the Nazis to build some of the barracks at Auschwitz-Birkenau.

Slovak government pay a fee of 500 Reichsmark per deported Jew for "vocational retraining." On June 23, 1942, Tiso, drawing on confiscated Jewish assets, paid Berlin some $1.8 million. Between March and October 1942—and over an unusual protest from the Vatican—58,000 Slovak Jews were herded by local ethnic Germans and members of the Hlinka Guards—the Slovak militia named for the late anti-Semitic nationalist leader Father Andrej Hlinka—onto trains and shipped to the Polish border, where German guards then took over for the final destinations: Auschwitz, Majdanek, and the Lublin, Poland, region. Another 15,000 were deported later in the war. Including those Jews who lived in the areas annexed by Hungary, some 130,000 Slovak Jews ultimately perished.[5]

Of the 25,000 to 30,000 who survived and returned, few would remain in Slovakia. "There was an enormous amount of hostility when people came back and asked for their homes and property—both from neighbors and the new government," says Alexander. Indeed, in some cases there were violent attacks on Jews and anti-Semitic demonstrations. Those brave enough to demand their rights ran into bureaucratic nightmares. Just before the war, the family of Martin Rodan, who now lives in Israel, had taken a bank mortgage in order to purchase a house in their hometown of Zilina in northwest Slovakia. The house was "Aryanized" and the Rodans deported with the rest of Zilina's 3,200 Jews. But the new "owners" failed to keep up the mortgage payments. At the war's end, those Rodans who'd survived demanded their home back. But it was soon seized by the bank because the family had

---

[5] In an attempt to stave off the 1942 deportations, a small group of Slovak Jewish activists tried to bribe the Slovak government's adviser on Jewish Affairs, SS officer Dieter Wisliceny. In fact, there was a hiatus in deportations. The group, hoping to expand their scheme and stop all deportations in Nazi-occupied Europe, appealed to Jewish organizations in Switzerland and Turkey to raise funds for what they dubbed "The Europa Plan." The organizations replied that they were unable to receive permission to send such funds to an Axis country. While there is no clear-cut evidence that the SS was ever ready to make such a deal with the Jews, failure to try to fund the plan remains a subject of debate.

not kept up its mortgage payments while they were in the concentration camps.

By 1949, with Slovakia now part of a Soviet-controlled Czechoslovakia, most surviving Slovak Jews had emigrated to the new state of Israel. Those who remained faced the confiscation of much of what little property had been restituted to them. The family of Pavel Frankl, leader of Zilina's tiny Jewish community, which today numbers fewer than a hundred souls, owned a well-known wholesale-textile business on the town's main National Street, whose other shops Frankl says were almost entirely owned by Jews. The textile business was returned to his family in 1946, he says, but after the 1948 Communist putsch, the shop was nationalized; the three-story turn-of-the-century building in which it was located remained in the family name. "The state paid us rent—but only 5 percent of it was to be divided among the five owners. The rest went to 'maintenance.' . . . They kept pressuring us to 'give' the state our building."

Slovak Jews fared no better with communal property. The postwar Czechoslovak Communist regime had repossessed more than 600 Slovak-Jewish communal properties and turned them over to the state. Religious schools became warehouses, and synagogues were transformed into everything from garages to giant storage bins for wheat and other grains. As for the private property of émigré Holocaust survivors, it was often seized by the Communists simply by their classifying the true owners as "Fascists or Nazi collaborators."

Soon after the Communists fell and Slovakia broke from Czechoslovakia, the country's new democratic government entered into negotiations with the World Jewish Congress and its affiliate the World Jewish Restitution Organization (WJRO). Ironically, it was Slovakia, which on its own initiative had once orchestrated the spoliation and ultimate destruction of its Jewish community, that became one of the first nations in Europe to agree in principle to return Jewish-communal property.

Nonetheless, the families of many of those individual Slovak Jews who decided to stick it out and remain in their country after the war are still struggling to recover family belongings. The Frankls are battling to recover a small plot of land that was taken from them. Tomás Lang, fifty-six, who now runs a successful business wholesaling machine tools in southern Slovakia's wheat belt, wants the small hotel in Nove Zamky that his family built and that first the Slovak Nazis and then the Slovak Communists confiscated. He can have it, he's been told, only if he pays taxes that accumulated during the years it was state-owned. "The new democratic government of Slovakia has promised justice," says Lang, "but we're still waiting."

Meanwhile, some Slovaks continue to attempt to rewrite the history of their wartime ignobility. In a 1997 book destined for elementary schools and published by the Education Ministry with funds from the European Union, the Slovak forced-labor camps to which Jews were shipped are described as "companies of an economic nature." Worse yet, in speaking about the deportation of almost 70,000 Slovak Jews, the book's author, a priest and Tiso apologist Milan Durica, insists that the puppet Slovak government decided to ask the Nazis to take along family members of "resettled" young Jews merely as "a charitable means of keeping families together and preventing children from becoming orphans."

"Durica maintains the view that the concentration camps were a paradise. That is simply not the truth," says historian Valentin Bystricky of the Slovak Academy of Sciences. Despite his and other protests, Durica's book is still in distribution in Slovak schools. In Zilina, whose right-wing mayor recently called for the deportation of Gypsies from Slovakia, a new statue of anti-Semitic leader Andrej Hlinka stands in the main square.

4

The Netherlands

Loot Thy Neighbor

Terrible things are happening outside. At any time of night and day, poor helpless people are being dragged out of their homes. They're allowed to take only a knapsack and a little cash, and even then, they're robbed of these possessions on the way.
—ANNE FRANK, January 13, 1943

Like the people who speak it, Dutch is a precise language. There are terms to denote the specific turn of a tulip petal, words for differing depths of winter ice on Holland's canals. The language of the Lowlands may also be the only one in the world with a specific verb for the systematic looting of a house: *pulsen.* It is derived from Abraham Puls & Sons, the name of the notorious Amsterdam moving-van company that Nazi-directed Dutch police employed to pillage and empty the homes of the 140,000 Jews of the Netherlands who were forced into hiding or shipped to their deaths during the Nazi occupation.

No Jewish community in Western Europe suffered more during the Holocaust than the Jews of Holland. Out of a prewar population of 140,000 (including 15,000 refugees from Nazi Austria and Germany), barely 15,000 Dutch Jews survived the four years of Nazi terror. A lucky handful escaped the death camps by fleeing before the invasion. But most of those who survived the war in Holland did so by hiding with the help of a network of brave countrymen who risked their own lives for the sake of others—usually total strangers.

The heroism of Holland's savers is legendary: the anonymous volunteers who waited outside the internment center at Amsterdam's Hollandsche Schouwburg theater to catch children literally tossed over the wall in a frantic last-minute attempt to save them from deportation; the underground railroad of workers, housewives, students, and clergy who passed fugitive Jews from one to the other, then sheltered them in attics, in basements—or in the case of the smallest children, raised them as their own; the brave souls like the gentle Miep Gies who at enormous risk to herself and her own kin helped hide three Jewish families, among them a young girl named Anne Frank.

But Holland's Anne Franks were few in number, and even the twelve-year-old diarist whose notebooks came to symbolize the Holocaust ultimately was betrayed by a Dutchman. For every Dutch Jew saved, ten others were shipped to their deaths for lack of neighbors willing to help—or for the abundance of those eager to collaborate and collect the seven-guilder reward the Germans offered per hidden Jew. Other Dutchmen and -women took their rewards from the Nazis in kind. Within hours of their arrest on August 4, 1944, the hiding place of Anne Frank and her family was ransacked and looted—some say by her Dutch neighbors, others by the Dutch-owned, Nazi-hired Puls moving company.

"This country took care of very few Anne Franks," says Dutch economist Victor Halberstadt, himself a hidden child during three years of the war. "The government did not protect us during the war. And when those of us who survived came back, the government was not particularly interested in us."

For the Jews of Holland, the Holocaust—and widespread Dutch inaction in response to it—was a brutal awakening. For centuries, the Netherlands had been the New Jerusalem, the European continent's only truly safe haven for Jews. While Spain and Portugal enthusiastically burned Jewish "heretics" at the stake, the State of Orange cautiously opened its gates to them. By the sixteenth century, Holland had become one of the rare nations in Europe to allow the sons and daughters of Israel to thrive and live in peace within its borders. The first to come were Marranos from Spain and Portugal, Sephardic conversos suddenly able to return to the faith of their fathers in Holland. Groups of Jews from Germany and Eastern Europe soon followed. Six months after the Batavian Republic was established in 1795, Jews were among those granted civil rights. "Until World War II," says Dutch-communal leader Henri Markens, the rector of its most prestigious Jewish school, the Maimonides Lyceum, "Holland was the only country in Continental Europe that had never forced its Jews to live in ghettos."

So free and liberal was the atmosphere in Holland that its Jews became an accepted part of the landscape, thriving religiously, financially, and culturally and living in a climate that produced Baruch Spinoza and inspired Rembrandt to use the elders of the Jewish community as the models for his biblical paintings. Artifacts at the Jewish Historical Museum in Amsterdam attest to the richness of life they enjoyed: a playful painting of a family of eighteenth-century Sephardic grandees, a tulip-decorated silver Hanukkah menorah, a delicate Torah crown of inlaid gold from Utrecht, and volume after volume of learned works.

By the nineteenth century, Dutch Jews held political positions and were numbered among Holland's bankers and industrialists as well as its farmers and proletariat.

The Nazi invasion on the night of May 10, 1940, changed all that. Holland, which had remained neutral in World War I and hoped to do so again, capitulated to Hitler's surprise attack within five days. Eventually the Führer planned to incorporate the Netherlands into his pan-Germanic Reich, much as he had done with Austria. With that in mind (and Queen Wilhelmina in exile), Hitler ordered that a civil rather than a military government be established in the newly conquered Netherlands—but under SS auspices. To maintain order, he appointed one of his most trusted lieutenants, Austrian Nazi leader Arthur Seyss-Inquart. On May 19, 1940, Seyss-Inquart became the Netherlands' Reichskommissar with five commissioner-generals under him. Ominously enough, a branch office of IV B 4, Adolf Eichmann's section in the Reich's Security Main Office, was immediately attached to the Amsterdam-based Nazi police apparatus. A Dutch administrative council was appointed by the Nazis to work in tandem with them. There was no problem finding members.

Most historians believe that the Nazis had hoped to gain broad popular Dutch support for their pan-Germanic plans. Eager, therefore, not to alarm the Dutch population, Seyss-Inquart waited until September 1940 to declare the first harsh legislation separating Dutch Jews from their Christian countrymen. At that point, Jews were systematically removed, then totally banned from holding any public office. Among the first to be ousted, Lodewijk Ernst Visser, president of the Dutch Supreme Court, who would eventually become chairman of the newly formed Joodse Coördinatie Commissie, the Jewish Coordination Committee that ironically joined Holland's Ashkenazic, Sephardic, and Liberal communities together for the first time in the community's long history.

The Germans and their growing number of Dutch collaborators soon pulled out all stops. By the autumn of 1940, Holland's non-Jewish government employees had all been ordered to sign "Aryan declarations," sworn statements that no Jewish blood ran in their veins. Those who refused to do so were presumed Jews under the same criteria as the Nuremberg racial laws of 1935 and summarily expelled from the Dutch civil service.

Other Aryanization measures soon followed. On October 22, 1940, decree #VO189/40 ordered the immediate registration of all Jewish enterprises as well as that of any other businesses in which Dutch Jews held large shares. The administration of some 20,960 Jewish enterprises was turned over to a Nazi "Commissariat General for Finance and Economy."

Desperate to maintain as much of their family possessions as possible, many Dutch Jews turned over assets to Christian neighbors, business partners, and lawyers for safekeeping. The safekeepers soon won the Dutch slang sobriquet *bewariërs,* or "Aryan guards." "There was an unwritten understanding that [the property] would be returned after the war," says Dutch historian Gerard Aalders, a premier researcher of the period. "However, the fact is, much of the property was never returned, and the Jewish owners, if they survived, were unable to do anything if they could not prove ownership."

Dutch Holocaust survivor Yohanan Heimans, who now lives in Israel, puts it more bluntly: "The property we left with the guardians was so well protected that they didn't return it to us."

Under decree #VO189/40, January of 1941 was the deadline for all Dutch Jews to register as either full Jews, half Jews, or quarter Jews. A total of 159,806 persons registered, according to Dutch-Jewish historian Jozeph Michman. Of these, 140,245 were "full Jews." The remaining 19,561 were *halfbloeden,* the children of mixed marriages.

To the Jews of Holland who shared the pedantic sense of orderliness of their Dutch-Christian neighbors, the Germans' rules were to be obeyed, no matter how odious. "The typical Dutch Jew was traditional, little inclined to fanaticism, emancipated yet keeping largely to his own kind. Above all, he was a loyal subject of the Dutch state," explains Socialist parliamentarian Judith C. E. Belinfante, a historian and the former directoress of Amsterdam's wonderful Jewish Historical Museum. Yet, tragically, it was this very sense of a "protected situation," insists Belinfante, that caused the "Jews of Holland to [tend] to be trusting of their government." It was that trust that "blinded them to the real meaning of the restrictive measures now enacted by the Germans."

Not all Jews remained complacent. Young activists organized resistance within the Jewish quarter, and in February of 1941, non-Jewish workers staged a nationwide strike to protest Nazi brutality—especially in regard to Jews.

A furious Seyss-Inquart ordered the establishment of the Nazi-controlled Joodsche Raad—"Jewish Council"—and on March 12 declared that Jews were not part of the Dutch people. The latter, he said, would have a clear choice: sympathy for the Jews or collaboration with the Germans.

In the summer of 1941, as in Austria in 1938, Jews were barred from public places—from transport, parks, swimming pools, theaters, and museums—in effect, from any contact with their gentile countrymen. Jewish children were barred from Dutch schools.

These isolating restrictions coincided with the first in a long series of heavy-handed confiscations of Jewish property. The first pack of vultures to descend on the Netherlands was the Einsatzstab Reichsleiter Rosenberg—the Rosenberg Special Operations Staff, named for Nazi Party ideological chief Alfred Rosenberg, to whom the Führer had given a free hand to steal whatever he deemed necessary to promote the Nazi cause. In the Netherlands, this began with choice Jewish libraries, both public and private. Among the prizes plundered: the famed Rosenthal Collection of precious books.

As they would elsewhere, especially in France, the Nazis soon turned their attention to art and the noteworthy collections belonging to wealthier members of the Dutch-Jewish community. Hermann Göring himself made more than one trip to Amsterdam to visit the best dealers and collections and make his choices. Some of the art was legally purchased, if under duress and/or at bargain prices. But other works were simply confiscated, packed, and transported to Germany.

Later, Rosenberg's gang turned its attention to more mundane but no less lucrative prey: the household furniture and other belongings of Jews deported to the death camps. Dubbed "Aktion M" (for Möbel or furniture), it was an operation of staggering proportions. No sooner had a family been arrested and deported than one of a fleet of German-made trucks belonging to the Amsterdam-based Puls moving company would arrive and empty the apartment—that is, says one Dutch Holocaust survivor, "if neighbors hadn't gotten there first." According to Michman, "in a single year, 17,235 apartments were emptied of their contents, and loads totaling 16,941,249 cubic feet [479,725 cubic meters] were crated and sent to Germany or to Eastern Europe to be divided among the ethnic German population being settled there.

First, says Hague-born period scholar and Holocaust survivor Isaac Lipchits, "they took away our radios, then our bikes, our cars, our savings, our art, our furniture. Before we were deported, they even took our backpacks and wedding rings. And at Auschwitz they finally took the gold from our teeth. It was a demonic system."

To organize and centralize this massive plunder, the Nazis established a highly specialized banking institution with main offices near the Amstel River just around the corner from the elegant Amstel Hotel. To "reassure" the Jews, they cynically named the depository "The Lippmann-Rosenthal & Co. Bank," the same name as that of a midsize, prewar Dutch-Jewish bank of impeccable reputation. In point of fact, the four-story redbrick building at 13 Sarphatistraat—which soon came to be popularly known as "Liro"—no longer had anything to do with the original bank or its Jewish founders. It had been seized from its Jewish owners in 1940 and given to a Nazi sympathizer as a prize for his loyalties to the Reich. "Had the two fine gentlemen who founded Lippmann-

Rosenthal known what their bank came to be used for," says Lipchits, "they would still be spinning in their graves."

To start the financial ball rolling, the Nazis first ordered all other Dutch banks to immediately transfer "known Jewish accounts" to the Liro. They followed in August 1941 by issuing *Verordnung* (Decree) 148/41, which blocked all Jewish-owned bank accounts and instructed all Dutch Jews not only to transfer their accounts and securities from other Dutch banks to the Liro but to deposit all cash holdings and checks of more than 1,000 guilders as well. The massive proceeds thus assembled were then to be turned over to the Vermoogensverwaltungs-und Rentenanstalt (Office of Property Administration and Pensions). It was this central German institute that administered the Liro's loot.

Jews were subsequently ordered to turn in gold and silver, jewelry, bonds, and insurance policies. Again Lippmann-Rosenthal was the central repository. By this time, the Nazis' Amsterdam bank was staffed with more than eighty Dutch employees, all drawn from respectable Dutch banks and other Netherlands financial institutions.

At first Jewish depositors were told they'd be allowed to withdraw up to 250 guilders per month per family of their own money from their Liro accounts. But this Nazi magnanimity soon ended. The Liro, says Lipchits, "became a bank where you could deposit but not withdraw."

On April 29, 1942, the Jewish Council was advised that as of May 1, all Dutch Jews over the age of six would would have to wear the yellow *Jodenster* on their clothing, a move that was intended not only to isolate and further humiliate them but to make it harder for them to hide. A shipment of 570,000 stars was distributed across the Netherlands.[1]

---

[1] For years it was presumed the *Jodensterren* had been printed in Poland's Lodz Ghetto. In fact, researcher Daniel Swetschinski recently discovered, they had been secretly prepared in advance in the Netherlands, at De Nijverheid, a small textile factory expropriated from Dutch Jews.

Roundups of Jewish "volunteer workers" began to be part of an almost daily pattern—first to camps within the Netherlands and then to Eastern work camps, the Nazi euphemism for death camps. Anne Frank described what she saw happening from her attic window: "Night after night, green and gray military vehicles cruise the streets. . . . They often go around with lists, knocking only on those doors where they know there's a big haul to be made."

For Dutch Jews, the Holocaust had begun in earnest.

The coffers at the Liro grew heavier each day. By the end of its first year, some 6,540 depositors had established 7,458 accounts totaling 25 million guilders (about $130 million in today's equivalent). It was far less cash than the Reichsbank had expected. But the shortfall was made up by the forced deposit of stocks and other securities. By the end of 1942, Lippmann-Rosenthal had soaked up Jewish-owned securities nominally valued at 213 million guilders—about $1 billion today.

Cash, stocks, and bullion constituted only a part of the booty. In the spring of 1942, another decree (VO58/42) ordered Dutch Jews to deliver anything they had of value—jewels, bonds, gold coins, stamp collections, antiques, paintings, etc. The items, they were told by the bank's Dutch staff, would be placed in "storage" in the safety-deposit vaults of Lippmann-Rosenthal Bank. Deposit stations were set up across Amsterdam as well as in Rotterdam and the Hague. Long lines of obliging Dutch Jews tramped through the streets to stand before the redbrick Liro headquarters, their family treasures clutched in their arms. After Lippmann-Rosenthal's clerks efficiently relieved them of their parcels, they then carefully issued worthless receipts.

Each painting, each piece of jewelry taken from the Jews was painstakingly itemized on catalog cards that also noted the object's value. The cards would eventually also carry the names of those to whom the plundered items were sold or transferred by the Liro.

Even real property became part of the Liro booty. Some 19,000 Jewish-owned buildings, with a value of 200 million guilders, were confiscated by the Nazis and their Dutch helpers between 1940 and 1943. Moreover, says Lipchits, "Once turned over to Liro, a Jewish-owned house would be mortgaged to the hilt and the money given to Liro, which of course then turned it over to the Germans." In this way alone, the Germans "raised" another 26 million guilders for their war effort.

Liquidated Jewish-owned businesses and real estate were then placed under *Verwaltung*—administration—or sold for bargain prices to "friendly" third parties, some of them German, many of them Dutch. The Jews had nothing to worry about, the Germans solemnly proclaimed through their Dutch puppets. The received purchase price, the Germans announced with a straight face, would be paid to former Jewish owners in twenty-five yearly installments. In point of fact, most of the owners were soon deported and no payments were ever made to anyone, nor had they been intended.

While property and businesses were distributed to a wide variety of people and organizations within the Netherlands and to Germany, most of the tons of gold and silver that the Liro confiscated was sold at preferential prices to the Deutsche Gold- und Silberscheideanstalt (DEGUSSA), a German smelting and precious-metals firm that exists to this day. However, exact records and invoices of the wartime Dutch gold sales were either lost, never kept, or more likely destroyed when it became clear in 1944 that the Nazis and their helpers were losing the war.

The Germans and their Dutch collaborators had little trouble disposing of looted stocks and other securities. They went on sale in 1942 on direct orders of Seyss-Inquart. And despite warnings broadcast over the Dutch government-in-exile's London-based Radio Oranje that anyone buying stolen property could be held criminally responsible, the Beurs, Amsterdam's stock exchange, was filled with eager bidders and buyers. Indeed, the Nazis and their collaborators found an easy answer to charges that they were fencing. Securities, they said, would be sold with special (and largely fictional) declarations that they were "bona fide"—in other words, that they had been "voluntarily" sold by their previous, and in most cases, Jewish owners. With time, the Nazis didn't even bother issuing what some Dutch Jews now refer to sarcastically as "phony kosher certificates." Nor did Dutch buyers ask for them.

The Beurs did a thriving business selling Liro's offerings of Jewish stocks. "To obtain a parcel of paper for a client," writes historian Raul Hilberg, "the interested bank had only to request an official in the Kommissariat to direct Liro to free the securities for sale."

Dutch banks participated in the trading, but it was the German Handelstrust West (a subsidiary of the Dresdener Bank) that did the lion's share of business.

Given the large quantities put on the market, most of the looted securities were sold at prices well below their actual value. "It was a buying spree," says one Amsterdam stockbroker. "The stolen stocks went like fresh herrings on a sunny day."

Most Dutch buyers would later claim that they hadn't known that the confiscated stocks had been stolen or extorted from their Jewish co-citizens. But Gerard Aalders, of the Nederlands Instituut voor Oorlogsdocumentatie (NIOD)—the Netherlands Institute for War Documentation—and other experts say that such denials were hardly credible. "It was well known," says Aalders, "that any stock offerings from Liro were 'tainted.' "

In the immediate aftermath of the war, many Amsterdam stockbrokers would try to claim that it was one of their colleagues, Otto Rebholz, a German who'd acquired Dutch citizenship in 1932, who was "the worst collaborator among the collaborating stockbrokers." But Aalders and other experts believe that the German-born Rebholz was singled out as a scapegoat for the sins of other stockbrokers who, while possibly not operating on the same scale as Rebholz, nonetheless grew wealthy on the sale and transfer of stocks stolen from Jews.

Stolen Dutch stocks were also sold on the exchanges of many of Europe's neutral countries. And it is clear that it was Rebholz's

Rebholz Bankierskantoor that handled the bulk of these foreign sales. Rebholz was also given responsibility for the conversion of foreign stocks into cash, especially Swiss and Portuguese stocks, whose disposal offered the Reich the possibility to acquire usable and badly needed neutral currency. As elsewhere in occupied Europe, it was that foreign exchange that helped greatly to defray the cost of the raw materials and goods the Reich required for its continued war effort, particularly the minerals and other goods it imported from Portugal.

At the suggestion of Adolf Buhler, the German commissioner appointed to run the Nederlandsche Bank (Central Bank of the Netherlands), Rebholz actually set up shop in Switzerland in early spring 1942 and began to unload stolen stocks there. He found a willing market.

The neutral Alpine nation was already a beehive of espionage and counterespionage. And word of Rebholz's shady Swiss operations quickly reached the British and American embassies. Both warned Swiss banks they would be placed on an Allied "blacklist" if they continued dealing with Rebholz. Some complied; others found ways to camouflage the sales, or did them via willing bankers in Liechtenstein. Another part of the stolen Dutch-Jewish stocks were traded in Spain. The profits from all these millions in sales, says Aalders, were put at the disposal of those Reich agencies and war industries that had special need for foreign currency.

In September 1944, with the Allies in advance, Buhler had the balance of unsold foreign stocks shipped to Berlin—about 12 million guilders' worth, according to Aalders. Some were sold; the rest, Aalders surmises, were probably taken by the Soviets when they captured Berlin less than a year later.

According to researchers, a total of 350 million guilders in stocks expropriated from Jews were sold in the Netherlands by Liro. At least 100 million guilders of that amount were used by the Nazis to pay off outstanding debts of the stockholders (to non-Jews, of course) and for the "maintenance" of the now captive and impoverished Jewish population of Holland. At least 25 million guilders of the stock money, says Aalders, was allocated to pay for the construction and operation of the concentration and transit camps at Westerbork and Vught, where Dutch Jews were held prior to their shipment to Auschwitz and other death camps. The Liro itself skimmed from the profits to pay its administrative costs.

Liro's mechanisms were as malevolent as they were relentless. Like some evil sorcerer's apprentices, its clerks even followed Jews on their final road to extermination. A team of Liro officials was assigned to the bleak Westerbork internment camp. There the Liro clerks established a campsite office in a frantic attempt to collect whatever anyone had failed to turn in—even wedding rings. Survivors recount that Liro officials would try to convince arrested Jews that depositing their last valuables with Liro was the "safest" thing they could do before they left for "the work camps in the East." When that argument failed to convince people to part with a precious family heirloom or keepsake, they were cajoled or threatened. Many were simply told their knapsacks were too big for the train trip: "You won't need that much clothing in the Eastern work camps." It might have been the only truth the Liro clerks uttered.

Some of the Liro clerks used their work there to protect their own families. "My mother was Jewish," says famed Dutch writer Harry Mulisch, whose Christian father was among the Liro's senior employees. "His work at Liro saved her life." But for most of the Dutch employees of Liro, it was just a job. A period photo, now in the collection of the Netherlands Institute for War Documentation in Amsterdam, shows a team of Westerbork Liro clerks in shirts and ties sitting around playing cards to while away the time between departures of the death-camp trains.

By the end of 1942, the monthly withdrawal allowances from Liro that many Jews used to survive had been completely halted. In any case, as per the German master plan, the Nazi noose had tightened, and there were simply fewer and fewer Jews to make withdrawals. "Labor camps" in the Netherlands had been opened as early as 1941 for "unemployed" Jews who, according to Dutch authorities, would be sent there to be "employed by the Dutch police." At the beginning of 1942, the Nazis began centralizing Jews in a ghettolike area they established in Amsterdam as well as in a new camp near Vught in the south of Holland. Stateless Jews—and those who'd failed to observe the Nazis' strict rules—were shipped directly to Westerbork.

By 1943, the Nazis had begun wholesale roundups. Rewards were offered for information leading to the arrest of Jews in hiding, and the Germans together with units of Dutch collaborators carried out "Jew hunts" through the narrow, canaled streets of Amsterdam, in The Hague, in Rotterdam, and into the most obscure villages of the Netherlands.[2] Jews were dragged from attics and basements, or simply picked up on the street when they dared venture forth in a search for food.

For months on end, entire families were shipped first to Westerbork, then crammed into trains for the horrific trip to Sobibor and Auschwitz. At Auschwitz, many of the deported Dutchwomen became special prey for the medical savagery of Dr. Josef Mengele and his team of "experimenters."

Even in cases where wealthy Jews managed to bribe officials to delay their deportations, it was only a question of time. Eventually, with but rare exceptions, all Dutch Jews were destined for deportation. The most the wealthier and best-connected could hope for was to be shipped to Theresienstadt, the Czech town near Prague, where the Nazis maintained their so-called model Jewish city—a cruel hoax that in effect was actually a ghetto and transfer camp for Auschwitz and the gas chambers.

"The removal of entire families," wrote Michman, "left no

---

[2] Two groups of Dutch collaborators were particularly active in rounding up Jews: the Groene Politie—or Green Police, so named for the color of their uniforms—and the Vrijwillige Hulp-Politie—the Volunteer Auxiliary Police—a body formed in May 1942 with a subdivision that specialized in ferreting out hidden Jews.

doubt that the term 'employed by the police' was no more than an effort to camouflage what was really the [total] deportation of Dutch Jewry."

There were some protests about the mass arrests and forced deportations of the Jews, notably from the Dutch Catholic Church. But next to nothing was heard from either the Dutch government-in-exile or from Queen Wilhelmina herself. Certainly there was never any definitive call for her subjects to help their Jewish countrymen. Worse yet, as elsewhere in Europe, the German plot to exterminate—and plunder—Dutch Jewry was, as Michman later wrote, "facilitated by the willingness of Dutch agencies to cooperate." Specifically, Dutch municipal administrations, railway workers, and the collaborating Dutch police.

Clearly aware that most of their clientele would never return from the destinations to which they had been deported, Liro quietly canceled all private accounts and consolidated all the deposits it had into one central "Jewish account."

The Liro also continued a process it had begun in 1942: cashing in Jewish-owned life-insurance policies. Local companies willingly obliged. The take was sizable. Though most of the Dutch-Jewish population was far from wealthy and most rented, not owned, their homes, "every poor Jew," says Lipchits, "had some sort of insurance policy."

Just how much cash and gold ended up in the Liro coffers as the result of the plundering of the Dutch-Jewish community? The most extensive postwar studies of this nagging question were carried out first by A. J. Van Schie, an official of the Netherlands National Archives and more recently by historian Gerard Aalders from the NIOD department of research. Both academics—and neither of them Jews—reached similar conclusions. Van Schie's figures, which he first presented in a paper delivered at a conference on Dutch-Jewish history held in 1984 at Tel Aviv University, were based on Dutch government statistics and records. "I estimate," Van Schie told the Tel Aviv assembly, "that the Jewish section of the population as a whole was deprived of about 650 to 700 million guilders, judged by the sales figures during the occupation." He added, "On the basis of the replacement value after liberation in 1945, this amount must have been considerably higher."

Aalders's figures varied only slightly from Van Schie's. "During the years 1940–45," wrote Aalders in a report on the plundering of Jewish assets, "the Jewish community in Holland was robbed of approximately 700 million guilders. Around half of this total (350 million guilders) consisted of securities of which about 250 million guilders was eventually traded."

To convert these sums into current values, Aalders used the basic ten-times formula (1 1945 DG = 10 1998 DG). Accordingly, the 110,000 Jews of Holland had been robbed of a monumental 7 billion guilders—or $3.5 billion. A 1946 American intelligence document described the Nazi plunder operation in the Netherlands as the "most ruthless large-scale robbery modern Holland had ever seen."

As Lipchits points out, while much of that capital was transferred to Germany, large amounts remained in Holland and were drained from the Liro to finance the train-transport costs for the 100,000 Dutch Jews the Nazis and their helpers shipped to their deaths. Lippmann-Rosenthal was also the owner of record of the transit-cum-concentration camps at Westerbork and Vught in south Holland. More than 26 million guilders were "appropriated" for the running costs of the two camps. After the war, the Dutch government transformed the two camps into internment centers for captured Germans and Dutch collaborators and paid Liro a coincidentally macabre figure of 6 million guilders. That notwithstanding, "in spite of moral and political pressure," wrote Van Schie, the Dutch government persisted in its refusal to compensate Liro for the other 20 million guilders that the Nazis had stolen to pay for the wartime camps. Once again, the Jews had paid for their own deportation.

By the end of the war, more than 90 percent of Dutch Jewry

had perished. The remnant of 15,000 Dutch Jews who'd successfully hidden from the Nazi net—or managed to survive the savagery of the concentration camps—began to return home ill at heart and in body. Most found little to return to—and little official succor. During five years of occupation, the Nazis had drained the Netherlands, and during the last harsh winter of the war, the Dutch population had been reduced to chopping up furniture for firewood to heat their houses and in more than a few instances to eating tulip bulbs to forestall starvation. Moreover, during the battle for liberation, Holland had been among the heaviest-hit nations in Europe. German artillery and Allied bombings had destroyed much of what remained of the nation's industry, ports, and infrastructure.

To the leaders of the financially bereft and economically hobbled Netherlands, its surviving Jews were of no special interest. They were received with ambivalence, often open coolness. Officially, this noninterest reflected democratic Dutch policy. "We will not be like the Nazis," said a proud government-in-exile official even before the war ended. "We will not differentiate between our Jewish and non-Jewish citizens."

Indeed, that "no special treatment" concept became official policy even while the Dutch government was still working out of its London exile base. But whether the hands-off policy was an honest expression of Dutch egalitarianism or merely the expression of a polite form of anti-Semitism, its practical result was a reverse discrimination that would scar Holland's already heavily wounded survivors. "Our government did not treat us especially well before the war, did not protect us during the war, and did little to help us after the war," says Dutch-Jewish banker Joop Krant.

In fact, Dutch Jews, who had suffered far more than any other of Queen Wilhelmina's subjects, were given no special considerations, no government rehabilitation services geared to handle their specific needs. The handful of Jews returning from Auschwitz and Bergen-Belsen or from Westerbork transit camp found no government-welfare committees to greet them at Amsterdam's Central Station—with the exception of some limited assistance from the American Joint Distribution Committee. "You got off the train and basically you were on your own," says Lipchits. "Survivors did not receive special rights; you were equal before the bureaucracy and its taxes." As Victor Halberstadt puts it, "I remember no welcome-home banners."

Most other Dutch survivors of Nazi labor and concentration camps returned to prewar homes and families and were quickly able to pick up the pieces of their lives. True, there had been widespread suffering and losses. But in most instances there were families waiting for them, jobs ready. It was a far cry from the situation of most of the surviving Jews who found themselves starting from scratch, often with as many as fifty or a hundred relatives now dead. "We were homeless, furnitureless, clothesless, and moneyless," says Halberstadt.

Worse yet, some of Amsterdam's press was openly anti-Semitic. "They were hard times, and right-wingers made it clear that we Jews had no special rights. If anything," says Lipchits, "they told us we were lucky to be alive at all—and to be in the Netherlands."

It did not make the task of trying to regain stolen assets any easier. Nor was that the first concern of most survivors. "What you really wanted to know was who else had survived," says Lipchits. "Were you totally alone. So you searched lists and went to the railroad station, you looked, and more often than not you did not find anyone."

To add to the tragedy, some Dutch Jews who sought to claim children of relatives who'd been hidden by Christians found that some foster families refused to return them. The result was a series of bitter court cases over "what was best for the children."

In this atmosphere, when restitution did begin, the process was slow and racked with bureaucracy. For those Dutch Jews who had direct claims against the Liro, it was a particularly painful procedure. Many of the people dealing with their claims proved to be the very same Liro employees who had dutifully helped confiscate their assets.

Other Dutch Jews found their homes occupied by strangers—or even former neighbors. And those who had turned over belongings to "Aryan guards" found that it had been easier to entrust them than to collect them. "My father and his non-Jewish partner owned a successful men's-clothing factory in northern Holland," recalls Shimon Cohen, sixty-six. "So before we went into hiding, Father turned his share of the factory over to him. We were lucky; we survived the war. But when we returned alive to Amsterdam, it was as if the partner didn't know who we were."

The elder Cohen went to court and eventually won back his share of the business. Nonetheless, says Cohen, now an oil engineer living in Houston, "the aggravation and the disappointment were too much for my father, and he died in 1951."

Other Jews returned to find that their property had been looted and their shops and businesses emptied of their stock and machinery. "My father's butcher shop was emptied of everything—all his equipment, everything. It was his competitors," says Cohen's wife, Fina.

The late Dutch sociologist and writer Gerald Durlacher, the only survivor of his entire family, returned to the family's prewar home in Arnhem to find strangers living in it. Embarrassed and bewildered, Durlacher later reported, he knocked on a former neighbor's door and asked if he knew what had happened to his family's belongings. "I know nothing," said the neighbor, whom Durlacher quickly noticed was now wearing a suit of clothing that had once belonged to his father.

In some cases, non-Jewish neighbors and friends proved honorable. Veteran Dutch-Jewish journalist Henriette Boas recalls with Dutch pride that most of a large collection of rare books belonging to her father, a renowned classics scholar, as well as a portrait of him that now hangs on the wall of her archive-crowded Amsterdam apartment, had been carefully hidden by her father's friends and colleagues at the University library—and quickly returned by them after the war. "We did less well with our house. Before the war, most Dutch Jews rented their homes and apartments, but we owned ours. In 1942, just before she was shipped to Theresienstadt, my mother 'sold' it for a symbolic amount to a close friend and neighbor in order to prevent it from being taken by the Germans. When we returned after the war," says Boas, now eighty-five, "the woman claimed that since real-estate prices had soared, she now wanted much more money before she'd 'sell it back' to my mother. We had no money at all, so we lost our home.

"I was angry," adds Boas, "but in a way grateful that we did not have to return to our old home. None of our Jewish neighbors had survived; it would have been too painful to move back in."

Not everyone responded with open anger. Victor Halberstadt, hidden as a child by Dutch-Catholic miners and today one of Holland's leading economic analysts as well as chairman of Europe's prestigious Bilderberg Conference, recalls being reunited with his father, who had also survived in hiding.

Returning to Amsterdam, Halberstadt and his father set out for their old apartment in southern Amsterdam's prewar Jewish quarter. "There was a Dutch family living there with a son who was about my age. We could see they were in our house, and they sat on our furniture and they ate from our plates."

Halberstadt doesn't remember whether his father even knocked on the door. "Basically my father turned his back and walked away. I'm sure he was angry, but he had other things on his mind—searching for any other surviving relations, starting to build a new life."

It was not easy. As with many other small entrepreneurs, Louis Halberstadt's prewar jute business had disappeared. "His clients were gone, his stock was gone, he had no money—just debts. The only things we got back from before the war were a few silver spoons and forks which had been buried in the garden of some acquaintances. We dug them up, and I still have them. Otherwise nothing was left—no trinkets, no jewelry, not even photos. Not that we had much; I come from a long line of relatively poor people."

The Dutch authorities displayed little sympathy for these problems and made scant if any effort to force looters to return stolen property. To this day, some Dutch officials dismiss it in terms of the harsh realities of the war years. "The Jews were away," says one member of one of the government commissions currently reinvestigating the war's aftermath. "People had no homes. They took over the homes of Jews. The Jews return and want their houses and apartments back. [But] seven or eight families are living there. Naturally there was a conflict."

Nor was there much in the way of rapid settlement or restitution. "After the war, it was possible to receive compensation for property taken by the Germans," recounts Wilma Stein, former head of Amsterdam's Jewish Welfare Association, "but the compensation was somewhat limited, generally only half of the value of the property. The claimant had to prove what exactly was in his home, and whoever was unable to do so received a minimal payment: enough to purchase a table, four chairs, a bed, and so on."

According to testimony from Stein, one Auschwitz survivor told of asking for the return of the Amsterdam apartment where his family, of which he was the only survivor, had lived before their deportation. "After a dispute with the bureaucracy, he received permission to enter the home. He received the apartment without gas or electricity—but with a bill for three years of unpaid consumption left behind by the previous lodgers. He went to the Town Hall, threw the bills on the table, and demanded that they furnish him with gas, saying, 'I didn't give you a gas account for the murder of my family!' The clerks called the police, who threw him out."

Historian Michman insists that even when there were clear

records, "a determined struggle had to be waged by the Jews to gain recognition of their claims to the property that had been stolen from them." This proved especially true with money that had been taken by the Liro. At first the government proposed reimbursing surviving holders of Liro accounts at a rate of 70 percent of whatever was found in the bank's coffers at the war's end. There was a public outcry and a vehement denunciation of this short-changing of the Dutch Jews. Eventually the government relented, finally agreeing to refund at 90 percent. "But," points out Lipchits with a sardonic smile, "it was 90 percent of what was *left* in the Liro accounts—not 90 percent of what had been taken from the Jewish depositors!"

By the end of 1949, Dutch auditors had compiled a list of some 70,000 Liro accounts. (It was not a complete list; some records had been destroyed by German officials and Liro employees when it became clear the Nazis were losing the war.) There were applicants for the return of only 23,000 accounts; all the other Liro depositors and their immediate heirs had apparently perished in the Holocaust.

Victims whose property and belongings had been stolen faced particular difficulties. According to Van Schie, even when the Committee for Property Return determined that property "sales" had been coerced, ownership was not automatically restored to claimants. This was especially true in cases where third parties claimed they had made a "bona fide," good-faith purchase of purloined objects, land, and buildings.

The same held true for the enormous wealth of stolen stocks and securities that had flooded the Amsterdam stock exchange in 1942. Initially the postwar Dutch government ruled that in order to receive compensation from the first rank of stock and bond purchasers, claimants would have to prove that purchasers had known they were buying stolen goods, a difficult task at best. When the Dutch Supreme Court overruled that decision, the otherwise staid Dutch Beurs responded first with outrage, then with panic, and went out on strike—the only time that had ever happened in its history.

Fearing major bankruptcies of stockbroking houses and/or of those firms and individuals who'd illegally purchased stolen stocks, the Dutch government eventually agreed to take the pressure off the Beurs (and the illegal stockholders) and in 1953 began to compensate the original Jewish owners of the stocks with a government payment of 90 percent original worth. The only condition: Ownership claims would be abandoned.

It worked out well for everyone except the Jews. Van Schie has estimated that while the claimants were paid 41 million guilders (about $150 million today), the stolen securities were valued at 8.5 times that amount in 1953. Furthermore, any securities that had been neither sold nor claimed after the war were simply absorbed into the Dutch state treasury, as were other heirless Jewish properties.

Some voices in the Jewish community objected that the arrangement was less than equitable. Besides, they said, heirless property should benefit the remnant community, not the government that failed to protect its Jewish citizens. Nonetheless, the governing boards of Dutch Jews meekly went along with the government's proposals, then remained silent. "It was the end of the war," recalled the late notary public Jacob Van Hasselt, who had been involved in postwar discussions with the government as part of a delegation of Dutch-Jewish survivors. "Most people thought it was better not to make waves."

In 1985, a new, bolder generation of Jewish community leaders screwed up enough courage to ask the government to reopen the issue and transfer to the community another 4.5 million guilders of heirless property, only part of the treasure. "They arrived at the figure this way," says historian Lipchits, wetting his index finger and raising it to the wind. The Dutch government, not pleased at this turn of events, responded as though it were bargaining in a prewar Amsterdam street market; it countered with an offer of less than half: 2 million guilders. They subsequently added an additional 100,000 guilders "to make it easily divisible by three." The Dutch-Jewish Community Council agreed to the offer. One third of the funds was divided among the various Jewish communities throughout Holland, one third went to Holland's Jewish Welfare Association, and the final third went to Amsterdam's Joods Historisch Museum—the Jewish Historical Museum—then planning to build an impressive new building on the site of three old and unused Amsterdam synagogues.

After that, the issue of heirless Jewish property dropped out of sight, save for scattered requests from individuals. The 1996 opening of investigations into the fate of Holocaust assets in Switzerland triggered new interest in the Netherlands, and several of the younger and more prominent members of the Dutch-Jewish community, such as economist Victor Halberstadt, now an adviser to Queen Beatrix, and Tom de Swaan, managing director of the Dutch Central Bank, urged the Dutch government to launch its own investigations before there was a public outcry to do so.

If the Dutch government needed any more incentive, it arrived when documents came to light indicating that in 1968, a group of Dutch finance-ministry employees charged with the custodial care of unclaimed Nazi spoils had auctioned off—among themselves and at sweetheart prices—jewelry belonging to Dutch Jews who'd never returned. Then, in 1997, an Amsterdam resident discovered a cache of long-hidden Liro file cards in an upper floor of a house on the Keizersgracht Canal. The building, it transpired, had been used in postwar years as an archival storage room for the Ministry of Finance. The finder went to both the Ministry of Finance and the nearby War Documentation Center with his find. But officials seemed uninterested in his discovery. Frustrated, he contacted two young journalists at the freewheeling Dutch weekly the *Groene Amsterdammer*. The two, Joeri Boom and Sander Pleij, quickly realized that they had a historic bombshell in their hands. The yellowing cards contained the names of "depositors" and specified the jewels and other personal property that they'd turned over to Liro. The cards also indicated something else: Much of the property was still unaccounted for.

In 1997, four government commissions were established to investigate Liro claims, looted gold, missing art, stolen insurance policies, and other financial matters stemming from the war—including the poor treatment of Dutch citizens repatriated from Japanese prison camps. The commissions would be headed by some of the Netherlands' leading civil servants and public figures, who as of this writing are still preparing final reports.

But it was left to the World Jewish Congress to produce the first lengthy and most scathing condemnation of the wartime and postwar behavior of the Dutch. Prepared by Israeli economic-affairs editor/journalist Itamar Levine and published in 1998, the report proved especially harsh in dealing with the fate of the Liro accounts. Using the Van Schie report as his basis, Levine concluded that "the whole process seems somewhat incomprehensible. Let us recall the figures: After the war, Liro located 70,000 accounts, of which 45,000 (65 percent) were heirless. Considering the scale of the *Shoah* in the Netherlands, this is a reasonable calculation. Assuming that the investigations were very efficient, and Liro clerks managed to identify some 12,000 heirs so that the percentage of heirs fell to 50 percent—this is still a feasible rate. But how is it possible," asks Levine, "that the value of the remaining accounts fell by 80 percent? Is it feasible that the bank managed to locate only the heirs of larger accounts? And what became of the securities which were not sold and were left heirless?"

Gerard Aalders belittles claims that vast amounts of stolen Jewish money remain in Dutch government coffers or in Dutch banks. Such claims, he says, "are nonsense." But Professor Isaac Lipchits, and others, are convinced they do and that they were absorbed by the Dutch state, which invoked its own law: Heirless property belongs to the state. Dutch Jews who had not enjoyed their nation's protection during wartime were now considered full citizens in every respect.

Unfortunately, in preparing the Levine report, the WJC made no real effort to contact either most leaders of the Dutch-Jewish community or members of the Dutch investigating commissions— including its prominent Jewish members, like Halberstadt and de Swaan. This outraged many in the community.

Yet there seems little indication that even if the WJC had tried to make contact, there would have been much cooperation from Dutch Jews. The community, which has grown to 30,000, has become fiercely independent, and many of its members are still bitter over what they felt was lack of concern by American Jews for their postwar plight. "We just don't need them," said educator Henri Markens, who also serves as chairman of the Coordinating Committee of the Dutch-Jewish Community Council. "We have a government that's eager to help, and a community that wants to get at the truth." Parliament member Judith C. E. Belinfante was blunter: "I don't remember the World Jewish Congress anywhere in sight when we came home from the camps in 1945."

Yet as fiery as this debate became, few battles are proving more emotional than and as complicated as the struggle over stolen Dutch art. It continues unresolved to this day. More than 20,000 art objects taken from the Netherlands by the Germans were recovered in the aftermath of the war and turned over to the Dutch authorities (thousands of others, including at least 10,000 paintings, have never been found). Under the auspices of a special commission called The Netherlands Art Property Foundation (SNK), most of the recovered art was returned to its original owners or to the institutions from which it was stolen. But to this day, some 3,000 works—paintings, sculptures, and antique furniture—remain "under custodianship" and form part of the state-owned Netherlands Art Property Collection, or "NK Collection."

Today's search for stolen assets has triggered intense new interest in their true ownership. In some cases, heirs have recently come forward demanding the return of works of art family members legally sold to German buyers, albeit for wartime bargain prices dictated by the pressures of occupation, if not outright coercion. "We have lots of claims from people who sold art at the time," says Rick Voss, who heads the NK and sits on the official Dutch committee dealing with the art problems. Voss's response to such claimants is unequivocal. "We tell them you can keep the money," he says, "but we will keep the paintings."

This is particularly true in the case of great-master paintings that once belonged to Jacques Goudstikker, Amsterdam's premier prewar Jewish art dealer. Goudstikker himself had already fled Amsterdam in May 1940 and died in a mysterious accident aboard the ship on which he was sailing to England. His wife and son went to New York, leaving his aged mother, Emmy Sellisberg, and two employees to deal with the Nazis—among them Reichsmarschall Hermann Göring, who made an early trip to the Goudstikkers' canalside gallery to make his choices.

In the end, the Goudstikker shareholders' board, which included Mrs. Sellisberg, voluntarily "sold" the collection to Göring for DG2 million. Goudstikker's mother became one of the few Dutch Jews who did not hide and was never deported. And the DG2 million remained intact throughout the entire war, despite the Liro confiscations. At the war's end, the Dutch government offered the Goudstikkers their recovered paintings in exchange for the money the family had received from Göring. Goudstikker's widow refused. But her heirs now say the price paid by Göring for these great-master paintings was "robbery" and had been forced on the family by Nazi threats. They have brought suit against the Dutch government for the return of their paintings.

Voss is far more understanding of heirs who have come forward claiming that until recently they were ignorant that family-owned paintings had been stolen or that their families had simply failed to ask for their possessions back at the end of the war. "There was not exactly a warm welcome-home for the surviving Jews. In the atmosphere of the Netherlands of 1945–46, some clearly declined to put in claims for fear it would draw attention to them. Some were even ashamed."

Unlike the directors of the French government network of museums, who still arrogantly insist they did "all that was required" to locate surviving owners of art and/or their heirs, the Dutch admit that their postwar searches were inadequate, at least by today's standards. "We didn't have computers then, and there were a handful of working color cameras," insists Voss. "People worked by memory, and I think they did their best."

An art commission is now among the central features of Holland's investigative process into stolen assets. "We have a team of art historians," says Voss, "and we're assembling period catalogs where we can, checking the provenance of everything in our possession."

Members of the other three commissions claim they are equally dedicated to uncovering the truth. Willem Scholten, the highly respected former deputy to the Queen and the effective executive head of Holland's Raad van Staten, its Privy Council, denies there was ever any "decision to enrich the country with Jewish money. If we made mistakes, it is time to acknowledge them. Society is asking for this, and time is pressing." But sitting in the sun-filled study of his modest apartment near the Hague, Scholten warns, "You cannot repair history. You can only study it and make some amends. Nor can you look at history with the eyes of today."

Scholten himself recalls events in his own small hometown in eastern Holland. "We had Jewish neighbors; the father was a butcher. One day the whole family disappeared, and I remember my father saying they had been shipped to Germany—at least that's what we thought at the time. So we and all the neighbors divided up their belongings to give them back when they returned. But they didn't return."[3]

Did the postwar Dutch government do everything it could to acknowledge the immediate suffering of its surviving Jews, to welcome them home and to reincorporate them into Dutch life? Did it do everything feasible to locate the heirs of unclaimed Liro accounts and art objects? Did it find a way to distribute heirless amounts equitably to the Jewish community? The answer to all three questions is clearly no.

It is also clear that many Dutch Jews, like Louis Halberstadt, simply refused to make claims. Their efforts were directed at starting another life and finding other survivors—if any—a tragically unsuccessful task for most in a country where entire families had been obliterated by the Nazi terror.

The details of survival and renewal in the wake of such soul-searing events are keys to any attempt to understand how survivors responded to the Holocaust. Entire sociopsychological studies have been devoted to the subject. Each story is different. Some defy description. That of Victor Halberstadt and his father, Louis, is both unique and typical, and worthy of telling. "In 1939, Mr. Pohl, a Dutch business friend who was Holland's Volkswagen dealer, told my father, 'You know, Halberstadt, I like you. But you're Jewish, so plan to leave. It stinks over there in Germany.' He even offered to help us with money. Instead my father made preparatory arrangements to go into hiding.

"After the Nazis came and the deportation began, we received a coded message from my cousin Harry, who'd been the first in the family to be shipped to a Polish labor camp. 'Please send best regards to the brothers K. in Nijmegen for me,' he wrote. It was a pre-agreed message, Harry's way of saying, 'Get the hell out of there.' The [brothers] owned a farm at Nijmegen, on the German

---

[3] Scholten, who was ten years old at the time, says he believes that most of the items were later given to surviving relatives of the family.

border. It was there that my father, mother, sister, and grandmother had arranged to go into hiding.

"Because I was so small, I was to go to a family. So one day
they put me in a car driven by some underground people; my
cousin Max went in another. We were betrayed and stopped outside of Amsterdam. My car escaped, my cousin's didn't. He was
deported and gassed on his birthday in March 1943."

Over the next three years, Halberstadt was passed from family
to family. "I think I stayed with a total of eleven Christian families;
I don't remember. I know I was supposed to be a cousin from
Rotterdam." Hiding Jewish children was a crime. At one family,
the young Halberstadt mentioned the word Jews. That very evening, he was put on the back of a bicycle and brought to the next
family, where he stayed for two years.

At the war's end, Halberstadt's father and two cousins set
out by foot to try to find him. "The underground workers kept
the locations of hidden children secret, so that if they were
caught, they could not betray the children. My father knew
vaguely that I was in the south. I was playing on the street one
day when three men walked up to me. Remember, they hadn't
seen me in three years. One of them, my father's cousin Eli, took
my face and began to feel my bone structure. He had been a bar-
ber before the war and spent a lot of his time shaving dozens of
family members—he knew the family facial structure. 'It's Victor,'
he said. That night I shared a room with the man my foster family
told me was my real father.

"Hidden children like myself were left with certain survivor
skills and fears: of rejection and of being left alone, of being unwel-
come . . . of finding it very difficult if at all possible to cry. But
we also never talk to one another about those times. Until recently
I didn't even know that my sister hadn't been all the time with my
parents. We just never talked about it—just as my father never
talked to me about the things that happened before or during the
war. You never said, 'So-and-so is dead' or 'So-and-so was gassed

in Auschwitz.' You simply said, *'Er iz nisht gekumen zurik'*—'he never returned.'

"I cannot recall one single instance in the thirty-four years that my father lived after the war that he and I ever discussed anything that happened before or during the war. Perhaps my parents talked to one another in bed when the children weren't around. But around us there was a taboo on such subjects, and we copied the taboos of our parents."

One of the taboo questions was, What happened to everything they had owned before the war? But Halberstadt insists the real question is not why they didn't try to recover their assets but rather "why, having lost all brothers and sisters, cousins—five hundred members of the family all told—why they wanted to live at all? Where did they get the courage?"

To this day, says Halberstadt, he has no answers.

5

Norway

Traitors in Their Midst

Their physical liquidation was a prerequisite for their financial liquidation.
— Norwegian journalist BJØRN WESTLIE, 1996

Berit Reisel remembers hesitating "a long hard while" before ringing the bell at the well-maintained prewar building in the affluent Oslo neighborhood of Frogner. "But I thought, If I don't push the bell now, I'll never be able to do it."

When at last she did and the door opened on that dark autumn day in 1995, the old man who greeted her "was tiny and skinny with very clear, awakened eyes."

Instinctively, Reisel, an Oslo psychotherapist and Jewish community leader, took off her glove and put out her hand.

"How do you do," her host said, returning the hand gesture. "My name is Rolf Svindal, and I am a Nazi."

Even now, at age ninety-six, Rolf Svindal unabashedly clings to his Nazi ideology. He also remains steadfastly proud of his wartime job as head of the Oslo region's Liquidation Board for Confiscated Jewish Property, the body established by the Nazi government of Norwegian traitor Vidkun Quisling for the express purpose of stealing the property of Norway's tiny but prosperous Jewish community. From 1940 to 1944, Svindal and his colleagues systematically looted anywhere from 450 million to 2 billion Norwegian Kroners' worth of assets, commercial and private.[1]

At the war's end, 40 percent of Norway's 2,173 Jews had been slaughtered. The 1,368 who survived received but a small portion—if anything—of what had been stolen from them and their families.

For Berit Reisel, a leader of a small group of Norwegian activists—both Jewish and non-Jewish—finally seeking restitution for Norway's Jews, the 1995 meeting with Svindal was part of a necessary if painful process. "I found it difficult even to look around his very large apartment, because he soon told me that some of his furniture and some of his paintings had belonged to Jews. But he had some of the facts we needed."

Svindal had carefully laid them out on a table in an orderly collection of books and files of the work he had done during the war. "He had no regrets, no shame for what he had done or for his Nazi ideology; he still believed in it," says Reisel. But if Svindal was unrelenting in his Nazi ideology, he expressed sorrow about one thing regarding his wartime activities. "He said he was angry," says Reisel, "that after the war the Norwegian authorities had mixed up the property files of the Jews and non-Jews—that's what bothered him the most. He was a very good clerk, and he had done everything right with the system down to the last centimeter. And

---

[1] Only 24 million old Norwegian Kroners' worth of assets have been traceable—an amount now worth 450 million Kroners by today's Krone values. But because so much of the expropriated assets had been pilfered or cloaked, experts estimate that this traceable figure represents as little as 20 percent of the true total.

someone had made a mess of his beautiful orderly system! It was awful to hear."

Norway had never been a particularly welcoming land for Jews. Until 1851, Norway's rulers effectively banned Jewish settlement within their borders and even barred Jewish traders and travelers from entry without special letters of safe conduct. Jews who ventured into the northland without such permits were imprisoned and deported (among them, one poor soul who was shipwrecked in 1817). The ban was relaxed for wealthy "Portuguese" Jews in 1844. But even after the nineteenth-century Norwegian writer Henrik Wergeland convinced the Norwegian Parliament that free immigration was an international right, few Jews chose to move to that harsh northern land. With the massive waves of emigration from Russia and Poland at the turn of the twentieth century, a Norwegian-Jewish community began to grow—largely Russian or Lithuanian Jews who reached Norway and then didn't have the heart or money to continue the difficult transatlantic journey to America.

By 1939, there were more than 2,000 Jews in Norway, including some 200 refugees from Central and Eastern Europe, many of whom had been helped by the humanitarian refugee commission founded by Norway's legendary Arctic explorer, Fridtjof Nansen. The community boasted a growing number of professionals—doctors, lawyers, and university professors; many others were traders of textiles, watches, jewelry, and furs. Their communal lives, if lonely, seemed secure. While there was some anti-Semitism, Norway's homegrown Nazi Party—the National Samling (National Union), the NS—had little public support and enjoyed little political influence on the eve of the war. On April 9, 1940, that changed when German troops landed at Oslo and German Foreign Minister Joachim von Ribbentrop announced that the Reich was assuming "protection" of Norway. Within hours, NS leader Vidkun Quisling, whose name would come to epitomize treason, was summoned to assume the German-made mantle of "Fører" of Norway.

A former member of the Norwegian General Staff, and a co-founder of the Nazi-oriented Nordisk Folkereisning (Nordic Folk Awakening), Quisling could goose-step with the worst of them—including Josef Terboven, the man Hitler appointed Germany's Reichskommissar in occupied Norway. Persecution of Norway's Jews began immediately.[2] Their radios were confiscated, they were forced to adopt Judaic names and forbidden to have "Aryan-sounding ones," and a committee of Quisling's party faithful began to draw up a program of anti-Semitic legislation. Yet Norway's Fører faced a serious problem, says historian Bjarte Bruland. "With so few Jews in Norway, Quisling was hard-pressed to prove that this tiny 'impure' community represented a danger to the country."

Quisling soon found an answer: He employed the myth that in fact there were at least 10,000 "spiritual and artificial Jews" in Norway, which meant not only "racial" Jews but anyone whose ideas were incompatible with Nazism.

In March 1941, new identity cards were issued to Norwegian Jews, all of them stamped in red with the letter J. By May 18, 1941, all Norwegian Jews had been dismissed from state and public institutions. Six months later, they were banned from teaching and other free professions. In November, Quisling ordered the Norwegian police to register all Jews—and all Jewish-owned property. There was talk of exile. In June, all Jewish-owned businesses were placed under the control of specially appointed commissars, most of them handpicked from the ranks of Quisling's own personal storm-troop organization, the Hird.

Some Norwegians reacted with protests. The National Theatre and Symphony Orchestra threatened strikes when ordered to sack Jews who worked there. Most remained silent.

---

[2] Ironically, Quisling had once served as an aide to Fridtjof Nansen during his tenure as refugee commissioner at the League of Nations in Geneva. On the day after Christmas, 1942, Quisling ordered the Nansen refugee-aid office in Oslo closed. Nansen's son, architect Odd Nansen, was arrested and imprisoned in a German concentration camp, but survived the war.

It was soon too late to protest. In the autumn of 1942, the SS, together with Norway's Nazi Statspolitiet ("state police"), began rounding up every Jew they could find: first all men over sixteen on October 25, then all women and children on the night between November 25 and 26. Thanks in large measure to the Norwegian Resistance—as well as to a handful of profiteering smugglers—some 930 Jews managed to escape being caught in the Nazi net and fled through the frozen forests to neutral Sweden. At least one of them, Helene Ehrlich, a member of the Norwegian underground, made her escape on skis. Another small number managed to hide in Norway, and another group, mainly Jewish men married to gentile women, was sent for forced labor to the ghetto camp of Sydspissen in the Arctic town of Narvik. All the rest were eventually taken to Oslo's grim Bredtveit Prison.

Eighteen-year-old Julius Paltiel of Trondheim and his widowed mother were among them. "We were gripped with despair . . . saddened to see Norwegians parading around in their Hird uniforms and playing 'SS.' . . . Some thought maybe it would be better if they sent us all to Germany. It was a naïve, angst-ridden belief that if we were all together we can help each other."

On November 26, a ship called the *Donau* sailed from Oslo's Pier 1 carrying 532 Jewish prisoners. It was followed by another shipment of 158 Jews on February 25, 1943. No attempt was made to hide its purpose or its passengers from the Norwegian public. In his Norwegian-language memoirs, *Against All the Odds,* Paltiel recalls the scene:

We are driven to the Oslo docks. The *D/S Gotenland* is berthed there. The great ship looms above us. The lorry turns in by the gangway, stops. . . . We are quickly rousted from the back . . . and have to fall in on the quayside. Then we get our marching orders: "Aboard!"

Wind and snowflakes buffet us from the fjord. Out there the frost mist forms small, white clouds. Whether the tears that fill our eyes are from the wind or from something inside us, no one cares. . . .

Heartrending scenes are played out as women and men are separated from one another and sent to their different holds. . . . The children cling to their parents' necks and want to stay with both of them. The elderly are taking too long to get aboard. The Germans beat them hard. Many cry out for help. But there is nothing here but cruel parting. The oldest on board is 80, the youngest just one and a half.

It is a sad departure from Oslo. . . . Farewell, my precious homeland!

Paltiel and other deportees in the second shipload were taken ashore at Stettin on Germany's Baltic coast and then brought by closed train to Berlin. Imprisoned in one of the few synagogues in the city not yet destroyed by the Nazis, they were forced to sign declarations turning over everything they had left behind in Norway—all their money and property—to the German state. In return, Paltiel recalls, "We were told the Reich will look after you until you die."

Paltiel was later sent to Buchenwald.[3] Most of the other Norwegian deportees were sent to occupied Poland and to Auschwitz, where the women and children were murdered immediately. Out of a total of 739 Norwegian-Jewish deportees, only 26 men survived the war. Of the approximately 1,400 Norwegians sent to Nazi concentration camps, more than 50 percent were Jews.

The liquidation of Norway's Jewish community was the green light for the massive appropriation of its property. The Quisling government's act of October 26, 1942, legalized the thefts. But the confiscations had been preplanned and the order to carry them out

---

[3] In 1945, Norwegian concentration-camp inmates were repatriated thanks to the efforts of Sweden's Count Folke Bernadotte. Norwegian-Jewish prisoners, however, were excluded from the arrangement.

was contained in a telegram sent by the head of the State Police on October 25 to every police authority in the country. In the telegram, Norwegian police are ordered to seize all assets belonging to Jews. It added that those most readily negotiable were to be "secured immediately."

During the weeks that followed the deportations, crews of lawyers and clerks attached to the Liquidation Board drew up detailed lists of all and any assets that the Jews had left behind: bank accounts, securities, the contents of safes and safety-deposit boxes, private possessions in their homes, and—in cases where people owned stores or enterprises—inventories and stock lists. Everything, says Reisel, who has discovered copies of the Nazi and Quisling committee lists, was noted down in detail, "down to the contents of kitchen drawers." One list, obtained after the war by Norwegian Jew Kurt Valner, who happened to be safely abroad when the deportations took place, includes the following notation: "one silver spoon, bent."

There was a clear pecking order for this organized theft arranged in negotiations between Norway's Nazis and their German masters. Items of high value, such as jewelry, watches, and gold, were sent to Gestapo headquarters at Victoria Terrasse in Oslo. Parts of the loot were used to pay the transport costs for the deported Jews. Cash, securities, and life-insurance policies were deposited into special government-controlled accounts. Much of the rest (that wasn't pilfered by Quisling's agents) was sold by the government at public auction, with the funds going into the government's "Jewish Account." As elsewhere in Nazi-occupied Europe, the disappearance of Jewish company owners and shopkeepers provided bonanza opportunities for their non-Jewish competitors, who were always among the first to bid at what became bargain prices.

In order to drive home the horrifying mechanics of the plunder—and the culpability of many Norwegians themselves—both Norwegian writer Bjørn Westlie and later, respected Swedish journalist Arne Ruth retraced the story of one Jewish family, the Plesanskys from Tønsberg on the southeast Norwegian coast. "Nothing has come to symbolize the conflict more," says Ruth, "than the fate of their family belongings."

Fifty-year-old Isak Plesansky, the founder and proprietor of the Tønsberg Clothing Company, had been among the first Jews in his town to be arrested and sent to a newly opened concentration camp in Berg. At dawn on November 26, 1942, the Quisling police returned to Plesansky's home and arrested his wife, eleven-year-old daughter, and twelve-year-old son—both of whom, records show, were sick in bed at the time with measles. Several hours later, says Ruth, the entire Plesansky family was among the 532 Norwegian Jews who boarded the *Donau* en route to Auschwitz. "Within a month, they had all been gassed to death."

The ship had hardly sailed out of sight when commission members began assembling their lists of Plesansky belongings. By December 19, 1942, new tenants had moved into the house where the Plesanskys had once lived. And within three weeks, many of the clothes from Plesansky's warehouse had been requisitioned by the superintendent of the Berg concentration camp, Alf Kjølner, who not so coincidentally was the son of one of Plesansky's prime competitors, a Tønsberg haberdasher named Emil Kjølner.

On February 13, 1943, the entire stock of the Plesansky family's clothing shop at Møllergaten 12 was snapped up by the Kjølner family for 6,356 Kroners, a fraction of its actual value. One of Kjølner's clerks kept careful contemporary notes of the chain of events: "The Tønsberg Clothing Co stock was sold via Alf Kjølner to Emil Kjølner. The goods were collected on 3/2 by Kaare Stang and Alf Kjølner. The following day at 9 A.M. all the goods were driven down to Emil Kjølner's (articles of every kind! Suits, coats, winter coats, lots of shoes and ties)."

On November 20, 1943, the Plesanskys' personal furniture and other household articles, which had been stored in their now empty shop, were publicly auctioned off for a total of 24,000

The day after Kristallnacht, removing the name from a Jewish-owned store.
(Stadtarchiv Hof, Germany)

Twelve-year-old Helga Weissova's drawing of her parents listing
possessions for the Nazis on the eve of the family's expulsion from their
Prague home, drawn in Theresienstadt Ghetto in 1943.
(Helga Weissova-Hoskova)

Scrip "money" issued to Jews in Theresienstadt in exchange for parts of the cash they were forced to hand over. *(author's collection)*

QUITTUNG ÜBER HUNDERT KRONEN

100

WER DIESE QUITTUNG VERFÄLSCHT ODER NACHMACHT ODER GEFÄLSCHTE QUITTUNGEN IN VERKEHR BRINGT, WIRD STRENGSTENS BESTRAFT.

100

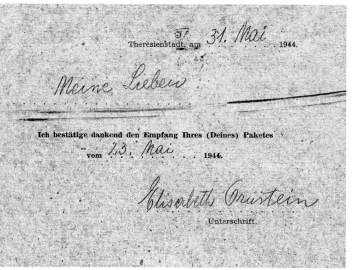

Theresienstadt, am 31. Mai 1944.

Meine Lieben!

Ich bestätige dankend den Empfang Ihres (Deines) Paketes vom 23. Mai 1944.

Elisabeth Ornstein

Unterschrift.

A form postcard from Theresienstadt to Vienna thanking a friend for a package. The Nazis severely restricted correspondence. *(author's collection)*

A moving van owned by the Dutch Puls company, which confiscated Jewish property for the Nazis and their Dutch collaborators. The sight of Puls vans became so common in the Netherlands that the term *"pulsen"* was coined to denote the looting of a house. *(Rijksinstituut voor Oorlogsdocumentatie, courtesy of USHMM Photo Archives)*

TOP: Dutch agents from the Property Administration and Annuities Institute, the organization established in 1942 to "Aryanize" Jewish enterprises, speak with a Jewish businessman whose establishments are being confiscated. (*Rijksinstituut voor Oorlogsdocumentatie, courtesy of USHMM Photo Archives*)

RIGHT: Hermann Göring leaving the Goudstikker Art Gallery in Amsterdam after a selecting visit, 1940. (*Rijksinstituut voor Oorlogsdocumentatie*)

BELOW: Nazi scrip for use in the Westbork detention center, the Dutch holding camp for deportation to Auschwitz and other death camps. (*author's collection*)

ABOVE: Lippmann-Rosenthal clerks confiscated any remaining valuables from Dutch Jews being deported to death camps, then whiled away their time playing cards between train transports. *(Rijksinstituut voor Oorlogsdocumentatie)*

BELOW: Dutch Jews being loaded aboard trains for transport to death camps. *(Rijksinstituut voor Oorlogsdocumentatie)*

Norwegian Nazi Rolf Svindal, one of the central figures in the plundering of Norway's Jews, on trial in Oslo after the war. (*Norsk Telegrambyra*)

ABOVE: French guard at the Pithiviers Camp south of Paris, where Vichy authorities interned "foreign" Jews before handing them over to the Germans. (*Archives du Centre de Documentation Juive Contemporaine*)

Anti-Semitic exhibit in Paris, 1942. (*ACDJC*)

RIGHT: In 1942, French Jews were ordered to wear the yellow JUIF star. *(ACDJC)*

BELOW: German and French authorities work together during an August 1941 *"rafle"*— roundup—of Parisian Jews. *(ACDJC)*

Vichy authorities seal the door to the confiscated Paris apartment of a French Jew—in this case, the former Colonial Minister Georges Mandel. *(Bundesarchiv, courtesy of USHMM Photo Archives)*

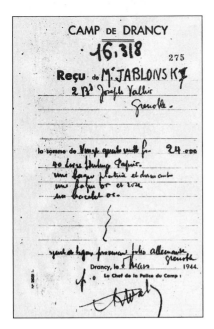

A receipt issued by Vichy authorities at the Drancy internment camp for property confiscated from Monsieur Jablonsky of Grenoble in March 1944. (ACDJC)

Fanny Cukier and her Paris-born children, Ginette and Irene. Because she was less than six years old, Irene was excused from wearing the yellow JUIF star. Fanny and her children were deported to Auschwitz on August 17, 1942. (From French Children of the Holocaust, by Serge Klarsfeld [The Beate Klarsfeld Foundation], courtesy of the Museum of Jewish Heritage, New York)

Paris photographer Joseph Zajdenberg with his wife Anna and infant daughter Claudia, in 1936. Joseph and Anna were arrested by Vichy authorities and perished in Nazi camps. Claudia, hidden by a French family, survived and lives in New York, where she is now part of a class action seeking return of family property stolen by the Vichy authorities. (Claudia Carlin Collection)

The Austerlitz camp warehouses in Paris where confiscated Jewish property was sorted and stored before being shipped to Germany. *(ACDJC)*

A German truck loaded with confiscated Jewish furniture stands on a street in Krakow, Poland. Armbanded Jews walk nearby. *(National Archives in Krakow, courtesy of USHMM Photo Archives)*

Kroners (the sum was reduced after one buyer complained that he'd "overpaid" for a dining set).

For the Kjølners it was an added wartime windfall—their connections to the Nazis had already helped them profit handsomely. Yet when the war ended, the family was barely punished. The Kjølner sons—Alf, the Berg camp commander; Per, one of several hundred young Norwegians who'd volunteered for a "Nordic" SS company that saw action on the eastern front; and a third son named Trygve—were all convicted for their membership in Nazi organizations. But, says Ruth, "their father, Emil, who reaped the profits from the elimination of the Plesansky family, was never called to account. He was not a party member, and what he did during the war could not be legally defined as theft—he'd had the Norwegian government behind him."

Indeed, it was the Norwegian authorities who fixed the 6,356-Kroners price he paid for his rival's stock. And it was the postwar Norwegian government that imposed a meager punishment on Kjølner: He was made to pay a special tax on his wartime "purchase"—an additional 6,356 Kroners, collected by the government. Kjølner himself remained unscathed by scandal. And several years later, he used his fortune to found one of Scandinavia's largest and most successful fashion chains, an eighty-six-shop network called Adelsten.

The only surviving member of the Plesansky family, an elder son named Bernhard, fared less well in the wake of the war. Warned in November 1942 by the Tønsberg chief of police of the impending arrests, the teenaged Bernhard had escaped the Nazi dragnet that tore away his parents and siblings by first hiding in Oslo and then by eventually making his way across a border lake to Sweden with the help of the Norwegian underground. In Sweden, he hitched a ride aboard an RAF plane to London, where Norway's King Olav and many of his officials had fled, and where the young Plesansky spent the duration working for the Norwegian government-in-exile.

A month after liberation, twenty-one-year-old Bernhard Plesansky, proudly wearing a Free Norwegian uniform, returned to Tønsberg to discover that his parents, brother, and sister had been gassed. He was greeted warmly and sympathetically by some of his old neighbors, several of whom returned a few of his family's belongings to him. "The family doctor had some money he said my father had asked him to look after," Bernhard later recalled. "Another friend told me, 'There are a couple of suitcases in our attic and some paintings that your father stored up there." Among the items he found: his parents' wedding photo. "For me," says Plesansky, "this was a bridge to a life that no longer existed."

Indeed, the family clothing store at Møllergaten 12 was no more. And any attempt at compensation from the Kjølners was rebuffed, as were Bernhard's attempts to borrow money from a local bank to restart his father's confiscated business. The bank told him, recounts Ruth, "that in contrast to his father, he could not be considered a financially reliable client."

Norwegian authorities eventually calculated that out of all the assets stolen from the Plesanskys, only 33,000 Kroners remained ($8,300 at 1946 values) in Norwegian government coffers. "Of this," says Ruth, "Bernhard was able to recover only 68 percent—21,000 in 1947." The balance was absorbed by the Norwegian government against "administrative expenses, etc."[4]

Faced with all this, Bernhard Plesansky left his native Norway and returned to London, where he changed his name to Bernard Prydal, learned to speak near-accentless English, and, while never giving up his Norwegian passport, tried to put the Holocaust chapter of his life behind him. For more than fifty years he never spoke of what had been done to his family—or to him in the aftermath of the war.

---

[4] The Reparations Office based its reduced payment in part on a claim that the Wartime Liquidation Board had used 32 percent of the funds it confiscated for its own administration. That included extravagant expense account budgets for board members.

Many of Norway's other surviving Jews fared no better. For those who had been unable to acquire Norwegian passports before the war, it was even worse. When the Nazis were defeated, the Norwegian government refused to allow Jews without Norwegian citizenship to return. "This included almost five hundred of the survivors—almost one-third of them," says Berit Reisel. "They had also been stripped of their property and belongings by the Quisling government and had been able to flee, but they were not allowed back because they were not Norwegian citizens."

Even those who were Norwegian nationals and could return ran into constant difficulties in their attempts to seek restitution. Norwegian Jews who survived soon discovered that many if not most of the records were incomplete—or missing. "In principle," says Berit Reisel, "all the assets of the Jews should have been registered and sold by the Liquidation Board. A postwar Reparations Board was supposed to return all these funds. In fact, it turned out that at least 70 percent of the assets had been looted after they had been stolen and before they ever got to be registered."

Berit Reisel adds, "The Nazi liquidation process involved reducing the total assets of a religious and cultural minority, in this case the Jews, to a quantifiable unit by treating all forms of ownership as bankrupt estates. And while there had been 1,381 seizures of such estates of Jewish property, there were estate files for only 1,053. The estates were treated as juridical persons, which meant they were taxed at the highest possible rates."

According to Reisel, this type of heavy-handed taxation often depleted whatever was left. "My uncle has two large shops. After the war, the taxes he was assessed were larger than the assets that were left."

Worse, the government made little effort to help returning Jews find those of their assets that did still exist. While there were government committees to do that for a variety of groups in the country—from seamen to residents of specific areas of Norway—there were none for Jews. And it soon became clear that there would be none. Nor were matters made easier for the Jews by the fact that many of the employees of the government's Reparations Board included some of the same people who had worked for the Confiscation Committees. "They had been released from prison for their new jobs," says Reisel. "The government's logic was that these collaborators had 'valuable experience.' "

In the end, many people, though certainly not all, did regain their prewar homes and apartments.[5] But cash, business assets, and personal belongings became steadily harder to trace and claim successfully. The Settlements Division of the Ministry of Justice, for example, referred claims for compensation for the loss of bank deposits to the banks themselves. But in a circular dispatched in April 1947 by the Norwegian Bankers Association, member banks were advised that they had to be careful that allowance was made for any compensation claimants might have received from another source and that "lawful expenses" were to be deducted. The net result, the Norwegian government would admit fifty years later, was that few bank accounts were fully restored. "One Jewish family from Oslo," says Bjørn Westlie, "whose assets had been fixed at NKR2 million in 1942, was informed in 1947 that only NKR19,000 would be returned to them."

The same principles were applied to life-insurance policies and to confiscated stocks and bonds. "Not all survivors even knew what their parents or relatives had had or what companies they owned stock in," says Berit Reisel. "No one was offering them the information."

In the case of one family, only two people out of eight had survived Auschwitz. The two sole heirs claimed compensation from

---

[5] Confiscated property was often registered in the name of a husband. In cases where only a wife and/or children survived, they received no reimbursement unless they could provide the impossible concentration-camp death certificate—or could wait several years until they received a court judgment of presumption of death. In the interim, estates were administered by trustees, who naturally deducted fees.

Norges Brannkasse, the large company that had been the family's life insurer. But the company claimed it would pay the survivors each only one-eighth of the estate—the amount to which they would have been entitled if the rest of the family had survived. After all, argued Norges Brannkasse, they should not benefit from "undue profit" because of war.

Save for the decency of some fellow Norwegians, personal belongings were almost impossible to find. Even communal property became difficult to retrieve. The synagogue in Trondheim, which the small local community traditionally boasted was "the northernmost in the world," had been used as a Wehrmacht barracks during the war and was then requisitioned again by the postwar Norwegian government's Løsørevernet (Custodian of Movable Property) as a storage depot. It took until autumn of 1947 for the remnant of the Jews of Trondheim to get back their house of worship.

Julius Paltiel, who had been sent to Auschwitz from Buchenwald and survived, returned to Trondheim to discover that everything in his family's shop had disappeared during the war.[6] He received a onetime payment of NKR12,000 for the loss of his mother. But the Reparations Office refused to assist anymore, claiming he didn't need their help.

Even more damning was the fact that while there had been pilferage from the Liquidation Board's accounts—and while the argument of "administrative costs" was morally dubious at best— there were vast amounts still available at the end of the war to help compensate Norway's surviving Jews. Records show that in 1947, at least NKR3 million was transferred from the Reparations Office to a state-run welfare scheme. Yet most Jewish restitution claimants received little if anything.

---

[6] Almost fifty years later, the widow of one of the Paltiel family's gentile employees gave Julius a "receipt" for NKR20,043 in cash that her husband had been forced to hand over to the Norwegian Nazi who'd been appointed the shop's Aryan commissar. Paltiel estimates that at today's values, the amount stolen was close to NKR750,000 (or about $100,000).

Nor did many openly complain. "When it became clear that not much was going to be returned," says Berit Reisel, "people clammed up. There would be no loud protests."

"The Jewish community had been decimated," explains Norway's chief rabbi Michael Melchior. "Two hundred and thirty families had been completely annihilated. The survivors for the most part were unwilling—or afraid—to ask for what had been theirs or their families'. People simply kept quiet and tried to build new lives."

At the war's end, Vidkun Quisling and twenty-three of his Norwegian Nazi colleagues were executed for their treason. Nineteen thousand other Norwegian collaborators received prison sentences, among them Rolf Svindal and several other Nazi Party members of the Confiscation Committees, who were each sentenced to two years in prison. It would take more than fifty years—and the work of a handful of determined Norwegians, both Jews and non-Jews—for Norway to finally come to terms with a shameful past.

Rolf Svindal is still alive and reachable only via a cellular-phone number. He did not return my call.

6

France

Les Biens des Juifs

*The offer of economic advantages much more easily excites
French sympathy for the anti-Jewish struggle.*
—SS Standartenführer HELMUT KNOCHEN, Paris, 1941

In his 1964 history of the medieval Duchy of Uzès on the western
edge of Provence, a local historian named Gaston Chauvet describes an event that he says took place in that exquisitely beautiful
town in the year 1297: "An Israelite and his wife had seized a
Christian child and by cutting the veins of his throat, had drained
all his blood, which they gathered in a glass vase; the officers of
[Gancelin] the Lord [of Uzès] then imprisoned the authors of this
ritual crime." Meanwhile, recounts Chauvet, the Bishop of Uzès,
Guillaume, arrested "several of their accomplices."

Nowhere does Chauvet, a much honored regional dignitary,
question the veracity of these accusations against the Jews. Nor

does he point out to his readers that the calumnious charge of ritual murder, something totally abhorrent to Jewish religious practice, numbered among the deadliest anti-Semitic libels of the Middle Ages.

Chauvet, however, does go on to describe a lively debate between the lord of Uzès and the local bishop regarding who actually had jurisdiction over the Jews. It was an important question, eventually won by the *seigneur*. For, as Chauvet recounts, in the aftermath of "this ritual crime," all the accused Jews of Uzès as well as those Jews living in nearby Beaucaire were "arrested and their assets confiscated."

The story—and the unquestioning rendering of it by historian Chauvet (for whom, ironically enough, a street is now named near La Juiverie, the medieval Jewish quarter of Uzès)—goes far to explain why so many Europeans, especially the French, allowed the World War II pursuit and plunder of their Jewish neighbors to pass with little if any protest. Eight centuries of authorized demonization of the Jews, of accusations of everything from ritual murder to deicide, had resulted in both a conscious and subconscious "justification" for almost any act committed against these eternal aliens. The Jews had become a people not above the law but beneath it; not a people to be protected by normal law but a people deemed unworthy of it.

Nowhere was this truer or more pervasive than in France, where since Gallo-Roman times Jews had lived a seesaw existence of guarded acceptance and often violent rejection by the Christian kings, nobles, priests, and peasants around them. Carolingian rulers welcomed Jewish settlers, allowed them to pursue studies and prayer, and gave them privileges in trade and agriculture; even the wine for mass was bought from Jewish vintners. But medieval church leaders began to rail against these "blind Christ killers," charging them as rich oppressors of the poor, poisoners of wells— and ritual murderers of children. Crusaders on their way to the Holy Land robbed them, then slaughtered them. Both Church and state burned their books, forced them to wear yellow badges, then restricted them to ghetto living and moneylending. As in most of Europe, the Jews of France became a people to be reviled, to be arbitrarily expelled and brought back only when rulers and Church officials needed to extort more gold from them. It must have been confusing; though banished from Paris and the rest of France, Jews were welcome, at one point, in southern Avignon and the adjacent area of Comtat-Venaissin under the protection of the Pope (and his treasurer), who "owned" the region.

Yet despite the uncertainty of their existence, the Jews of medieval France produced a wealth of scientific literature and religious philosophy, from the eleventh-century Rashi of Troyes, considered by some the greatest biblical commentator the Diaspora has ever seen, to physicians and translators who labored in Provence.

Liberation for French Jews came with the Revolution of 1789 and a proclamation granting them equality under law, a declaration that Jewish historian Nathanel Ausubel once called "the most momentous event in Jewish history since the destruction of the Temple in the year 70."

Despite spurts of bitter public anti-Semitism—notably the infamous 1894 Dreyfus Affair, in which a Jewish army officer, Captain Alfred Dreyfus, was falsely accused of treason—the Jews of France managed to find their place in the republic. Part German in origin, with others rooted in Spain and Portugal, the French-Jewish establishment produced political thinkers like nineteenth-century Minister of Justice Adolphe Crémieux and twentieth-century Prime Minister Pierre Mendès-France, bankers and businessmen like the Lazard brothers and the Rothschilds, artists like Camille Pissarro, writers like Marcel Proust, and composers like Camille Saint-Saëns.

By the turn of the century, "living like God in Paris" had become a popular Yiddish expression for doing well. One result: Scores of thousands of Jews fleeing pogroms and revolutions flocked to France from Eastern Europe, adding to the community's size. So too did the first Nazi persecutions in Germany and Austria. In the mid-1930s, on the eve of World War II, there were almost 350,000 Jews in France—immigrant and native-born—among them its first Jewish-born premier, Socialist leader Léon Blum.

Yet, with the fall of France in 1940 and the establishment of the Vichy regime of Marshal (Henri) Philippe Pétain in the southern half of the country,[1] France slid quickly into its old tradition of judeophobia. Few facts are more damning of Vichy's collaborationist enthusiasm than the speed with which France's new morally bastard government slavishly abandoned the Republic's 150 years of egalitarianism and made official anti-Semitism the law of the land. Indeed, on October 3, 1940, well before the Nazis ever asked them to, the Fascist lawmakers in Vichy promulgated a special "Statut des juifs," a "Jewish status" that placed Jews beyond the pale by "legally" excluding them from the limits and protections of France's most basic laws.

The definition of who was and who wasn't of *la race juive* exceeded even the extremes of the Reich's absurd biological rules: Vichy's rules included the non-Jewish spouses of Jews, again more than the Nazis asked of them.

France's best-known Nazi hunter and its leading advocate for Holocaust victims, Paris lawyer Serge Klarsfeld, says, "Anti-Semitism was not just a feature of Vichy rule. It was incorporated as an integral part of this so-called *révolution nationale*—the Vichy policy that was to turn France into a corporate, nationalist, and Fascist dictatorship."

---

[1] Under the terms of the Franco-German armistice, France was divided into two unequal parts: the occupied zone, under Reich military rule, and an unoccupied "free" zone under the rule of the new Vichy-based regime of Pétain. The German zone included Paris, the entire Atlantic coast, and most of the more fertile regions to the west, north, and east; Pétain was in full control of the remaining two-fifths of the nation, including Lyons and Marseilles. German military decrees took precedence in the occupied zone, but French Vichy law remained valid throughout the entire country, and French police functioned in the occupied zone under German direction.

Some scholars of the period, like Richard Weisberg of Yeshiva University's Benjamin N. Cardozo School of Law, lay much of the blame for France's pro-Fascist *esprit de corps* not only on anti-Semitism but on an almost perverse attachment to what Weisberg calls "a 'dessicated Cartesianism,' a uniquely French desire to see the elaborate interpretation of the religious laws through to every logical conclusion." Weisberg believes that it was the determination of the French legal establishment—almost more than the laws themselves—that brought about "the pervasiveness and ultimate acceptability" of the Statut des juifs.

The Statut des juifs provoked a bitter response from French Jews, many of whom thought of themselves first as Frenchmen and only then as "Israelites." Influential Paris banker Georges Wormser, who traced his French origins to well before the revolution and had been one of World War I Prime Minister Georges Clemenceau's closest associates, penned a public letter of protest to Marshal Pétain. Invoking the memory of his brother, André Wormser, who had been awarded a medal by Pétain himself and died defending France in World War I, Wormser wrote, "Yesterday, I suffered the humiliation of having to declare my wife, four children and myself separate from the French community. I would be lacking in dignity if I did not cry out in protest."

Pétain's response to Wormser and to anyone else who questioned Vichy's Jewish policies was silence—followed by a tidal wave of laws that further restricted the rights of French Jews. From October 1940 to December 1941, just over a year, the Vichy government carefully prepared and published a list of no fewer than 109 edicts affecting Jews in France, foreign and French-born. The Statut des juifs, says French analyst Dominique Gros, gave birth to "a new branch of law." It would set the French chapter of the Holocaust in motion. Chief among its purposes, the confiscation of Jewish-owned property and assets.

The eventual deportation to death camps of close to 87,000 of France's 350,000 Jews—and the death there of 77,000 of them—

did not begin in a vacuum. As historian Michael Marrus[2] puts it, "It was the culmination of two years of aggressive legislation and persecution, including the passage of laws defining who was to be considered Jewish, isolating Jews in French society, taking away their livelihood, interning many, and registering them with the police."

No less damning is the fact that so very much of the foul work of registration, confiscation, roundup, and finally deportation to death camps was done by French authorities, not German. The Nazis never stationed more than 3,000 German military police in France. But Vichy authorities maintained a police force of 100,000 that operated in both the occupied and "free" zones. It was the French police and their counterparts in the Vichy's paramilitary *milice* who ultimately were charged with implementing many if not most anti-Jewish policies.

Nonetheless, from the day Wehrmacht troops marched down the Champs-Élysées, the fate of the Jews of France became the ultimate bailiwick of SS Hauptsturmführer Theodor Dannecker, a trained lawyer who became one of Adolf Eichmann's central accomplices in the Final Solution and reported directly to the Berlin office of Eichmann's deadly Bureau IV B4. Until the end of 1942, when he was transferred back to Berlin, it was Dannecker who was Hitler's voice to the Vichy on Jewish questions. His insistent message: "Deport the Jews."[3]

Acting on Eichmann's instructions, Dannecker advised the Vichy leadership that he planned opening a Zentraljudenrat—a Central Jewish Office—in the occupied sector. The French, ever

---

[2] Marrus, together with another American, Columbia University's Robert Paxton, would become the first to thoroughly examine the Vichy regime's anti-Semitism *(Vichy France and the Jews,* New York: Schocken, 1981). Until recently, the subject was not one any French academic wished to tackle.

[3] The German occupation also brought the inevitable Nazi plunder brigades: the Einsatzstab Reichsleiter Rosenberg (ERR). Their four-year orgy of avarice would set new records for looting.

eager to maintain the fiction of their "sovereignty"—and to gain access to Jewish property—suggested instead that Vichy authorities be the ones to establish a French-directed Jewish bureau, whose authority would eventually extend to both the occupied sectors as well as the southern free zone. The bemused Germans agreed.

This newest cog in France's bureaucratic wheel: Le Commissariat Général aux Questions Juives (CGQJ)—the General Bureau for Jewish Matters—officially opened its doors on March 29, 1941. It was charged with coordinating and activating all anti-Semitic legislation and propaganda. Admiral François Darlan, then head of the Vichy government, named as its director French war-veterans' leader Xavier Vallat an ultranationalist who intensely disliked the Germans but just as intensely shared their virulent anti-Semitism.

Vallat and his staff were soon enthusiastically codifying new laws in an attempt to close any loopholes still open to the Jews. Rules for *aryanisation économique* were announced that would set Jews apart from the general population and deprive them of both their assets and their property. And just as the Nazis would establish Judenräte—Jewish councils—in Eastern Europe, Vallat established the Union Générale des Israélites de France (General Union of Jews of France, UGIF), a Vichy-coordinated group intended to "control Jewish activities and communal affairs." The term "Jews of France" as opposed to "French Jews" meant that the UGIF would be all-inclusive; it would oversee both French and foreign Jews in France.

On November 17, 1941, Vichy expanded the Aryanization rules to exclude Jews from any employment beyond menial labor. Jews were forbidden to engage in banking, merchant shipping, financial brokerage, publicity, capital lending, commercial brokerage, real estate, sales on commission, or wholesale trading in grains, horses, or livestock. They were expelled from medical and other professional organizations—and from the veterans' organizations. In addition, Jews were banned from trade in antiques, from forestry, gambling, news services (with the exception of a small

Nazi-authorized Jewish press), publishing, filmmaking, theater, and radio. (Vallat hoped eventually to prepare a third Statut des juifs, which would have allowed a certain number of Jewish artisans to practice their trade as long as they did not employ others.)

Exclusions from jobs and professions as well as the theft of their property quickly pauperized many members of a community that had previously prided itself on being largely self-sufficient and highly productive. As was their wont elsewhere, the Nazis and their Vichy allies agreed that the Jews would have to pay for their own poor. Article 22 of the July 22, 1941, Aryanization law provided that part of the assets from the liquidation of Jewish properties would go into a "common fund" to help support this new and growing class of Jewish poor. On December 14, 1941, a German proclamation announced an overall fine on the Jewish population of 1 billion French francs. The funds were drawn from blocked Jewish accounts in French banks. The banks cooperated, including the seized local branches of British and American banks.[4] It was a far cry from their stance when Jewish clients who'd fled to the "safety" of the Vichy-controlled areas and were left without means to support their families asked for transfers from their accounts in Paris or other places in the north. "They just ignored my father's written requests to withdraw funds," says François Lévy, who was then twelve.

Nor had French banks, who'd been given advance notice that Jewish-owned assets were to be frozen, notified their Jewish clients that it might be wise to withdraw at least part of their money. To the contrary. A May 23, 1941, memo signed by Roger Lehideux, chairman of the Bankers' Union, advises the banks that he has received advance notice of plans to block Jewish accounts. Lehideux tells the French banks not to wait for the official order and to freeze Jewish-owned accounts immediately.

---

[4] These French branches continued operation even after the United States entered the war, which in the case of the Vichy regime was only in 1942.

The reappointment in April 1942 of the comically mustached Pierre Laval as the Vichy government's premier signaled a rapid rise in measures against the Jews. Laval, who saw France's future within the Reich's realm, was determined to strengthen collaboration with Hitler. That meant still tougher measures against the Jews. Xavier Vallat, while no lover of Jews, had nonetheless been anti-German and legalistic to the point of pain. But Louis Darquier de Pellepoix, whom Laval appointed Vallat's successor at the CGQ in May of 1942, had no such scruples. He was even more rabidly anti-Semitic than Vallat and more than prepared to cooperate to the hilt with any Nazi plan "to cleanse France of its Jews."

On June 11, 1942, plans were launched in Berlin for the deportation of Jews from France, Belgium, and the Netherlands. Laval was asked to do his share and to assume transportation costs; he agreed. All Jews in the German zone of France were ordered to wear the yellow stars to make it easier to identify them (the Jews were even forced to use scarce clothing-ration coupons to pay for their stars). In another ominous development, the Wehrmacht was ordered to yield authority on maintaining "public order" to the SS, headed in Paris by Polizeiführer Carl Albrecht Oberg.

The first targets for arrest were foreign Jews, either refugees from Nazism or immigrants who'd been in France for years but never received French citizenship. There were soon arrests and deportations.

But the most brutal *rafles,* or roundups, began during the long summer days of 1942. On July 16 and 17, 9,000 members of the French police force descended on the Marais and other working-class quarters of Paris, blocked off streets, and arrested 12,884 Jews, among them the old and handicapped as well as some 4,000 children, many of whom had French nationality.[5] Dragged from

---

[5] Some 10,000 Jews on the roundup list managed to escape arrest thanks to advance warning—in some cases from sympathetic French officials. But even some of those warned ended up in the net; they had no place to hide.

their homes, 7,000 of the deportees were crammed into the "Vél d'Hiv," the Vélodrome d'Hiver sports arena, with little food, water, or adequate sanitary facilities. There they were held incommunicado, had their possessions inventoried, and were processed for shipment to hastily built transit camps.

To show their determination to cooperate with the Germans, Vichy authorities simultaneously carried out their own roundups of foreign Jews in the territory they controlled. The largest one took place in August, when close to 10,000 foreign Jews were netted in various cities of southern France and turned over to the Germans.

Those rounded up were first shipped to two holding camps: Pithiviers and Beaune-la-Rolande south of Paris, where conditions were sparse at best. Ten smaller camps were eventually installed throughout both occupied and Vichy France, including Les Milles near Marseilles. There soon were deaths from disease and exposure. "The first Jewish victims of the Holocaust died on French soil, not Polish or German," says Serge Klarsfeld. Based on departmental and prefectoral archives, Klarsfeld has compiled a list of more than 2,000 Jews who died in French transit camps. The total, concludes Robert Paxton, "is probably closer to three thousand."

But the largest and most appalling of the holding pens was established at Drancy, just a short, sad ride north of central Paris. Built just before the outbreak of the war as a workers' housing project, it was transformed into an overcrowded dispatch station for Auschwitz. It soon came to symbolize the despair and betrayal of French Jews on their own soil.

Of the 87,000 men, women, and children eventually shipped to the camps from Drancy and the other French detention centers, only 2,500 returned at the war's end. Approximately two-thirds of the deportees were non-French citizens. And while collaborators would later try to claim that by helping the Nazis "rid France of foreign Jews" they were saving "real" French Jews, almost 30,000 of the deportees were in fact, as Michael Marrus puts it, "citizens of long standing."

Years later, former Vichy functionaries would also try to accuse Jewish leaders of complicity in choosing just who was to be deported. During his 1997 trial, Maurice Papon, the onetime Vichy secretary-general of the Bordeaux Préfecture, tried to use that argument in defending himself against charges he committed crimes against humanity by ordering the deportation of 1,560 Jews—among them several hundred children—from the Bordeaux area to the Nazi camps.

In fact, UGJF officials were forced at times to help draw up lists of potential deportees for both the Vichy and German police. But if they did so, says Arno Klarsfeld, Serge's son and one of the lawyers who prosecuted Papon, it was because they "had a knife to their throats, whereas the only knife M. Papon had was the one with which he sliced cake when serving tea to German officers in his office."

France also holds the shameful distinction of being the only nation to have voluntarily turned over Jews to the Nazis from outside areas of German military occupation. (Bulgaria deported Jews from areas it conquered in Macedonia and Thrace, but protected its own Jews.)

There were attempts by some Vichy officials to help individual French Jews (especially wealthier, influential ones), and in the earliest years, deportations were limited largely to non-French Jews.[6] But, says Paxton, official "interventions did nothing to deflect the general bent of Vichy policy." As Vichy Justice Minister Joseph Barthélémy put it in a speech in 1941, "one must not let personal regrets stand in the way of cruel necessity."

---

[6] As in other parts of occupied Europe, an unconnected network of brave souls also did its best to hide and save French Jews—and sometimes smuggle them to safety in adjoining neutral countries. Among them: underground Resistance groups, individual Catholic nuns and priests who opened monastaries and convents to Jewish children, and frequently farm families who either helped for pay or out of conscience. Among the most noteworthy in the latter category: the tiny Protestant farming village of Le Chambon-sur-Lignon, which successfully hid more than 2,000 Jews during the war.

Xavier Vallat was even more specific. "We have tried to be surgeons and not butchers," he wrote in 1942, but "France was stricken with a Jewish brain fever of which she almost died."

The deportations were devastating to the community. And while the fiction was officially maintained that the Jews were being sent to "labor camps," there was growing unease on the part of the French public. At the same time, there seemed little opposition to Vichy's project to "eliminate all Jewish influence from the national economy." No aspect of its anti-Semitic policies had a wider effect on the general public than "spoliation." Once the July 22, 1941, laws had been promulgated, CGQJ agents had immediately begun to force Jews to register their property, and Vichy agents quickly swept down to grab it and place it under the control of state-appointed *administrateurs provisoires*—temporary trustees.

"Vallat," says Paxton, "wanted to prove to the Germans that he could organize as effective an economic purge as they could." He also wanted to block any German attempt to extend the influence of occupied-zone administrators and military personnel into the Vichy zone.

The French trustees were charged not only with taking over Jewish offices and businesses but with submitting reports on their economic worthiness. Under the Vichy law, expropriated properties that were considered important to the French economy were sold or transferred to new, non-Jewish owners. If they were unimportant, "they were to be liquidated and the assets auctioned off."

According to period records, by May 1944, 42,227 Jewish enterprises had been placed in trusteeship. Of these, 9,680, including 1,708 apartment buildings, 4,869 shops and businesses, and 1,930 artisan concerns, had been sold to gentiles (among them: 1,954 enterprises in the Vichy-controlled areas). A total of 7,340 enterprises had been liquidated by the trustees. According to Paxton and others, more than 200 million francs had been realized by both sales and liquidations. The funds were deposited into blocked accounts numbered 501 and 511 that were kept by the French public bank, the Caisse des Dépôts et Consignations. By 1943, together with other seized Jewish deposits, the amount plundered from the Jews of France totaled some 3 billion francs.

"The net of Aryanization kept widening," note Marrus and Paxton, "and more and more ordinary business and professional people were drawn into it by the feelings that life must go on, that they must try to obey a novel and confusing law, and that these new arrangements were probably permanent."

The arrangements also proved profitable for the greedy, who were quick to organize. A group calling itself The Affiliated Owners of Aryanized Goods established headquarters not far from the Arc de Triomphe, at 24 avenue Friedland and announced plans to "protect their rights."

Then there were those thieves stealing from the thieves, albeit official ones. Vallat, a fanatic who believed he was serving France, remained squeaky clean financially and according to most experts probably never earned a personal sou from his zealous campaign of "Aryanization." But he did worry that others were trying to profit. "Given the delicacy of the Jewish question in France," he told a fellow Vichy official in the spring of 1942, "it is important to keep personal considerations or commercial rivalries from becoming involved with the measures taken concerning the Israelites." He had an independent auditor assigned to each expropriated business and even devised a system of sealed bids for Jewish property—already an object of struggle between French and German interests. Shortly thereafter he warned that the program of Aryanization "has unleashed greed."

It certainly had among many of it *administrateurs provisoires.* Some, like Gaston Capy, appointed to take over the venerable Paris publishing house of Calmann-Lévy, turned out to be known felons (Capy had served two prison terms for burglary and pimping). Others "acquired impressive strings of Jewish enterprises to manage." One of them, Ambroise Désiré Guy Augustin de Montovert de la Tour, "scion of an ancient and authentically [sic] French family, Catholic and Aryan, from the beginning" as he described himself, had been empowered to administer no fewer than seventy-six different Jewish enterprises—skimming, it was charged, large sums in the process.

So pervasive was the dishonesty that in May 1944 the French asked Louis-Gabriel Formery, the Vichy inspector of finances (auditor), to carefully investigate the entire Commissariat Général aux Questions Juives. Formery, who had no moral objections to the theft of Jewish property, simply wanted the system to work. He concluded that there were "innumerable and incredible abuses," not differentiating between those who were stealing from both the system and the Jews and those who had entered into "secret deals with Jewish proprietors to camouflage false Aryanizations."

Like the French banks, many of the Vichy-sponsored trade and professional associations *(comités d'organisation,* or COs), saw the anti-Jewish legislation as a golden opportunity to get even with competitors. This was particularly true in those industries, such as crafts and trade, where Jews had been the dominant force. The French fur industry, which according to some sources had been 80 percent Jewish before the war, was quickly "cleansed." Then, at the behest of its trade association, Jewish enterprises were liquidated rather than sold to "outsiders." Diamond merchants were advised to form a cooperative to buy the stocks of the 75 percent of their trade that had been in Jewish hands.

Ironically, some French economic interests were less than happy with the results of the anti-Jewish legislation. As in the old story of the Swiss hotel manager who when asked whether he was anti-Semitic replied, "Not in season," hotel owners and casino operators along the Riviera pressed to keep the business of the same wealthy Jews whom Vichy and the Nazis wanted to ship to French internment camps.

Slightly different complaints were heard from other parts of the French business world. Leather-goods manufacturers might not have wanted Jewish competitors, but they desperately needed the skills of Jewish artisans who traditionally had been their primary cutters and sewers. According to one French National Archives document uncovered by the Marrus-Paxton team, the Limoges branch of the watch industry even applied to have some Jewish watchmakers released from detention to help the industry meet its quotas. But Vichy official Darquier de Pellepoix refused, claiming that the jobs should go to French skilled artisans. "The [watch-industry] official then felt obliged to assure Darquier de Pellepoix that 'I'm an old anti-Semite,' but that it took a long time to train a watchmaker" and demand was high.

In November 1942, German and Italian forces rolled into southern France to occupy the Vichy's so-called free zone. And for a brief moment, Jews could dramatically enhance their chances for survival by seeking refuge in those sectors controlled by the Italians. More than 50,000 flocked to the eight southern departments east of the Rhône, where Italy maintained a liberal and remarkably humane occupation force. Though Mussolini had slavishly legislated his own anti-Semitic laws, many of his officers had little appetite for their enforcement. In Nice, carabinieri stood guard outside the local synagogue and gave leaders of the local Jewish community permission to issue identity cards. More important, and to the absolute dismay of the Germans and Vichy alike, the Italians intervened to stop deportations of both French and foreign Jews.

The downfall of Mussolini in April 1943 ended the brief respite. Not inclined to cooperate with Nazi demands, Italian troops had already begun to withdraw from southern France. Italian-Jewish leader Angelo Donati had hoped to arrange an emergency evacuation of as many as 30,000 Jews to Italy and North Africa. But when Nazi forces marched into Nice on September 8, Donati's plan went up in smoke. Tens of thousands of Jews who thought they were safe were now caught in what the French prefect of the

Alpes-Maritimes would later describe as a "veritable climate of terror."

Lawyer Serge Klarsfeld agrees: "The roundups in Nice were the most savage in western Europe."

Klarsfeld knows. He was there. The son of Polish-Jewish immigrants, he and his sister had been taken by their mother to the southwest of France when the Germans entered Paris in June 1940. "My father was a volunteer in the French Army. When France fell, he became a POW, but he escaped from Germany and came to find us. We eventually all made it to the Côte d'Azur, to Nice, where we felt safe with the Italians. It was the only part of occupied Western Europe where Jews were living completely free."

That freedom ended one night shortly after the Italians left. "My father had built a double wall in the closet of our apartment. When the Germans arrived to round up the Jews of the house, he put my mother, my sister, and me behind [the false wall], and he remained in the apartment to open the door to the SS. They looked around, but not carefully enough. Then they took him away. The next day, we escaped to another place and hid again."

"So our family," Klarsfeld says dryly, "is an example of what happened in France. One-quarter of the Jews were deported, my father among them. My mother, my sister, and I, we survived."

As if the raids and roundups by the Germans and their ever-acquiescent friends in the French *milice* were not bad enough, the Jews found themselves victimized by French gangs who demanded protection money—and then turned them in anyway for bounty.

Those Jews rounded up in the *rafles* throughout France immediately had their apartments and possessions confiscated. "What the German and French police didn't take," recalls Claudia Ann Carlin, who lost her parents to deportation when she was barely seven, "neighbors usually stole." Those Jews who managed to leave with a few small, personal possessions or cash had it taken from them at Drancy, where there was a systematic stripping of all possessions of value. True to form, the Germans and their French bureaucrat assistants kept orderly records in small notebooks and in receipt-voucher ledgers. Discovered after the liberation, they are preserved today in a drawer in the archives of the somber Center for Jewish Documentation in the Marais district of Paris. Almost every entry speaks a multitude of sadness.

275: March 5, 1944
Monsieur Jablonsky, Grenoble
Twenty-four thousand francs (24,000)
40 pounds sterling
one platinum and diamond ring
1 gold wedding ring
1 gold bracelet

With the liberation of Paris in August 1944, the contents of the Drancy depository were transferred to French government safes where, *en principe*, survivors could come to make claims. But what of the tens of thousands of Drancy alumni who did not return? According to newly available records, by 1951 most of the unclaimed jewelry, watches, and keepsakes had been put on the public block by the French government (without any indication that Holocaust victims were the source). The profits from these auction sales of "unclaimed items" were deposited into the French government treasury.

Drancy's officially appointed bookkeeper, Maurice Kiffer, had also kept assiduous records, not only of the items confiscated in Drancy but of cash and other objects of value confiscated when Jews were first arrested. Soon after the camp was liberated in 1944, Kiffer turned in a report to the new Gaullist government with the details and sums of all the amounts he'd recorded. All told, said Kiffer, FF12,039,892.85 had been confiscated from the Jews imprisoned at Drancy. Almost all this money, he reported, had been transferred to the French national banking institution known as the Caisse des Dépôts et Consignations.

No less astounding were the amounts of property and objects that the Nazis themselves confiscated in France under the stewardship of Alfred Rosenberg, the Nazi Party's chief ideologue and its leading plunderer. As cover for his thievery, the Estonian-born Rosenberg, who also headed the party's foreign policy department, had established an Institut zur Erforschung der Judenfrage—Institution for the Investigation of the Jewish Question—in Frankfurt in 1939. Its primary mission, according to Holocaust historian Lionel Kochan: "to ransack the libraries, archives, and art galleries of European Jewry in order to promote 'research.' " The Einsatzstab Rosenberg, Rosenberg's operational staff, had already begun its work in the Netherlands. Now it descended on France. On December 18, 1941, three months before the deportations of the Jews in France began in earnest, Rosenberg himself requested Hitler's personal authorization to seize all the household effects and personal possessions belonging to Jews and to distribute parts of them among party members and Wehrmacht staff. Hitler issued his own personal seal of approval in a memorandum dated December 31, 1941.[7]

As in the Netherlands, the Einsatzstab Reichsleiter Rosenberg's (ERR) first targets were France's most prestigious Jewish-owned art collections. Paintings and sculptures belonging to the Rothschild family, for example, were estimated then to be valued at more than 2 billion francs. Other noted collections included those of wealthy Jewish art patrons like Alphonse Kann and the David-Weills. Jewish art dealers, like Paul Rosenberg (no relation to Alfred), were also singled out for special treatment. At first they were shaken down to force them to turn over their stocks. Eventually their precious artworks were simply confiscated.

---

[7] On June 8, 1944, two days after the Allied D-Day invasion at Normandy that heralded the fall of the Reich, Rosenberg issued a comprehensive report on the Einsatzstab Reichsleiter Rosenberg's achievements. "After four years of operation, dear Führer, I can report that we have executed your orders to the best of our ability."

European collections that had been sent to France for safe-keeping before the actual outbreak of war also fell prey to German avarice. The wealthy Dutch-German banker Friedrich Gutmann, the youngest son of the founder of Germany's Dresdener Bank, had consigned thirty of his best old master and impressionist paintings to a Paris gallery. Most of them were seized by Alfred Rosenberg's agents. Works by Degas and Renoir, considered too "modern" for Nazi taste, were sold or exchanged in the European art market. At least one of the Gutmann-owned paintings, a portrait by Dosso Dossi, joined the growing Göring Collection.[8]

In a disgusting display of greed, many Paris dealers collaborated in this Nazi plunder, cashing in on their Jewish colleagues' misfortune. But the French weren't the only villains. Dealers and collectors in nearby Switzerland were as eager to traffic in looted Nazi art as wartime Swiss bankers were ready to traffic in looted Nazi gold. And according to American investigative reporter Hector Feliciano, at least one of the most prominent Jewish-owned galleries in Paris, the Wildenstein Gallery, seems to have collaborated with the Nazis both before and after the occupation. (The embarrassed Wildenstein family has denied the charge and is suing Feliciano for damages, a suit that was rejected by a French court.)

To accommodate their loot, the Rosenberg units transformed the Jeu de Paume Museum on the broad place de la Concorde into a vast Nazi storage chamber. The best of the looted pieces, especially the old masters and great classics that Hermann Göring planned on shipping back to Germany, were sent. Closed and carefully guarded, the museum was also a holding hall for important works of the "degenerate" impressionist and modern art that the

---

[8] Gutmann and his wife remained in Holland. Promised safe passage through the efforts of an Italian diplomat, they left by train for Florence in the spring of 1943. When their luxury car stopped in Berlin, German officials removed them and shipped them to Theresienstadt. The Nazis still wanted that part of Gutmann's collection that remained beyond their reach. When Gutmann refused to "legally" sign it over, he was beaten to death. Two of his looted paintings, a Renoir and a Degas, would show up fifty years later in American collections.

Nazis scorned but planned to sell in Switzerland and other neutral nations in order to trade for old masters or raise cash for the German war effort. Eager streams of dealers—French, German, and Swiss—were among the frequent callers, with Parisian art dealer Gustav Rochlitz one of the major "exchange organizers"—the term used for brokers.

Fortunately for the French, several of the Parisian curators assigned to help in the enormous task of cataloging and safekeeping the art loot kept careful, secret notes on what passed through their hands (one of them, the legendary Rose Valland, became the subject of a popular postwar film). After the war, their records would be of invaluable help in recouping at least parts of what had been stolen.

The amounts of internationally significant art devoured from French Jews by the Nazi plunder machine are staggering. According to an Einsatzstab Reichsleiter Rosenberg report dated July 15, 1944, between October 1940 and July 1944 some 21,903 truly great works of art were shipped to the Reich from France. Among them: 5,281 canvases including works by Rembrandt, Rubens, and Fragonard, as well as 2,437 historic pieces of furniture and 583 Gobelin tapestries. At least 137 freight cars were eventually used to transport the loot to Germany. The largest single shipment, filled with Gobelin tapestries, as well as paintings and other precious items, consisted of 35 freight wagons and reached Germany on March 15, 1943.

While their primary interest in Paris was great art, the ERR also turned its attention to lesser-known Jewish-owned art and antiques, as well as furniture, jewelry, furs, and precious books. Entire Judaica libraries were looted and crated. Among those seized: the 60,000-volume collection of the Alliance Israélite Universelle, considered among the finest Judaica libraries in Europe; the 30,000-book collection of the École Rabbinique; and some 28,000 volumes and 760 crates of archival material from the Bibliothèque Rothschild. Like other great Jewish libraries the Nazis plundered in every city they occupied, the rarest of the books were shipped to the Frankfurt Institut zur Erforschung der Judenfrage and to other anti-Semitic research and propaganda institutes in Berlin. Many of the rest were sold for pulp.

Nor was music immune from the Nazis' reach. In August of 1940, just a month after Reichsleiter Rosenberg had established the first ERR office in Paris, a special Sonderstab Musik division of his operation was opened under the direction of Haupstellenleiter Herbert Gerigk. Its assigned task: to confiscate ancient French musical manuscripts as well as anything connected to music that belonged to Jews—instruments, books, scores, and recordings. Berlin's instructions to Gerigk were "to process music literature, music paraphernalia, and music manuscripts . . . and . . . to prepare [them] for shipment to Berlin, Leipzig, and Upper Bavaria."

The Sonderstab Musik raids on apartments in Paris and homes in the countryside, many of them abandoned or sealed, swept up not only pianos, violins, and other instruments belonging to individual Jewish families but also the personal collections of such international musical luminaries as Wanda Landowska, Darius Milhaud, and Artur Rubinstein. A special series of music warehouses was established in Paris and equipped for storage and inventory of the instruments prior to their shipment to Germany. Three of the warehouses were devoted only to pianos. Another, on the rue Bassano, was expressly created to house "small musical instruments."

It was an enormous, if evil, task. According to a comprehensive study of Sonderstab Musik by Amsterdam University's Willem de Vries, 1,500 workers were employed at the height of the Musik Aktion just to empty the homes of musically inclined French Jews. An average of two loot-laden trains departed for Germany each week—and at least one freight car in each shipment was loaded with musical instruments, gramophones, and music books. In addition, furniture vans belonging to French firms such as Crassier and Bailly carried out overland-shipping work for the Nazis. Even

D-Day couldn't stop the musical plunder. The final train shipment of instruments left France as late as July 21, 1944, with thirty-four upright pianos and twelve grand pianos. German records indicate that they arrived seriously damaged, apparently because of the haste with which they had been packed.

Just how much did the Germans and their Vichy allies steal from France's Jews? According to French historian David Douvette, the total take was gargantuan. "The Rosenberg Brigade, which was directed in France by Colonel [and Baron] Kurt von Behr, had a normal procedure. Once a home had been emptied of its inhabitants," says Douvette, "the Einsatzstab Rosenberg would appear and systematically empty it of its belongings." According to Douvette, this included "everything"—furniture, linens, clothing, toys, decorations, kitchen utensils, photos, and personal files—everything. All the stolen goods would be taken for temporary storage in the vast warehouses of an organized French furniture company called Lévitan, which had been seized from its prewar Jewish owners. Rosenberg's crew of "experts" would then classify the stolen goods before shipping them to Germany. "In 1942, the Germans shipped 40,000 tons of stolen furniture from France to Germany."

The haul was indeed staggering. According to an August 8, 1944, report detailing German expropriations in occupied France, Belgium, and the Netherlands, the Rosenberg Brigade had "cleansed" a total of 69,512 Jewish apartments of all their furnishings. To transport them, the report said, the Germans had commandeered 674 trains—a total of 26,984 freight cars. Douvette notes, "They used greater care in packing the furniture into the trains than they did in packing the Jews they deported to the death camps."

Though three-fourths of French Jewry had survived the war, the liberation in 1944 saw the Jewish community devastated and disheartened. "There were some gentiles who had helped," recalls one survivor. "But there were so many who hadn't and so many who had turned on us. None of us would ever be able to fully trust our French neighbors again."

Others who'd survived the horrors of the camps found that when they returned, many Frenchmen refused to believe the brutal realities they'd witnessed. One woman recently interviewed by French television says that after hearing her describe Auschwitz, the government physician who examined her in 1945 recommended she be sent to a Paris psychiatric asylum. "He thought my story was a madwoman's."

Yet in some ways the war had strengthened French Jewry. "We had learned to rely on a new self-unity during the war," says Serge Cwajgenbaum of the French branch of the World Jewish Congress, himself the son of French Holocaust survivors. "We knew we had to stick together, and this meant both the old established community of French Jews and the new immigrant community."

While almost entirely consumed by the immediate care and feeding needs of returning survivors, refugees, and war orphans, the Jews of France also devoted efforts to recouping expropriated and stolen property, especially those of deportees. Many survivors who had owned homes and apartments before the war received them back with some bureaucratic difficulty and almost always devoid of their possessions and furnishings.

"Our country home in Normandy, which overlooked the Seine, had been emptied of everything—including my father's precious collection of first-edition books" recalls André Wormser, whose father, Georges, had penned the famous open letter to Pétain. "Everything was gone; it was all empty."

So too was the Wormser family's sprawling full-floor apartment on the elegant rue Spontini off the avenue Foch. "Fortunately, a cousin who was married to a non-Jew remembered having stored some of my grandmother's belongings in a warehouse before the war. So at least we had tables and chairs. But my parents could find no trace of anything else," says Wormser.

"We considered ourselves lucky to have survived. But there

was one possession my mother truly mourned: the grand piano she'd been given by her mother as a wedding gift."

By chance, a source in the new De Gaulle government tipped off the Wormsers to the existence of one of the repositories north of Paris where the Nazis stored stolen instruments before shipping them to Germany. "Apparently they hadn't managed to get everything out of France before the liberation," says Wormser, who now heads Banque Wormser Frères, the same family bank his father and uncle had founded. "I took my mother to that place, and we were taken into a vast warehouse room. It was filled with hundreds, thousands of pianos in every size and shape—all in neat rows and all without their legs. They had been removed to facilitate shipment, but had been carefully numbered so that they could be re-attached to the pianos when they reached Germany. It was a staggering example to me of the scope and depth of the plunder."

Amazingly, Mme. Wormser found her wedding piano. Today, its legs intact again, it stands once more in the apartment on rue Spontini.

Not all received their homes and property back so easily, even empty. Albert Finel, a hatmaker who'd emigrated to France with his wife and children from Poland in 1933, had been in the first wave of deportees despite the fact that he'd served France in the Foreign Legion and won the Croix de Guerre. Still without French citizenship, he had been summoned to the mayoral office near his apartment and atelier in the *Pletzel*—the "little square"—that narrow-streeted quarter on the Paris Right Bank that has been a center of Jewish life since the Middle Ages.

"They told him it was just to verify his identity," recalls his son, Lucien Finel, later a deputy mayor of the city of Paris. "But they also told him to bring a blanket and three days of supplies."

Finel's mother warned her husband not to go. "But he believed in France, in the Republic, and he had his Croix de Guerre."

Sent first to the teeming detention camp at Pithiviers in the

Loire region, Finel was turned over to the Germans and deported to Auschwitz on July 13, 1942, never to be seen again. When his son returned to their apartment after the war, another French family from the north was living there. It took a lengthy court battle to recover their apartment. But hundreds of other Holocaust survivors who also returned to find their prewar apartments taken never won their struggle to reclaim them—or never even went to court to assert their rights. "In those first years after the war," says the popular French-Jewish author Marek Halter, "many French Jews refused to even discuss the issue. Who talks of money in a cemetery?" asks Halter.

Postwar French systems for restitution left a great deal to be desired. The Vichy Office for Jewish Affairs, the CGQT, ceased to exist and was reconstituted as a restitution-claims office—with many of the same bureaucrats who'd administered Aryanization. "There was an effort to make it seem as though the only ones to blame here were the Germans," says Douvette.

But the pillaging had also been carried out by Frenchmen. Primary among them, says Douvette, were those who worked in the French offices of the Gestapo, notably the infamous one on the rue Lauriston in the 16th arrondissement. Many of these collaborators, says Douvette, quoting French government records, "just helped themselves." According to Douvette's research, the booty in just one month, April 1941, included 142 million francs (of which 17.5 million were in British sterling and 9 million in U.S. dollars), 17 gold bars, 502 pieces of silver, "thousands of metric cubes of antique furniture and rare carpets," as well as 300 kilos of adult clothing, 150 kilos of children's clothing, and 3 kilos of "food ration tickets."

"Members of the Fascist *milice,* functionaries of the collaborationist parties, officials of prefectures, and even some *gardiens de la paix* [traffic policemen], didn't hesitate to pillage apartments."

Many others denounced Jewish neighbors to the authorities,

often in anonymous notes or phone calls. One file recently seen at the National Archives in Paris contains a letter from a Frenchman complaining petulantly that a Jewish immigrant egg seller, forbidden from doing any more business in the local *marché* by the Aryanization laws, had been "seen giving his sister-in-law and cousin six eggs." The man was arrested and ultimately sent to Auschwitz.

Once such Jewish neighbors were arrested, those who'd betrayed them often raced to their now empty apartments ahead of the authorities "to steal whatever they could."

"It didn't matter what level of society you were in," says Douvette. "During the occupation, every social category in France was contaminated by the temptation to inform in order to 'appropriate.'"

Douvette and other scholars of the period insist on differentiating between what they call "legal plunder" and plain old-fashioned plunder: in other words, the expropriation of Jewish property under Vichy's anti-Semitic laws on the one hand and the criminal looting of Jews by freelancing amateurs and semiprofessionals on the other. The former has been difficult enough to quantify; the latter is almost impossible. "We know that there were FFR1,289,139,035 blocked in the Caisse des Dépôts et Consignations," Douvette told a 1990 colloquium on the fiftieth anniversary of Vichy's Statut des juifs. "But how do you estimate the cash stolen from apartments, the monies confiscated from people rounded up, the amounts handed over to non-Jews for 'safekeeping,' the amounts taken from bank safety-deposit vaults? How do you value the tons of stolen jewelry? How do you estimate the value of the tons of furniture and personal effects stolen by one or another? At how much value do you place the contents of all those little ateliers, shops, and studios: the machines, the tools, the raw materials? What about the stocks, bonds, and paintings still held today?"

Because there was so much "private initiative" in Vichy's economic Aryanization, period officials may well have doctored their own figures to cloak private initiative.[9] An April 1944 census by the Director of Aryanization of the Commissariat General for Jewish Matters lists 42,227 Jewish industrial, commercial, and building enterprises. The report goes on to say that 9,680 Jewish enterprises and 11,000 Jewish properties had been "Aryanized" and another 7,340 Jewish enterprises totally liquidated.

But Douvette calls those figures "derisive" in the face of the reality and even questions the figures of Joseph Billig, one of the earlier researchers of the damage wrought by Vichy's thefts, who estimated that the Aryanization expropriations had cost French Jews some 8 billion French francs. "Without a doubt," says Douvette, "considering all the incalculables, [Billig's] figure is less than real."

What was returned? Major French-Jewish-owned enterprises—such as the Galéries Lafayette department store, Citroën autoworks, and the Rothschild Bank—could be easily balance-sheeted and returned to their original owners with little problem. Georges Wormser's bank actually turned a profit of more than a million francs under its wartime Vichy-appointed managers. But Wormser refused to ask the postwar French government to credit the money to his bank. "It was the furthest thing from our mind; it would have been shameful to do so," says his son André.

While the *grands seigneurs* of French Jewry could collect at least parts of what had been expropriated from them and their families, it was next to impossible to calculate damages for thousands of small and medium-size businesses, shops, and ateliers that belonged to Jewish proprietors many of whom, as Douvette puts it, "completely disappeared with their entire families."

Matters were not made easier by the French government, which until 1999 invoked state law to keep hundreds of thousands of Vichy-period documents safely under lock and key (the War

[9] Several of the greediest had been discovered by German officials, arrested, and were themselves sent to concentration camps for "stealing from the Reich."

Documents section of the National Archives contains no fewer than 62,460 file boxes relating to Vichy dealings with Jews). Until a scandal broke more than a decade ago, even the fact that the archives still contained almost all the Vichy-period registration cards of French Jews was kept secret, and the data deemed inaccessible.

Nor were the great banks of France eager to make amends. In 1951, when the Center for Contemporary Jewish Documentation, France's finest Holocaust-research center, presented a detailed list of confiscated Jewish assets known to have been deposited in the banks' coffers and asked that the banking industry search its records, almost all the banks refused, citing "banking secrecy rules."

Restitution conditions were especially abominable for the tens of thousands of French-Jewish children who, while themselves French nationals, had deceased parents who were not. The postwar German government had transferred reparations payments to France for the orphaned French children of deportees and for victims of Nazism—mostly Jews. But the French government used major chunks of the German money to compensate and reward active Resistance fighters and their families, ignoring the needs of the orphaned Jewish children. "When these French children of 'foreigners' approached the French government for assistance," says Serge Klarsfeld, "they were told, 'Your parents were foreigners; you should address your complaints to the German government.' When they went to the West German authorities, they were told to 'go to the French government.' It was a Kafkian situation, made all the more horrible by the fact that these were orphans in both moral and material distress."

Such was the case of Fernande Bodner, whose Polish-born father had been a furrier with a large apartment-cum-atelier at 7, rue Boinod in the 18th arrondissement of Paris. "When they arrested him," says Bodner, who now lives in Brooklyn, New York, "the Vichy sealed our apartment and took away all his business assets—

his fur stocks, his machinery, his equipment. They also took all our private belongings—our silver, china, paintings, and jewelry, everything we had, including bank accounts—and they made lists of it all."

After her father was deported in 1944, Bodner was placed in a Vichy-run home for French-Jewish children, where she was forced to wear a yellow Juif star. "I used to cover it with a book held to my chest so that I could slip into a cinema forbidden to Jews. I came back home one day and saw that the Vichy were loading all the children onto trucks. I ran and spent the rest of the war hiding." Despite numerous queries to the French government, she has never been able to discover what happened to her family's belongings.

There are hundreds of similar stories. Annette Zajdenberg, now Claudia Ann Ca•lin of New York, a publicist and writer, was the daughter of one of Paris's best known prewar portrait photographers, Joseph Zajdenberg. "My father specialized in theatrical portraits; he was an official photographer for the Comédie Française and signed his pictures 'Studio Charles.'"

In 1942, barely seven years old, Carlin-Zajdenberg says she remembers passing two men in long gray overcoats standing on the stairwell of her apartment building on the rue du Château-d'Eau. She later learned in horror that the two were French policemen who took her mother and infant sister away. Both were shipped to Auschwitz on November 11 and gassed upon arrival. The family's possessions and assets were seized.

She and her father managed to slip away and hide in Paris, until they were finally arrested by the French police in April of 1943. The Polish-born elder Zajdenberg was sent to Auschwitz on June 23, 1943, and perished there, one more victim of the Vichy. Claudia, first handed over to a French relative, was later sheltered by a Christian family and survived as a "hidden child" until liberation in August 1944.

With her immediate family dead and everything they'd ever

owned completely vanished, Carlin left France and eventually settled in New York. Despite numerous approaches to French authorities, she says, she has never been able to trace her father's rich photographic and art collection, his equipment, or his bank accounts.

Jews in the provinces often fared no better, nor, in the aftermath of the war, did their children. Polish-born Meijlach and Sara Levendel owned and operated a small *épicerie* in the town of Le Pontet in the southern Vaucluse. Their only son, Isaac, had been born in Avignon in 1936. In March 1940, Meijlach Levendel enlisted in the French Army. Captured by the Germans, he managed to escape to Switzerland, where he was interned until October 1944.

Back in Le Pontet, Sara Levendel continued to run the shop. When the mayor of Le Pontet ignominiously included the Levendels in a 1941 census of Jews in the region, their identity and ration cards were immediately stamped "Juif." Fearing for her son's safety, Sara hid him with a French farmer's family in the nearby countryside while she remained behind in Le Pontet.

On June 6, 1944—D-Day and a little more than two months before the liberation of France—Sara was arrested in her shop by French police, apparently on a tip from Marseilles-based bounty hunters. Severely beaten on the spot, she was taken to Avignon's Sainte-Anne Prison and then transferred to the French transfer camp at Drancy, where the chief of camp police signed a receipt indicating she had been relieved of 470 French francs and a gold Tissot wristwatch. On June 30, 1944, Mme. Levendel was loaded onto a cattle car. It was Drancy's convoy number 76—its next to last. She was gassed in Auschwitz on July 4, 1944, only six weeks before the German Army was defeated in France and Paris was liberated.

As for the contents of the Levendels' Vaucluse store, witnesses reported that everything, including cash, merchandise, and other valuables, had been carefully inventoried and then removed by truck within hours of Sara Levendel's arrest. It was part of the prize accorded the bounty hunters. According to court documents, the cash was deposited into a French bank trust—as was the expropriated property of 26,418 other Jewish victims who were arrested between June 18, 1943, and August 18, 1944.

Isaac Levendel, who now lives in Naperville, Illinois, finally discovered the details of his mother's deportation in 1990, thanks to the research carried out by Serge Klarsfeld. Like many of the survivors of France's plundered Jewish families, he is convinced that most if not all of the cash and valuables are still buried somewhere in the French treasury's account books. No French government has ever provided a reckoning.

Lawyer Klarsfeld, who is president of the Association of Sons and Daughters of the Deportees, a group he created, has fought for more than four decades on behalf of "the forgotten children." It has been part of a lifetime of struggle rooted in memory and a passion for historic justice, even if it is no more than setting the tragic record straight. Though most known for the dramatic work he and his German-born, non-Jewish wife, Beate, the daughter of a Wehrmacht soldier, have done in hunting down such notorious Nazi war criminals as Klaus Barbie, the Gestapo's "Butcher of Lyons," Klarsfeld arguably has done more than any other Frenchman to shake French consciousness out of its postwar stupor and into a recognition of the sins of the Vichy period—sins of both commission and omission. "De Gaulle was a great leader who wanted to unite France. He did not want to remind it of the terrible things Vichy had done—especially to the Jews of France. He turned the national page as quickly as he could."

As late as 1991, French President François Mitterrand, who himself had worked for the Vichy regime's Ministry of Veterans' Affairs in 1941 and in the postwar years continued his own personal friendship with René Bousquet, the man who had been the Vichy prefect of police, would insist that "Vichy was not France."

Indeed, for almost fifty years, most French historians concentrated on glorifying if not exaggerating the role of the French Resistance, all but ignoring the extent of France's collaboration and the ignobility of its treatment of its Jews, native as well as foreign. It was left to an American historian, Robert Paxton of Columbia University, to point out France's moral nakedness during the war years. In his landmark book on the Vichy years, *Vichy France: Old Guard and New Order,* and then again in his *Vichy France and the Jews,* written together with Michael Marrus, Paxton unleashed a torrent of detail that official France refused to face and many French still find difficult to absorb.

Still, Klarsfeld and others offer no blanket condemnation of the French. "There were different behaviors," he insists. "The French government and those who collaborated with it must be condemned for the actions they took against the Jews, actions they even took without the Germans demanding it. At the same time, there were many in the French population who deserve some kind of gratitude for their reactions against the Vichy ideology. These people did not respond like Vichy—they responded like Frenchmen."

Paris-based international lawyer Samuel Pisar, who as a young boy spent three years in Auschwitz, agrees. "There were the collaborators, there were the thieves, and there was the majority that simply watched with folded arms." But Pisar, who is today the French chairman of the Yad Vashem Holocaust Memorial, says there were others—certainly not the majority—"who proved they were righteous humans."

In 1996, the international scandal caused by revelations regarding Swiss banks began to have the same ripple effect in France as it had in other European countries. Questions long dormant were now asked in public and in the press, including France's. There were shocking revelations, including the discovery that apartments and buildings seized from deported Jews had been absorbed by the city of Paris and were now among the 1,389 low-rent, high-luxury apartments owned and controlled by the municipality. In some cases, new apartments had been built on land that once belonged to deportees. One particular fact greatly embarrassed the Élysée Palace: In a book called *Private Property,* French investigative reporter Brigitte Vital-Durand disclosed that the residents of one of the best low-rent city-owned apartments included President (and former Paris mayor) Jacques Chirac's brother-in-law and his family. The land on which the building stood had been seized from Elias Zaijdner, a Jewish antique dealer who died in Auschwitz in 1944, together with his three sons.

Another book, this one by Puerto Rican–born cultural-affairs writer Hector Feliciano, was no less shocking to the French public. Called *The Lost Museum,* it was the culmination of seven years of research on Feliciano's part—and stonewalling by French museum officials, who were not about to cooperate with an American in Paris.

Acting on a tip from a friend who worked in one of France's national museums, Feliciano embarked on an investigative trail to discover the fate of paintings looted by the Nazis and their agents, which were returned to France at the end of the war and never claimed or returned to their rightful owners.

According to the French ambassador to the United States, François Bujon d'Estaing, "the task of retrieving [looted] artwork started right after the end of the Second World War." In fact, it began as early as November 1944, when the French established a Commission de Récupération Artistique charged with recovering as many as possible of the artworks seized by the Nazis.

Working from prewar and wartime records, including the inventories covertly prepared by French curators like Rose Valland who had worked under the Nazis classifying and caring for the looted paintings they'd warehoused in the Jeu de Paume, the commission prepared a fourteen-volume catalog of stolen artworks, which they distributed internationally.

They met with relative success. Of the approximately 100,000 items listed as stolen, France managed to retrieve 61,257—including works from some of the most prestigious collections, such as the Rothschilds'. The balance disappeared, some of them occasionally popping up in auctions or in some cases even in American museum collections.

By 1949, 45,441 of the retrieved art objects had been returned to their rightful owners or the heirs of those owners. But looted paintings and the other artworks were returned only if owners or heirs of owners actively laid claim to the items and could prove ownership.

A total of 15,816 items were never claimed. Instead, by order of a discreet French governmental decree dated September 20, 1949, all unclaimed works were classified as "MNR"—*Musées Nationaux Récupération*—and placed in the care of the Museums of France. Shortly thereafter, a selection was made. The directors of the Musées de France chose 2,058 pieces of unclaimed art as "worthy of keeping" (1,029 paintings and the balance sculptures, tapestries, carpets, and antique furniture). The remaining 13,758 items were put up for public sale; the monies realized from the auction were deposited into French governmental coffers.

In 1950, most of the 2,058 unclaimed works that were kept were transferred to the National Museum of the Château de Compiègne, north of Paris and not far from the railroad siding in the Compiègne Forest where France had signed its humiliating surrender to Hitler on June 22, 1940. The French government would claim they remained "available for viewing" till 1954, which authorities said "allowed owners adequate time to make claims." (In fact, about thirty of them were claimed and returned.) But in the austerity of postwar France, Compiègne was hardly a convenient location for the exhibit. Nor was it a normal exhibit open to the general public; claimants had first to describe what they were looking for before being allowed to view anything. In the case of heirs of war and Holocaust victims, many had been children during the war and were not necessarily aware of what art had been looted from their families.

The damning fact is that from 1949 until 1997, French authorities never made any active effort, let alone a concerted one, to search either for the rightful owners of the MNRs or their heirs. And they failed to do so, points out Feliciano, "even in the case of rather famous paintings whose provenance was easily traceable, even in the case where German documents clearly stated who the paintings had been stolen from. They just weren't interested."

Instead, the "unclaimed" MNRs were spread among French museums for display or used to decorate government offices and embassies (one piece of sculpture, an eighteenth-century bust of a woman said to be Madame de Pompadour, found its way into France's presidential Élysée Palace; two other pieces were placed in the French mission to the United Nations and in the French consulate in New York).

French authorities would later assert that all of the unclaimed art items thus distributed were listed only in "provisional inventories," in that way carefully separating them from the permanent collections of the institutions now housing them; all of the works bore some sort of generic marking code to indicate their "recuperated" status.

But there was no explanation of what the codes meant, nor were the codes prominently displayed. Nor was there any annotation or plaque indicating that any given work had been looted by the Nazis, retrieved after the war, and never claimed by its original owner. How many millions of visitors to the Pompidou Center passed in front of Fernand Léger's 1914 cubist masterpiece *Woman in Red and Green* without ever knowing it had been stolen from the collection of Paris gallery owner Leonce Rosenberg? How many visitors to the Musée des Beaux-Arts in the Breton city of Rennes on the Brittany coast have admired Picasso's 1921 *Head of a Woman* without knowing that it had once belonged to Jewish collector Alphonse Kann? And where was the comprehensive catalog of the unclaimed works, a list that as late as 1998 the Museums of France still insisted was "in preparation"?

"For half a century," says Feliciano, whose book became a runaway bestseller in France, "these works have been in a sort of artistic purgatory with no huge effort to resolve what is a cultural embarrassment."

Some French officials readily admitted that no effort had been undertaken to find the owners of the lost museum. "It is a very bizarre story," said Hubert Landis, the head of the Administration of French National Museums from 1977 to 1987. "We never attempted to look for the owners. I realize how surprising that must seem. The weak point in the justification offered by museum administrators is that no one in the last fifty years has taken the initiative."

Yet even after Feliciano's revelations sullied France's tradition as the world's art capital, other French museum officials remained in denial. In a July 1998 letter to the *New York Review of Books,* Françoise Cachin, directoress of the Musées de France, vigorously denied they had done any wrong.

Feliciano himself came under personal pressure to drop his claims. According to Feliciano, both Cachin and Didier Shulman of the Pompidou Center called to urge him to let the Musées de France "handle the issue." And coincidentally or not, five days after a major interview with the American writer appeared in the influential French daily *Le Monde,* Feliciano received notice that the French income-tax authority was investigating him.

But the atmosphere in France had changed, and the "taboos of the black years," as one French journalist put it, "are gone." With the passage of time—not to mention the death of President François Mitterrand, the last of the wartime generation of French leaders—France finally seemed prepared to face up to the ignobilities of its Vichy past. The 1998 public trial of Maurice Papon, the Vichy secretary-general of the Bordeaux Préfecture who helped deport Jews to their deaths and then went on to serve as Minister of Budget under President Valéry Giscard d'Estaing, gave many of

France's younger generation new insights into a long-shadowed past.

On July 16, 1995, fifty-three years after the first major *rafle*, the infamous Vél d'Hiv roundup of Parisian Jews, French President Jacques Chirac finally issued a statement recognizing French complicity in the Holocaust. "This criminal madness of the occupying forces," Chirac told a memorial assembly in Paris, "was assisted by the French and the French state." And Cardinal Lustiger, himself a convert from Judaism, issued a statement of penance on behalf of French-Catholic leaders for the Church's failure to show more decisive action in helping French Jews during the Vichy years.

On January 25, 1997, under pressure from the World Jewish Congress and the French Jewish community, a French state commission was finally appointed to investigate the extent of Jewish property stolen by both the Vichy government and the Nazis and still in the treasury of France. Charged with cataloging everything from pilfered paintings to confiscated apartments, the Matteoli Commission (named for its highly respected chairman, Jean Matteoli, a Resistance hero and himself a survivor of Nazi camps) was also asked to put a price tag on the treasure trove of loot and to suggest ways to compensate victims.

An interim Matteoli report, issued in January of 1998, indicated that the work was going slowly but meticulously, as staff members plowed through hundreds of thousands of hitherto secret files and documents and tried to track down others they could not find. To speed up their work, the French government eventually announced that a "surveillance committee" would be created to oversee the work of banks and other French financial institutions in searching archives for evidence of assets either seized by Vichy or left behind by Jews fleeing persecution. Bank employees would do the actual work. "It will be a long and difficult task," declared French Finance Minister Dominique Strauss-Kahn, himself a member of one of France's foremost Jewish families. "But I am not at all worried about the banks' willingness to cooperate with the state."

But many French-Jewish leaders were not as rhapsodic. "What you have is a group of former banking officials looking into French banks," said Henri Hajdenberg, tough-talking president of the Conseil Représentatif des Institutions Juives de France (CRIF), the umbrella group of French-Jewish secular organizations. Hajdenberg and others called for an independent investigative body.

Barely a year later, when the commission prepared to present another part of its study to the French government, Jean Matteoli issued a statement that was surprising but not unpredictable in the light of France's postwar record: "One can conclude," he told Europe-1 Radio, "that there is a relatively limited number of Jews who didn't receive compensation."

Claudia Ann Carlin and thousands of others are not in agreement.

No less agreeable—but shocking nonetheless—was Matteoli's revisionist view of the events that had shaken wartime France. In an extensive interview with the Swiss French-language daily *Le Temps,* he warned the French Jewish community against seeking any global compensation specific to it. After all, he argued, "in France there is no difference between Jew and non-Jew."

When his interviewer pointed out that Jews in France had been deported during World War II only because they were Jews, Matteoli chose once more to ignore the history of the Vichy regime: "It was the Germans," he responded cooly, "who made that distinction."

7

Eastern Europe

Plundering the Killing Fields

*"Mezuzahs," she said ". . . Verses from the Bible in little niches
in the door frames. Every Jewish house had them."*

"They're still there?"

*"Covered up, mostly . . . they didn't want to look at them,
be reminded . . . that there are ones who were . . . who are
gone. Or that they were ever here. In these houses where they
now live. Who wants to remember that every time they go
through the door?"*

—From *In the Memory of the Forest,* a novel by CHARLES T.
  POWERS, 1997

Though they could be murdered but once, the Jews of Eastern
Europe have been robbed twice—first by the Germans who occupied their lands and the local collaborators who helped ship them
to slaughter, and then again in the wake of World War II when
Communist forces seized control of Poland, Hungary, Romania,

Bulgaria, and all of Europe that stretches from the Baltic to the Black Sea, destroying dreams of liberation and confiscating whatever property was left.

The theft did not end there. Eastern Europe's surviving Jews were also robbed of their chance at any material restitution, not only for their wartime suffering but as well for the loss and destruction of their families and of their entire world. The Russians never responded to any requests. While an estimated 300,000 Holocaust survivors in Western Europe, Israel, North and South America, Australia, and Africa received millions of Deutsche Mark in postwar reparations from the federal government of West Germany, such payments were categorically denied the Jews of Europe's Comintern bloc—a measure taken because of Western fears that any restitution funds would never reach them, but would be pocketed instead by the bureaucrats of their Marxist governments. "All the doors were closed to us," says retired Bucharest textile engineer Pero Kaplanescu. Until the fall of the Berlin Wall in 1989, most of Eastern Europe's Jews could turn for aid only to relief organizations like the American-based Joint Distribution Committee—and then only when Communist regimes allowed it to function.

Rather than survey each of the countries in this great swath of land that was the wellspring of so much of European Jewish life, I have chosen to focus on two nations that to my thinking epitomize the twice-written tragedy of Eastern Europe's Jews: Poland and Hungary.*

Poland: Forever Strangers

After the deportation of the Jews, the Germans posted guards in front of the Jewish homes to safeguard the property left behind so that all valuables could be shipped to Germany. However, the

* Details regarding Yugoslavia are discussed within the context of the Vatican involvement.

*local Polish population outmaneuvered the German guards and
looted the houses by breaking in through the back doors. While
looking for Jewish treasures, they would often come upon Jews
in hiding. To appease the Germans for their thievery, they would
hand over the Jews they found. Thus the Poles were allowed to
hold on to the looted goods, and the eradication of the Jews was
made virtually complete.*

—YAFFA ELIACH, *Hasidic Tales of the Holocaust*

It is the tallest building in Poland's capital city, a towering twenty-
four floors of blue-tinted glass and steel that dominates the down-
town skyline of 1990s Warsaw, glowing at night with a shimmer-
ing sign that reads, predictably enough, SONY. Some of Poland's
most prestigious companies maintain their offices there, and the
shops and cafés on the ground-floor level attract many of Warsaw's
most successful new entrepreneurs. Yet nowhere in the smart Blue
Tower that symbolizes post-Marxist Poland is there any plaque,
sign, or memorial commemorating the building that stood there for
almost seven decades, the handsomely domed Tlomackie Street
synagogue, the grandest synagogue in Poland and in prewar Warsaw, where fully one-third of the prewar population was Jewish,
the most important building in the Jewish community.

Rich with marble and hand-carved wooden balustrades, the
domed Tlomacka was built in 1875. The architect, influenced by
the new Paris Opéra, designed a classic basilica that bore greater
resemblance to great churches and theaters than it did to the hundreds of more modest Orthodox Jewish prayer halls and synagogues that once dotted Warsaw.

The rabbis at the Tlomacka translated Hebrew prayers into
Polish—a first in Poland. It was the pride of Polish-Jewish modern-
ists. And it came to symbolize the attempt by a growing number of
Polish Jews to preserve their Jewish identity yet put ghetto life
behind them and assimilate into a more secular Polish life. That
dream died with the Nazi invasion in 1939. And as fate would have

it, the Great Synagogue was spared by the Nazi bombing of Warsaw and even fell outside the boundaries of the wretched Warsaw Ghetto, into which the Nazis would later cram more than half a million Jews. But on May 16, 1943, Brigadenführer Jürgen Stroop, commander of the German forces that had destroyed the Warsaw Ghetto, ordered the Tlomacka Synagogue leveled. It was, he said, part of his "symbolic punishment" for the noble ghetto uprising that had lasted six weeks.

The synagogue was never rebuilt—even after the defeat of the Germans. Instead, the land on which it stood was confiscated by the state, then sold. And like thousands of other Polish-Jewish structures destroyed or damaged during the war, its memory—and the memory of the tens of thousands who once worshipped there—was all but erased by the bulldozers that rebuilt postwar Poland. "It was as if the Tlomacka Synagogue had never been there," says Grazyna Pawlak, the director of the nearby Jewish Historical Institute, one of the few antebellum Jewish buildings to have survived the war.

Few issues regarding the wartime spoliation of Jews and the restitution of their stolen assets conjure up more emotion than the question of Jewish property in Poland. The figures speak for themselves. Nearly 3 million Poles—almost 10 percent of the entire prewar population of Poland—were Jewish. Poland was Europe's single largest Jewish community, with more Jews than in all the other countries of Central and Eastern Europe combined. In fact, as World Jewish Congress scholar Lawrence Weinbaum points out, if one excludes the Soviet Union, "the Jewish population of Poland was greater than the entire population of many European countries such as Ireland, Norway, and the Baltic states."[1]

While many Polish Jews were engaged in rural farming and marketing life, many others had flocked to towns and cities. In

[1] An estimated four out of five American Jews trace their ancestry to pre–World War II Poland, which at times included within its boundaries much of what is today Lithuania, Belarus, and Ukraine.

1939, Jews accounted for more than one-third of the inhabitants of Poland's major cities. In the case of Kraków, it was closer to 50 percent. They were also, as anti-Semitic Polish nationalist groups would claim, often "overrepresented" in the ownership of urban real estate. In Warsaw, tax figures for 1938 indicate that Jews owned some 40 percent of all the city's residential real estate. In many small rural communities, where the proportion of Jews was sometimes as high as 80 percent, the percentage of Jewish property ownership was even higher.

Wealthier Jews were also heavily involved in the Polish economy and owned significant parts of the country's industrial and commercial complex, especially factories and companies producing and distributing leather, textiles, chemicals, rubber, food, and building materials. In 1938, Jewish-owned firms were believed to be employing more than 40 percent of the Polish republic's total industrial labor force.

Most important, Poland had also been the wellspring of almost a thousand years of Jewish history and creativity, cultural and religious. "Records of Jewish life in Poland," says Polish-Jewish historian Eleonora Bergman, "are as old as the state itself."

Among the few states in medieval Europe that welcomed Jews, Poland attracted Jewish settlement as far back as the tenth century. In her recent monumental book, *There Once Was a World,* historian Yaffa Eliach talks of traces of Eastern Jewish traders arriving in her small town of Eishyshok in the 1100s. The early Crusades and their vicious pogroms en route brought a sharp upsurge in Jewish migration to Poland, especially from Germany and France. By 1264, Polish rulers, who saw the Jews as a positive force in their land, began extending a form of religious autonomy to their Jews, a special ranking that established legal status for the Jews of Poland and allowed them to deal independently with their everyday communal issues, like religious, social, and economic concerns.

In the sixteenth century, a Jewish parliamentary body, Vaad Arba Haartzot—the Council of the Four Lands—was established in the central Polish city of Lublin and served as the representative body for the Jews of Poland and Lithuania. Poland's Jews were taxed heavily, not allowed to serve in the military, and required to live in specified areas of town, like Kazimierz in Kraków and Praga in Warsaw. But at least they were allowed to live.

That freedom also permitted rabbinical literature and Talmudic academies to flourish, providing platform and home for such major rabbinical figures as Moses Isserles and Shalom Shachna. Even the devastating massacres carried out in the seventeenth century by the Cossack renegade Chmielnicki failed to dampen Polish Jewry's religious fervor. It was in the kingdom's eastern stretches that the Hasidic movement of Israel ben Eliezer, the Baal Shem Tov—the Master of the Good Name—was born. Centered on the joy of life and revolving around the courts of charismatic, miracle-working rabbis, the magic of Hasidic faith soon spread among all the poor Jews of Eastern Europe and to this day remains a central force in Jewish faith on five continents.

Life for Poland's Jews grew harsher in the eighteenth century. Their council disintegrated when the Poles lost power to the Russians and both taxes and restrictions were increased. Nonetheless, when Polish national hero Tadeusz Kosciuszko invited Jews to join in his ill-fated 1794 revolt against Prussia and Russia, a regiment of Jewish volunteers led by Colonel Berek Joselewicz, a young Lithuanian-born Jew serving in the Polish Army, quickly answered his call.

Their zeal did little to impress Polish nationalists, who remained firmly opposed to emancipating Jews. Even Polish reformists conditioned offers to grant rights to Polish Jews on their dropping their distinctiveness and their agreement to "meld into the Polish culture." In the end, whatever rights Poland's Jews did receive during the nineteenth century were conferred by the European giants who had conquered Poland: Austria in Galicia and imperial Russia in the remainder of the land.

Relations with Polish gentiles were not improved by a new

influx of Jews escaping the harsh anti-Semitism of the Pale of Settlement, the areas of western Russia where the Czar suffered Jews
to live. Even massive Jewish emigration, especially to the United
States, did little to diminish a growing tide of Polish anti-Semitism.
"Despite an almost symbiotic relationship in many places," says
historian Yaffa Eliach, "to the average Pole, the Jew remained a
suspect outsider, an enemy."

It was a message that Poland's Roman Catholic Church did
little to deflect and a great deal to enhance. Railing against the
"Christ killers," local priests, bishops, and even Princes of the
Church helped stoke the fires of hatred that would later allow 3
million Polish Jews to be consumed without any widespread attempt—or even interest—by most Poles in saving them.

Those assimilationists among the Jews who did manage to
enter the Polish mainstream, like the great violinist and composer
Leopold Lewandowski, soon faded from any connection to the
community. Still, the isolation of Polish Jews—both self-imposed
and imposed upon them—spawned major new streams of Jewish
thought: the Haskala, the enlightenment that brought secular and
modern thought to Jewish life; Zionism, the movement for Jewish
national renaissance, many of whose major leaders, such as David
Ben-Gurion, would emerge from Jewish Poland; and socialism.

The birth, after World War I, of an independent Poland, only
exacerbated relations between Polish gentiles and Jews. With Poland increasingly urbanized, economic competition between gentiles and Jews increased. And while Polish leader Marshal Józef
Klemens Pilsudski, who seized power in 1926, was himself friendly
to his Jewish compatriots, the successors who followed his death in
1935 made up for it by turning anti-Semitism into an instrument
for furthering their political and socioeconomic policies. "The
years before the war," says Eliach, "were marked by anti-Jewish
economic boycotts, by *numerus clausus* restrictions on Jews in universities and technical schools, and very often by violence."

There were anti-Semitic riots in several Polish cities, and even a 1930s Polish government proposal that Poland's Jews emigrate to Madagascar. It was a troubling yet vibrant time for Polish Jewry. With Nazism crushing German Jewry and communism stifling Jewish life in the Soviet Union, Poland—with its 3.5 million Jews, its own vast Yiddish and Hebrew cultural-education systems, its thousands of synagogues and study halls, its thirty-eight Jewish daily newspapers and countless publishing houses, its political organizations ranging from Hasidic to Communist, its own theaters and cinemas—had become the center of European Jewish life.

It would all end on September 1, 1939, with the Nazi invasion of Poland. By September 2, 1939, German forces, and most especially the killer squads later known as Einsatzgruppen, had begun to line up Polish Jews before firing squads (some of them manned by ordinary German recruits and local Fascist militias). By September 3, the German authorities had begun to confiscate Jewish property.

Far from being different, the Nazi pattern of spoliation in Eastern Europe was simply more intense and even more brutal than it had been in Western Europe. By September 8, 1939, Hans Frank, Hitler's chief of German civilian administration in the newly established Generalgouvernement of German-controlled Poland, had ordered all Jewish stores to immediately begin displaying the Star of David. Once such stores were identified, the invading forces then either ordered their closing or forced the sale of their stock at nominal prices or against "receipts" that soon proved worthless. Jewish communities were pressured into making large "contributions" of cash, gold, silver, jewelry, and furs to their local Nazi commanders. "From almost every house," recounts Yaffa Eliach, "you could see families carrying furs for delivery to the Germans."

German officials, said one report from a representative of the American Joint Distribution Committee, took particular pleasure in "paying a visit" to the office of a local Jewish-community council, then demanding that all communal funds be handed over. In many places, says Eliach, local Jewish councils were forced to make compulsory contributions several times over. Wealthy individual Jews were the subject of particular extortion. But no amount of blackmail was sufficient. Sensing that the worst was coming, some 300,000 Polish Jews tried to flee east to the Soviet-occupied areas of Poland. Others, panic-stricken and unable to leave, had begun a frantic but futile attempt to hide valuables, which they thought they could later use to buy their freedom or even their lives from the Germans.

In the village of Stanislawów near the Russian border, at least one Jew understood that there was no hiding property from determined Nazis. Instead, Joseph Semel, a successful local businessman, sought out a German Army captain and invited him into the home Semel shared with his wife, Rosa, and infant son, Aron. On the dining table, Semel would later tell Aron, he had assembled all the family valuables—jewelry, silver, paintings—"anything of value, even the brand-new baby carriage they had ordered for me from Warsaw."

"My father," Semel recounts, "said he told the German to take anything he wanted, just to please leave us alive. The captain took it all—everything except my parents' wedding rings. Then he told my father, 'All right, you and your family are going to be the last Jews alive in this town—but when it comes time for you to go as well, you will go or I will come and shoot you myself.' "

The start of slaughter was the signal that that time was soon coming. "The Germans had ordered pits dug and then filled them with groups of Jews from the town. One after another, they shot them, then buried them. They let my father continue working, delivering bread to the German soldiers. When he passed nearby the next day, he said, there were still groans—even some movement—coming from the dirt-filled pits."

Soon after, Semel enlisted the aid of a Polish worker to whom he'd once lent a helping hand. The worker arranged for Semel, Rosa, and Aron to go to a local farmer, where they would survive the war living in an underground hideaway. "The last thing my father gave away were the gold wedding rings. He gave them to the farmer to help pay for our keep."

Those Polish Jews who'd not yet been murdered or gone into hiding found themselves subject to increasing restriction and financial deprivation. The Frank administration, which had quickly confiscated major factories and businesses belonging to Jews, also blocked individual bank accounts and stringently limited the amount of money Jews could keep in their homes. The punishment for noncompliance was death. In a move clearly intended to speed up the process of pauperization, Jews were forbidden any involvement in the textile and leather businesses, two mainstays of the community.

Within a year, the confiscation of everything Jewish in Poland had been almost total. It was formalized by a decree published on September 17, 1940, in the *Reichsgesetzblatt*, Part 1, page 1270. It stated quite simply, "The property of Jewish subjects of the former Polish State is to be sequestered in the public interest."[2]

At the same time, the wholesale slaughter had begun in the countryside. Roaming units of the Einsatzgruppen—the mobile killing groups—aided by SS and German police units as well as their willing assistants from among Estonian, Lithuanian, Ukranian, and other volunteer forces, orchestrated a genocidal campaign that left thousands dead. It would continue through the summer and early fall, while the ground was still unfrozen and soft enough for mass burials.

The murders became an excuse for looting. In town after town, village after village, the pattern was the same: The Jews were

---

[2] In a letter to Himmler, Frank would later proudly report that among the items confiscated from Jews and delivered to Germany were "94,000 men's watches, 33,000 women's watches, 25,000 fountain pens, and 14,000 propelling pencils." Most would be distributed, Frank said, among German troops and concentration-camp guards. But the more expensive ones with jewels, gold, or platinum would be melted down "for special use."

rounded up and then lined up against walls or in front of pits or in many cases—as in the cities of Przemyśl and Bialystock—locked in the local synagogue, which was then set ablaze by German troops.

In the immediate aftermath of each mass slaughter, the Nazis would often allow local villagers to pick through and loot whatever they and their helpers hadn't already plundered. It was a story repeated from the villages of northern Masury to the mountains of Zakopane in the south. And yet the sheer horror of it requires that it be brought down to a specific. Here is the story of the plundering of one such shtetl:

The wind blows almost constantly on the rise where they slaughtered the Jews of Eishyshok. Yet even now, Zvi Michaeli of New York says he still hears the words his father whispered as he pushed his sixteen-year-old son into the open pit of dead and dying. "Remember and avenge!" he said in that split second before the next round of shots rang out, in the micro-moment that saved Michaeli's life. "Remember and avenge!"

More than half a century has passed since the 4,000 Jews of the tiny town of Eishyshok, south of Vilnius,[3] were marched to their village cemeteries, forced to disrobe, and then systematically gunned down by SS-directed Lithuanian militia guards who'd lined them up along open pits so that their bodies would fall into the graves like dominoes.

Michaeli was among the handful who survived the September 25–26, 1941, massacre that ended nine hundred years of Jewish life in Eishyshok, a mixed village of Jews and ethnic Poles whose sovereignty shifted with history among Russia, Poland, and Lithuania. That night, naked and covered with blood, Michaeli had climbed from the pit. Fleeing into the forest, he found shelter with a frightened Polish peasant woman. "I convinced her I was Christ come down from the cross."

---

[3] Though now within Lithuanian territory, Eishyshok, which had a prewar population that was 80 percent Jewish and 20 percent Polish-Catholic, had been part of Poland for centuries.

No one else from the town noticed him. They were all far too busy looting what they could from the now empty houses of the Jews with whom they'd once lived and worked so closely. "They stripped the houses clean," says historian Yaffa Eliach. "The Jews were dead, and the vultures could descend."

As the killings and lootings progressed in the countryside, the Nazis continued rounding up urban Jews and concentrating them in a network of ghettos in every major city of the Generalgouvernement. It was a prelude to the deportations and camp killings that followed the 1942 Wannsee decision to unleash the Final Solution. For the moment, however, the ghetto system served Germany's needs to separate and isolate the Jews. Hans Frank, now living with his family in Kraków's elegant hilltop Wawel Castle, ordered the establishment of a Judenrat—a Jewish council—in every ghetto,[4] whose prime purpose was to maintain the order the Nazis imposed and to furnish the mechanisms for the forced-labor units that were vital to the German war effort and for eventual deportation of the ghetto Jews to the slaughter camps.

In the 840-acre Warsaw Ghetto, which was formed from two sections of the prewar city's largely Jewish quarter, 500,000 people were jammed into an area that had previously accommodated barely 100,000. Some 30 percent of Warsaw's population was packed into 2.4 percent of the city's area, with the average number of persons reaching as high as thirteen per room and a daily per capita food allocation of 184 calories (Polish gentiles received 634, Germans 2,310). Though some Jews were put to work in factories where they earned as little as fifty cents a day, most of the ghetto suffered from mass unemployment. It also faced a huge fuel shortage. As the already appalling conditions grew even worse, the streets became strewn with the corpses of those who each day starved to death—and with children half mad from hunger begging for food. By the summer of 1942, more than 100,000 had died of

---

[4] One had existed in Kraków since November 1939.

starvation and sickness in the place the Nazis preferred to call the *Jüdischer Wohnbezirk*—the Jewish quarter.

The situation was no better in the ghettos of cities such as Kraków, Lódz, and Lublin. While the Germans were forcibly rounding up slave-labor workers and others for deportation, some Jews volunteered, lured by the food the Germans promised and believing that by coming of their own free will to the Umschlag-platz—the assembly point for packing aboard cattle cars—they might win survival.

But as the Final Solution swung into full gear, there seemed little chance to escape. A small number of Polish Christians tried to help. More than 12,000 individual Poles have been honored by Jerusalem's Yad Vashem Holocaust Memorial for their efforts in saving Jewish lives. The legendary Polish nurse Irena Sendler and her comrades in the Żegota network of underground volunteers, for example, boldly smuggled more than 2,000 children out of the Warsaw Ghetto to safe hiding in monasteries and convents and with private families. But 12,000 out of a population of 28 million is not very many. And in the end, fewer than 50,000 Jews managed to hide safely in Poland throughout the war. Those who did often paid other Poles to conceal them, always fearing that they would be betrayed when the cash ran out. Yet another class of Poles earned their living during the war with rewards they received from the Nazis for spying and informing, or with blackmail extorted from frightened Jews.

Generally, however, most Poles simply turned their backs on the Jews, some because they feared brutal German retribution against themselves and their families (the punishment for helping a Jew in Poland was death). Yet beyond fear of the obvious risks, a growing number of Holocaust historians have concluded that so many Poles refused to try to help their Jewish neighbors primarily because they disliked Jews. At no time in Poland were there any public protests to the Nazi deportations. Sendler and other Żegota members cite virulent anti-Semitism as a major reason it was so difficult to find shelter for Jewish children. Even the Polish underground was less than enthusiastic about helping Jews; when the Warsaw Ghetto rose in rebellion in April of 1943, the Polish underground offered only token support. Moreover, many—though not all—of the Polish partisan groups subscribed to the slogan *"Polska bez żydów"* ("Poland Without Jews"). As historian Yaffa Eliach puts it, "The so-called White Poles hated Jews even more than they hated Russians and Germans—they actively sought Jews out to kill them and certainly weren't upset that the Germans were killing us." Members of Jewish partisan bands, or those "Red" groups that accepted them, confirm. "There were two wars fought by the Poles," says former Jewish partisan leader Reuven Paikowski, "one against the Germans and the other against the Jews."

As for the general population, Holocaust historians say that many Poles saw the Nazi policies, abhorrent as they might have been, as a convenient way to be rid of the Jews.

There is no doubt that the non-Jewish population of Poland suffered terribly during the war: 3 million non-Jewish Poles died. It is also clear that it was extremely dangerous to try to save Jews from the Nazis. But as the efforts of Irena Sendler and twelve thousand other gentile heroes of conscience prove, it was not impossible. The numbers speak for themselves. There were 3.24 million Jews in prewar Poland. Three million perished during the Holocaust. About 200,000 survived by fleeing to the interior of Russia. Some 50,000 may have survived by hiding in Poland. Of those, Yad Vashem estimates from records and testimony that only 15,000 to 20,000 were hidden by the several thousand Poles who were motivated by compassion and altruism (as opposed to those who hid Jews till their money ran out). The rest of Poland's 28 million gentiles clearly turned their backs.

Polish nationalists take great umbrage at these charges, and Jaroslaw Wolokanowski, the official historian of the largest of the Polish partisan groups, the Armia Krajowa—the Home Army, or

AK as it was popularly known—forcefully denies them. Some Holocaust scholars, particularly Dr. Yaffa Eliach, have come under fierce attack from Polish groups for their criticism of Poland's wartime record. Still, Dr. Mordecai Paldiel of the Yad Vashem Holocaust Memorial in Jerusalem says in his study, *The Path of the Righteous,* "The weight of evidence from eyewitness accounts and documentary material, it must be said in full candor, points to a widespread anti-Semitism that militated against a serious attempt to render succor to the afflicted Jews—difficult as such undertakings would have been in light of the Nazi terror machine which operated with a special brutality against the Polish population. In many quarters there was even sort of an eerie satisfaction that the Jewish question in Poland (an irritating 10 percent of the population) was at long last being solved for the good of the country, coupled with a revulsion among some at the methods used to achieve this end.

"The opinion that the Poles only stood to profit from the disappearance of the Jews was, however, commonplace. All the blame for this sordid deed would, for good measure, fall squarely on the shoulders of the German nation. This feeling—relief at the disappearance of the Jews coupled with revulsion at the methods employed—may be said to have been quite widespread, other than for those elements who openly gloated over the tragic demise of the Jews (and even participated in the killings) and the few others, at the other end of the spectrum, who risked their lives to save Jews from certain death."

Paldiel concludes as follows: "The threats faced by would-be [Polish] rescuers, both from the Germans and [Polish] blackmailers alike, make us place Polish rescuers in a special category. . . . The few thousand rescue stories emanating from Poland are of great significance to the student of the Holocaust, anxiously searching for traces of humanity in the immense hell of the Holocaust, for they exemplify a spiritual boldness hardly conceivable to the human mind. These Polish rescuers epitomize man as a loving and caring person. . . . Their deeds ought to serve as behavioral role models for future generations."

By August of 1944, Soviet troops and those Polish partisan units that supported them had managed to crush Hitler's forces in Poland. The toll was enormous for Poland, but for Poland's Jews it was beyond immediate belief. Fully 90 percent of the world's largest Jewish population had been exterminated. Fewer than 300,000 Jews remained alive in and around Poland, most of them those who had fled to the Soviet Union. The fabric of Jewish life and creativity had been destroyed. Jewish life had been shattered. Entire villages and entire extended family groups of hundreds had been annihilated. "Poland was one vast graveyard," says the World Jewish Congress's Israel Singer. "And one result," says Singer, is that because of the scope of the deaths, "in the immediate postwar period vast quantities of Jewish property went unclaimed."

Many of those who survived the camps had little desire to return to their former homes in Eastern Europe, preferring instead to turn their sights to the West or to Palestine. Those who did choose to trek back to the cindered shtetls of Poland, Russia, Romania, and Hungary often found that overt anti-Semitism had not died with the defeat of the Germans. Historian Yaffa Eliach, one of only 29 Jews who survived the slaughter of the 4,000 Jews of Eishyshok, remembers the chilling taunts of some of her Christian neighbors when, as a child of seven, she and her family finally emerged from their underground hideaway after "liberation" and came "home" in July of 1944. "You are like cockroaches creeping out from all the cracks," she says they yelled.

Four months later, a rogue gang of Polish partisans, accompanied by a neighbor, stormed the family house. Yaffa, hiding in an attic closet, watched through a crack as her mother held Yaffa's infant brother in her arms and pleaded, "Kill me first, not my baby."

In reply, recalls Yaffa, the Poles fired nine bullets into the baby's body before pumping another series of rounds into Yaffa's mother. "Anton Sharavei, the gentile neighbor who'd led the murderers to us," she says, "was the son of a local pharmacist, our family's major prewar business competitor. . . . Apparently he didn't want that to become the postwar situation."[5]

It was not an isolated incident. In Poland alone, at least 2,500 Jews were killed in random and organized violence *after* the Nazis had been routed. It was, in fact, a development that had been foreseen by the London-based Polish government-in-exile as early as August of 1943. Anticipating a defeat of the Nazis, Roman Knoll of the Polish Foreign Affairs Office wrote the following in an internal memo: "The return of the Jews to their jobs and workshops is quite out of the question, even if the number of Jews is greatly reduced. The non-Jewish population has filled their places in the towns and cities; in much of Poland this is a fundamental change, and final in character. The return of masses of Jews would be perceived not as an act of restitution, but as an invasion against which they would have to defend themselves, even by physical means."

Knoll went on in his memo to recommend that together with Polish Zionists, the Polish government take the initiative to create a future Jewish state in Europe (not Palestine). "Our attitude on this matter should be philo-Jewish rather than anti-Jewish."

Unfortunately, his benevolence was not shared by many of his compatriots. The worst single incident of violence against Jews took place during a pogrom at the southern city of Kielce on July 4, 1946, in which forty-two Jewish survivors were set upon and slaughtered by a mob who attacked a refugee hospice and accused the Jews sheltered there of ritual murder (fifty others were wounded).

[5] This event, which Eliach has written about extensively, most recently in her book *There Once Was a World,* became the fulcrum of bitter criticism from Polish nationalist groups in both Poland and the United States. They charge that her story is fabricated and initiated a Polish government investigation. But after a series of my own interviews and a visit to Eishyshok, there is no doubt in my mind that her story is painfully accurate.

The pogrom at Kielce and incidents like it signaled many surviving Polish and other East European Jews that the nightmare had not ended. Even with the defeat of the Nazis, there was little left for them in the lands of their birth. Tens of thousands languished in the liberated camps that had been their prisons, adding a new acronym to our lexicon: DPs—displaced persons. Yet others found a way to leave Europe. A desperate mass exodus of survivors began. Leaving their property behind, thousands, many of them led by volunteers from Palestine, trekked by foot over the Alps to the Mediterranean coast in hopes of catching a *Breicha* boat of "illegal immigrants" trying to break through the British government's blockade of Palestine. It was the heroic will of Jewish Palestine's people—and some significantly influential friends around the world—that ultimately led to Israel's birth. Yet in many ways it was the image of this desperate *sheerit ha-pleita*—the remnant of survivors—crammed aboard leaky freighters, braving the sea and the Royal Navy, that provided the turning point in world public opinion that led to the United Nations' decision to partition Palestine and the establishment of a Jewish state. By the 1950s, most of the surviving Jews of Eastern Europe had dispersed, many heading toward the newborn Jewish state.

The postwar Polish government moved quickly to consolidate its hold over whatever had been abandoned by Polish Jews who'd perished in the Holocaust or survivors who'd either failed to return or subsequently fled. According to a government decree on abandoned property dated March 8, 1946, all Polish property not claimed by December 31, 1947—a date later extended to December 31, 1948—automatically became state property. "The murders of survivors right after the war," says Naphtali Lavie of the World Jewish Restitution Organization, and himself a Polish-born survivor of Auschwitz "had intimidated many who might have sought their property back. Fearing for their lives, many made no attempt to retrieve their assets." Moreover, according to the WJC's Weinbaum, "many of the surviving Jews were only repatriated to Poland *after* the claims deadline had passed."

The enactment of a new Polish inheritance law on October 8, 1947, did not make their situation any easier. Succession rights were restricted to father, mother, direct descendants, and any surviving spouse. "Given the magnitude of Jewish losses in Poland, in which often entire immediate families were wiped out," says Lavie, "this clearly deprived more distant surviving relatives, and even lateral family members, of the opportunity to claim property."

Indeed, despite protests from Jewish leaders at the time, neither the postwar Polish government nor the governments of all other European nations made any provision for the transfer of major amounts of heirless and unclaimed Jewish property to appropriate Jewish successor organizations for the relief, rehabilitation, and resettlement of survivors. It would remain a sore point for more than half a century.

Worse yet, even when survivors did make claims for the return of property, they often found themselves cheated out of their legacies—sometimes under the most surprising circumstances. Efrayim Paz, a member of Kibbutz Tel Yitshak north of Tel Aviv, had been caught at the outbreak of the war while on a Zionist mission in his native Poland. Interned by the Germans as a British POW because of his Palestinian passport (the Germans hoped to exchange him and other British nationals for German nationals imprisoned in British Palestine), Paz managed to survive the war and returned to his kibbutz after he was liberated. There, officials of the Keren Kayemet LeIsrael—the Jewish National Fund (JNF), the Zionist land-procurement and reafforestation organization—approached him, as they did thousands of other European-born kibbutz members, and asked him to sign over to the JNF whatever property he might have inherited from his family, which had been completely annihilated during the Holocaust. The JNF, in turn, he was told, would lay claim to the property, dispose of it in Poland, and share the profits with him.

"My father had some valuable tracts of land before the war," says Paz, now a retired university instructor living near Tel Aviv. "So in my Zionist enthusiasm, I agreed and signed the papers. The next thing I was told was that the land had been reclaimed and sold, but that the new Polish Communist government had frozen all bank accounts and that the JNF could not repatriate the funds. Then some years later, after many letters, they told me the funds were available—but because the Polish zloty had been so sharply devalued so many times, it was now worth nothing. So I never saw anything."

Officials of the Keren Kayemet say Paz's story is essentially true and is shared by at least 18,000 other cases of land, property, and prewar bank accounts that had been turned over to JNF trusts in the years before and immediately after the war—not only in Poland but in Czechoslovakia and Romania as well. "When the Berlin Wall fell," says JNF co-chairman Avi Dickstein, "we thought perhaps we could finally recover something. But the banks in Poland conveniently said that they'd kept the money in old zloty accounts and that with all the devaluations, the total value of what we had deposited was less than a thousand dollars—when it should have been millions in terms of appreciated value."

Negotiations for some sort of settlement with Polish and Czech authorities have therefore gotten nowhere. JNF officials report that there is some progress with Romania, which has suggested the establishment of a Romanian-based (and owned) JNF corporation that could possibly access funds there at a repatriated premium. But until such settlements are made, the JNF denies that it has any responsibility to compensate those now aging Zionist pioneers like Paz, who put their trust in what after all was a sacrosanct Zionist institution.

And what of the enormous network of an estimated 30,000 pieces of Jewish-communal property in Poland? Synagogues,

schools, theaters, hospitals, social-welfare institutions, and cemeteries (a World Monuments Fund survey carried out for the United
States Commission for the Preservation of America's Heritage
Abroad, a presidential commission, identifies no fewer than 1,008
Jewish cemeteries within the territory of the present-day Republic
of Poland)? Under Communist rule, all were nationalized. As Poland's remnant Jewish community dwindled, thanks in large measure to an unmitigated twenty-year Communist campaign of anti-
Semitism,[6] most of the properties were transformed into store-
houses, offices, and even residential quarters. Jewish schools and
hospitals became Polish schools and hospitals. Cemeteries were left
to go to ruin, or in many cases, bulldozed over without any trace to
make room for other buildings.

When Eastern Europe's Communist regimes fell, together
with the Berlin Wall, there were those who hoped that the situation regarding Jewish property claims would radically and
quickly improve. They were sadly mistaken. Though the question
of restitution was among the first raised when Eastern Europe's
governments tumbled one after the other, few of the new demo-
crats were prepared to confront the issue beyond lip service. The
Polish government of Solidarnosc leader President Lech Walesa
established a special office of ownership transformation to deal
with questions of restitution. It was even accorded ministerial
status, and steps were taken to restore private property to the
powerful Catholic Church, as well as to a number of other Polish religious communities, including the Orthodox and Protestant
churches.

But legislation regulating the restitution of Jewish-communal

[6] Though many of Poland's postwar Communist leaders were of Jewish origin, Stalin and others soon discovered that Poland's traditional anti-Semitism
could provide the Communists with a strong cohesive weapon that would deflect
Polish public unhappiness with Marxist rule. The ensuing anti-Semitic campaigns
led to the emigration of those Jews who'd remained in Poland because they believed in the Communist cause. By 1968, the Polish-Jewish population had sunk
to a low of 5,000.

property—as well as the restoration of private property—simply dragged on under not only Walesa but also his successors.

The situation was further complicated by the role to be played in the management of Jewish-communal property by Poland's own surviving organized Jewish community, an aging and disparate group of perhaps no more than 5,000 people whose official leadership ironically included many veteran Communists. To the vast diaspora of Polish-born Jews, and to the leadership of international Jewish organizations, the situation was not acceptable. "It is impossible that a handful of aging Communists in Poland," declared the World Jewish Congress's Israel Singer, "would become the heirs of a thousand years of Jewish memory."

And yet it is in individual memories that the heritage still plays out its most poignant and telling reactions. In November of 1997, Yaffa Eliach led a small group of Eishyshok survivors—including both Zvi Michaeli and Reuven Paikowski—and their families on a pilgrimage to their native shtetl. There was little physical change. The rough village streets and slanty-roofed wooden houses still looked as if they had come straight out of a Chagall painting. But the Jews of Eishyshok were gone. The town market, which was once thronged with scholars, farmers, and market vendors, was now all but empty. The main synagogue had been transformed into a youth center, the "new" Jewish cemetery was now a schoolyard, Jewish homes now belonged to others.

In one such home, Eliach recognized the furniture that had belonged to her grandmother. "It is not anything that I want," she said, speaking for most of the returning pilgrims. "All we want is for the memory to remain."

Some of the Poles in the village surrounded them in friendly if bemused greeting. Older ones recalled "our Jews" fondly. One woman emerged from her home with a tired 78-RPM record of Jewish klezmer music and an embroidered picture of a house that she said her mother had found in one of the abandoned Jewish homes. "Take them, you should have them," she said.

But others in tiny Eishyshok were less enthusiastic about their visitors. One young man followed the group from the United States, Canada, and Israel as it walked through the town, handing out pamphlets denouncing Eliach for having "slandered" the Polish resistance. Most others peered apprehensively from their windows, their fears finally expressed aloud by a drunken woman who wandered up and down Eishyshok's old Vilna Street, shouting and madly gesticulating. "You know what they want?" she said to no one in particular. "You know what these Jews want? They want their property back! That's why they are here."

Hungary: The Bloody Danube

I am prepared to sell you one million Jews. . . . Blood for money, money for blood.
   —ADOLF EICHMANN in a conversation with Hungarian-Jewish leaders in Budapest, April 25, 1944

For more than three hundred years, the family of Shumi Schwarcz had worked the same sandy, windblown tract of land in Hungary's northern Szabolcs-Szatmár-Berg County. "Other Jews were always on the move," recalls his nephew, Washington-based writer Charles Fenyvesi. "They were traders and merchants, beggars and money managers—they bought wheat in the Great Plain, barrels of wine in the Tokaj region, and plates of tin and silver in Transylvania, and traveled the width and breadth of Europe seeking alms or giving financial advice. . . . Yet from generation to generation, my ancestors chose to stay put and till the soil in the vicinity of Derzs, a tiny village at the end of a seldom traveled road. What to others must have been the far end of the world was to my family a safe haven, if not a Garden of Eden."

Most of that paradise—and the sizable family fortune it provided—was drained away in the tangle of economic crises that followed World War I. Whatever was left was taken from Shumi's family, as it was from other Hungarian Jews, first by Hungarian Nazis and then by Hungarian Communists. Yet for Uncle Shumi, whose first wife, five-year-old daughter, mother, and dozens of relatives had all been murdered in Auschwitz, the peaceful memories of the place he'd once called home stayed ever sharp, almost magically enchanting. Fenyvesi remembers, "He would go back and visit. No Jews remained in Derzs, not a single one. But he made friends with the local collective farmers and Catholic priest."

Finally, one day in the 1960s, Shumi announced to the consternation of his second wife he wanted to be buried in Derzs. When he died in 1988 at the age of eighty-nine, his wish was fulfilled. Uncle Shumi was laid to rest in the old, long-unused family cemetery in Derzs. Once his unplaned wooden coffin was in the ground and covered with a mixture of soils from Derzs, Auschwitz, and the Israeli village where his two brothers settled, the Kaddish, the Hebrew prayer for the dead, was recited by a group of local Christian children reading from transliterated cards that Shumi himself had prepared for them in the final years of his life.

Shumi Schwarcz's ties to his native land were outstandingly strong. But so they had been for most of the Jews of Eastern Europe, religious and secular. Despite travails, despite bitterly painful periods of anti-Jewish terror, home had always been home, whether it was in the poverty or sophistication of urban life or the all-encompassing world of the smallest and simplest shtetl.

This was especially so for the Jews of Hungary, some of whose ancestors had arrived in the magyar lands in the wake of the Roman legions. "Many of us thought of ourselves as much as Hungarians, as we did as Jews," says Fenyvesi, who survived the war as a hidden child and then fled to America after the anti-Soviet uprising of 1956.

Still, for Hungarian Jews, the sense, real or not, of being Hungarian had not been easily won. The country's medieval rulers and church leaders had severely limited their rights and sometimes compelled them to wear the Jewish badge. While less prevalent than elsewhere in Europe, blood libels and scapegoating for plagues did sometimes lead to vicious pogroms and burnings at the stake, especially in areas under Habsburg rule, something that caused many Hungarian Jews to retreat to the Balkans with the more tolerant Turks after the short-lived Ottoman conquest of Buda in 1541.

The late-eighteenth-century reign of Habsburg Emperor II József brought some improvement to the lot of Hungarian Jews, while an authorized Jewish migration from Moravia and Poland helped swell their number. In 1783, Jews were finally allowed to settle in royal cities. Many actively supported Hungarian nationalism. By the time political reform came to Hungary in the 1830s and '40s, the country's new political leaders were granting Jews increasing doses of emancipation.

Hungarian Jewry flourished religiously as well, producing great rabbinical scholars such as Moses Sofer of Pozsony. And there was a major influx of the Hasidic thought and practice of the gentle Baal Shem Tov, with his philosophy of the harmony of heaven and earth. At the same time, growing numbers of emancipated Hungarian Jews began to speak the Hungarian language. Many turned to "neology," or reformed branches of Jewish worship; others turned their backs on the community and desperately tried to assimilate totally. During the 1880s, more and more Jews began to enter the country's liberal professions. Writers such as the poet Jószef Kiss contributed to national literary life. And Hungarian Jewry produced three of the Western world's most famous journalist/writers: Joseph Pulitzer, Theodor Herzl—the founder of modern Zionism—and Arthur Koestler.

As the multifaceted community prospered, Jewish capital played a significant role in the growth of Hungarian industry. Jews became major figures in the marketing and export of Hungarian agricultural produce. Political emancipation came in 1867. In 1895, the Hungarian state finally accorded the Jewish religion the same rights enjoyed by Hungary's Catholic and Protestant churches.

There were still periodic outbursts of anti-Semitism, especially after the defeat of the post–World War I Communist regime of Béla Kun, in which a considerable number of Jews figured importantly. As Nazism grew in Germany, there were ominous signs of political anti-Semitism that mimicked the mood in the new Reich.

In fact, some of these signs had surfaced in Hungary more than a decade before Hitler took power. A *numerus clausus* bill passed by the Hungarian Parliament in 1920 restricted the number of Jews in universities to 5 percent. It was mitigated—but not repealed—in 1928, and Jews were also allowed parliamentary representation as a religious community.

Nonetheless, as German influence grew among Hungary's ruling classes, so did anti-Semitism. In May 1938, just a month after the Austrian Anschluss, Hungary passed its first major anti-Jewish economic law. The "Jewish law" restricted the participation of Jews to 20 percent in the liberal professions, administration, and general economy. A second Jewish law, passed a year later, further reduced Jewish economic participation to just 6 percent. The source of livelihood for a quarter of a million people was slammed shut. The law also defined Jews in blatant Nuremberg-style racial terms. Under Hungary's homegrown restrictions, anyone born of Jewish parents, even the children of converts to Christianity, would be considered a Jew.

That rule alone added 100,000 Jews to the overall communal population. By the official count of the mid-1930s, there were now half a million Jews living in Hungary. That number grew dramatically when World War II broke out and Hungary, with the approval of Nazi Germany, was allowed to gobble up territory from Slovakia, Romania, and Yugoslavia. By January of 1941, the Jewish population of greater Hungary had grown from 444,567 Jews to 725,007—184,453 of them in Budapest. A third Jewish law extended the concept of "Jewishness" in even more radical racial terms. By mid-1941, the total number of people subject to Hungarian racial laws was estimated to be a minimum of 850,000.

Jews now found themselves discriminated against in almost every sphere of Hungarian life—economic, cultural, political, and social. Jews were also excluded from military service. Instead, they became subject to draft by the munkaszolgálat, a forced-labor service system specifically designed for Jewish men of military age. Tens of thousands were sent first to build defenses along Hungary's borders. But when Hungary dropped its modicum of independence and fully joined Hitler's war against the Soviet Union[7] and the West, the primary destination for the labor battalions became the eastern front.

Yet even the pro-Nazi, anti-Semitic policies of the government party, the Magyar Élet Pártja—Party of Hungarian Life—failed to satisfy Hungary's growing, fiercely anti-Jewish Arrow Cross Party. All but Nazi in name, the Arrow Cross demanded still tougher discriminatory policies against Hungary's Jews.

At least part of their wish was fulfilled in July 1941, when 20,000 Jews mostly from areas annexed by Hungary from Czechoslovakia were expelled by force to Kamieniec-Podolski in German-occupied Poland. Between August 27 and 28, 18,000 had been annihilated by SS execution squads assisted by Hungarian troops. Another thousand Jews were massacred by Hungarian gendarmes in the formerly Yugoslav Bácska region in January 1942. The killings had begun.

Nonetheless, when anti-Semitic Prime Minister László Bárdossy was succeeded by the more moderate Miklós Kállay on March 7, 1942, many Hungarian Jews presumed that their lot would improve. In some ways, it worsened. Kállay almost immedi-

---

[7] The initial Hungarian-Jewish labor battalions were established in May 1940, comprised some 14,000 men, and were primarily sent to the Eastern Front. But by 1943, the number grew to 50,000. When the Hungarian Army fled in panic from the advancing Soviet Army in January of 1943, as many as 40,000 of the Jewish slave laborers were killed during the retreat.

ately announced draft laws banishing Jews from the countryside, further excluding them from cultural and economic life, and expropriating Jewish property. As elsewhere, Jews were ordered to register their assets. "I remember long lines of people waiting to list their assets with Hungarian officials," says ninety-nine-year-old Hilda Barinkai.

Kállay also publicly pledged the "resettlement" of all of Hungary's 850,000 Jews. It would be "a final solution," he said, using the ominous German euphemism for their extermination. Nevertheless, Kállay emphasized that it was a plan that could be carried out only after the war ended.

Kállay's defenders, including a number of Hungarian Jews who knew him, would later claim that Kállay and the Hungarian regent Admiral Miklós Horthy were merely stalling in a heroic but futile attempt to fend off pressures from Berlin to begin deporting Jews.

According to Charles Fenyvesi, his grandmother Roza Schwarcz, who, together with her husband, Karl, had been close friends of Kállay's family, wrote to the Prime Minister in 1942 asking his guidance and help in the face of growing anti-Semitism. Kállay immediately responded, says Fenyvesi, urging his "Auntie," as he called her, to find some way to flee Hungary with her family. But Kállay offered no help in doing so. "By that time," insists Fenyvesi, "even Kállay's hands were tied."

Still, by 1943, Kállay—whom the Germans described as a "hireling of the Jews"—had already begun secret negotiations with the Allies to extricate Hungary from the war. However, restrictions were implemented limiting Jewish economic involvement to their percentage of the population (6 percent), liquidating all but a few Jewish agricultural holdings, and confiscating large amounts of assets.

None of these moves placated the Führer, who became increasingly impatient with the Hungarians. In a stormy April 1943 meeting with Horthy, Hitler condemned the regent for "irresolute and ineffective" handling of the Jewish question. Horthy protested that having already penalized the Jews with discriminatory laws, he could not be asked "to beat them to death." His reply infuriated both Hitler and German Foreign Minister Joachim von Ribbentrop. "The Jews," von Ribbentrop told Horthy, had either "to be killed off or sent to concentration camps—there was no other solution."[8]

On March 19, 1944, Germany took steps to assure that in a move they dubbed Operation Margaret, Nazi troops occupied Hungary. Nearly 63,000 Jews had already died in wartime Hungary; now it was the turn of those who remained alive.

In fact, German preparations for the annihilation of Hungarian Jewry had begun even before the occupation. Months before their troops crossed the frontier, Adolf Eichmann and his SS staff of the Reich Security Main Office had assembled a new Sondereinsatzkommando—Special Task Force—in Mauthausen, Austria. Most of its members arrived in Budapest on the very day of the occupation, March 19. Eichmann himself reached the Hungarian capital two days later. Hungary, he confided to associates, would be among his greatest challenges.

The new German-appointed government was led by the former Hungarian minister to Berlin, the notoriously pro-Nazi Döme Sztójay. And it included some of Hungary's other most outspoken pro-Nazis: László Endre and László Baky, who were both appointed state secretaries in charge of "the Jewish question." Both worked closely with Eichmann, and all, says historian Béla Vago, were "willing collaborators with Germany in the accomplishment of the Final Solution.

Thousands of Jews, especially communal leaders, were almost immediately arrested, and Budapest's Jewish organizations were dissolved and replaced by a German-appointed eight-member

---

[8] The only leading Nazi to have moved in Jewish circles before the Third Reich, von Ribbentrop often went out of his way to demonstrate his anti-Semitic zeal.

Zsidó Tanács—Jewish Council. Similar committees were set up provincially, not to help foster the continuation of Jewish life but in an attempt to reduce panic and drain the Jews of their belongings as efficiently as possible.

By the time the Provisional Executive Committee of the Jewish Federation of Hungary was appointed on May 6, Jewish community life had all but ceased to exist for much more than the purpose of assuring "the complete and unhindered transfer of Jewish assets and valuables." Banned from economic, cultural, and public life, Jews were dismissed by the Sztójay government. "Suddenly a lot of boys in my school disappeared," says Hungarian-born Robert Lándori-Hoffmann, now a merchant banker who divides his time between Montreal and Budapest. "When I asked my mother where they were, she told me that because they were of a different religion, some people didn't consider them Hungarians. I'd never even known they were Jewish."

Jews were also sacked from all public service and barred from practicing professions; their businesses were closed down and any assets over 3,000 Pengös (about $300 at the time) were confiscated, as were their cars, bicycles, radios, and telephones. They were also prohibited from using any form of transportation except streetcars, and eventually ordered to register all their assets.

"To describe what the Nazis did to the Hungarian Jews is heartbreaking," wrote Gemma La Guardia Gluck, who lived in Budapest with her Hungarian-Jewish banker husband, Herman Gluck, and was the sister of New York's legendary Mayor Fiorello La Guardia. "They took all the shops away from them; Jewish employees were forbidden to work in any offices. All the actors, artists, and musicians had to quit their engagements at once. Jewish doctors were allowed to practice only among Jews; Christian doctors were not permitted to treat Jewish patients. . . . A curfew was imposed, and Jews were allowed on the streets only between 11 A.M. to 3 P.M."

Nonetheless, few were ready to believe the worst. "Horrifying rumors of the ghettos, slave labor camps, gas chambers, and crematoria, where millions had already perished, came through underground channels," recalled Gluck, "but were received with skepticism."

The illusion quickly ended. On March 31, 1944, Hungary's Jews were ordered to wear the *sárga csillag*—the yellow Jew badge—and within a week, Hungarian Arrow Cross gendarmes had begun to force Jews into ghettos, particularly in areas outside of Budapest. The deportations in the countryside began, as always under the pretense of work in factories, and in fact some were. But the pretenses were dropped in May, when transports began carrying 2,000 to 3,000 Jews a day to Auschwitz—a number that quickly grew to as many as 14,000 per day. In eight weeks between May and July 1944, when Admiral Horthy ordered the transports halted, half a million Jews had been shipped to slaughter from the Hungarian provinces.

The arrest procedure was brutal. "We were driven out of our homes at night, allowed to take only a few personal belongings, and then sent to horrible conditions in factory areas, or just outdoors. These were our new homes," recalled survivor Lilly Levinson.

Among those arrested in Budapest: Gemma La Guardia Gluck—like her famous brother the child of an Italian-Jewish mother—her husband, and later her daughter, son-in-law, and grandchild. They were among the "lucky ones," even though the Nazis considered the outspoken Fiorello La Guardia among "Germany's greatest enemies." Because of her "prominence," they hoped to use his sister as a hostage. Gemma Gluck and her family were shipped not to Auschwitz but to the Mauthausen camp in Austria, where her husband perished and she survived. But not before the Nazis stripped them of their last possessions—her husband's gold watch and her wedding band.

The robbery process that came after deportation followed the same procedure—an immediate inventory of all movable Jewish property and the sealing of Jewish houses. Most property was officially confiscated by the state. But freelance looting was also rampant, by both Hungarian gendarmes and local civilians. By May 1944, 400,000 Hungarian Jews had been deprived of their homes and property and forced into filthy, overcrowded, makeshift ghettos. They would not remain for long.

Through the joint efforts of the Germans and Hungarians, by the end of July, 437,402 rural Jews had been deported. The process was excruciatingly cruel. Though each freight car was supposed to carry forty-five persons, generally eighty to a hundred were crammed into each car. During the three- to five-day journey, the already sick and weak died of lack of water or air. Ninety-five percent of those who survived went directly to Auschwitz, where preparations had been made for their mass murder. The strong were shipped to work camps, often in the Reich.

Lilly Levinson, then a young girl of fifteen from the northeastern Hungarian city of Sátoraljaújhely, was also among the "lucky ones." Separated from her family at Auschwitz, where her parents and grandparents were immediately sent to the gas chambers, Lilly was transported to the German town of Württemberg. There, together with 320 other Hungarian-Jewish women, she was a slave laborer working as a welder at a factory of the Württembergische Metallwarenfabrik (WMF), a housewares company that had been converted to munitions work. "It was a harsh winter, and even though the factory was receiving payment for us from the Reich, we had almost no food, no clothing, no hats, no coats. I don't even know how we survived. But it was better than the gas chambers."[9]

A few did escape both enslavement and the death camps

[9] Liberated at the war's end, Levinson returned to Hungary to find all but two of her family dead, her family's property all gone. In 1949, she emigrated to the United States. Like thousands of other Hungarian Jews who survived slave-labor work, she has never received compensation from the company that enslaved

through a perverse *"Blut für Ware"*—"Blood for Goods"—transaction. The Nazis, represented by no less than Adolf Eichmann, were ready to spare a substantial number of Hungarian-Jewish lives in exchange for badly needed war supplies, especially trucks. The deal had been struck by two Hungarian-Jewish leaders, Joel Brand, a onetime Communist, and Rezsö Kasztner, a Zionist functionary who had made contact with Eichmann in the early days of the German occupation of Budapest. With the Nazi armies hemorrhaging on two fronts, war supplies seemed suddenly more important than the murder of Jews, even to Eichmann. Brand traveled to neutral Istanbul, then to Aleppo in Syria in a vain attempt to convince the Allies to agree and to persuade the leaders of the Yishuv, the Jewish community in Palestine, to lend their voices to the idea. It was a mission doomed to failure. Zionist leaders in Palestine, while sympathetic, proved afraid of anything that might interfere with the Allied war effort. The Allies turned a deaf ear to Brand, who was ordered to travel to British-controlled Palestine, then to Cairo, where he found himself under arrest by the British authorities in Egypt.

Kasztner had some limited success. Sent to Switzerland, he met at the border with Himmler's envoy, SS Obersturmbannführer Kurt Becher, and Sally Mayer, a Swiss representative of the Joint Distribution Committee. The result was an agreement that eventually led to the liberation of three trainloads of Hungarian Jews to Switzerland at $1,000 a head—1,658 on June 30, 1944, 318 on August 18, and a final 1,368 on December 6.

Critics would later claim bitterly that Kasztner had shamelessly saved his family and friends, then the wealthy, the influential, and those affiliated with him in his Socialist wing of the Hungarian Zionist movement. They also charged that although he knew of the deportation and extermination plans for those without Kasztner

---

her, WMF, which maintains an American office in Huntington, New York, and now claims it is examining compensation possibilities.

train tickets, he had failed to warn the rest of the more than 400,000 Hungarian Jews who perished in the death camps. In his defense, Kasztner argued that his hands had been tied and that his choices were no less heartrending than those of other Jewish-communal leaders during the Holocaust period. In fact, he said, those saved included people from all walks of Hungarian-Jewish life and that the wealthy had often paid for the poor. Moreover, he pleaded, had he issued a general warning, it would have led to panic and prevented him from saving those that he did save.[10]

For most Hungarian Jews, the Kasztner trains had little meaning. Between the Nazi occupation of 1944 and the final Soviet defeat of the Wehrmacht in Budapest on April 14, 1945, more than half the Hungarian Jewish population was shipped to the death camps.

The final agony of Budapest's Jews began almost the moment the Germans and their Hungarian helpers had completed their *Entjuden*—ridding of Jews—in Hungary's provinces. On June 16, 1944, the 220,000 Jews of Budapest were ordered to leave their residences and move their families and the scant possessions they were allowed to take with them into some 2,000 "yellow star houses"—buildings designated for "Jewish habitation."

"The conditions were appalling," remembers eighty-two-year-

---

[10] The Kasztner Affair did not end with the war. In 1954, a Hungarian-Jewish immigrant to Israel, Malkiel Grünwald, charged in print that Kasztner, by then an Israeli government official and candidate for parliament, was "a traitor to the Jewish people." Moreover, it was hinted that Kasztner, who gave testimony after the war that helped save SS officer Becher from death, had then somehow retrieved much of the money paid to the Nazis and passed it on to the leadership of Israel's ruling Mapai Labor Party. Kasztner sued for libel, but the bitter, highly polemic trial became his own; Grünwald was largely exonerated and Kasztner, accused by the presiding judge of having "sold his soul to the devil," was found guilty by implication of collaboration with the Nazis. Kasztner appealed the decision, but he was assassinated by a nationalist fanatic before the Israeli Supreme Court reached its verdict. In the end, the Supreme Court found Kasztner guilty only of having helped Nazis escape from justice. He was the highest Israeli official ever to be charged with collaborating with the Nazis.

old Eva Kahn. "We were sometimes fourteen to a room, with barely enough space to breathe and never a moment without anxiety. But we were at least relatively safe for a while."

That ended abruptly on October 15. Angered by Horthy's attempts to extricate Hungary from the war and make a separate peace with the Allies, the Germans took Horthy's son Miklós prisoner, then replaced him with Hungary's Nazi Arrow Cross Party leader Ferenc Szálasi. Arrow Cross thugs became the lawkeepers of the land.

As Hungarian-Jewish historian György Ránki put it, "Total chaos seized Hungary. The Arrow Cross began a reign of terror, plundering, pillaging, and murdering."

Jews were their special targets. Thousands, many of them women, were force-marched to the Reich's border to build fortifications for the Nazis. Of those who remained behind, some 86,000 were ordered into a ghetto area in the old Jewish section of Pest near the great Dohány Street Synagogue. Arrow Cross gangs roamed the streets, beating, torturing, and killing indiscriminately. Those who they believed had hidden belongings were particular targets.

"It was a horrific sight," recalls Lándori-Hoffmann, then a boy of ten. "They were pulling Jews out of houses and shooting them. And when they were short of ammunition, they lined people up along the bank of the Danube and tied several together with wire so that even if one bullet only killed one person, it would drag the others under the water."

The same scene was witnessed from the Margit Bridge by then seven-year-old Charles Fenyvesi. "We'd taken refuge with false papers in a neo-Baroque villa that had once been the scene of lavish parties. Now, thanks to a Lutheran pastor,[11] it was a children's shelter. I saw murder for the first time: People lined up by the river

---

[11] Fenyvesi was among 1,600 Jewish children and 400 of their mothers who in the wake of the Fascist putsch of October 15 were hidden by Pastor Gábor Sztehló in a network of thirty-four homes.

were shot in the nape of the neck so they fell into the river head first."

Those who managed to avoid the Arrow Cross terror faced a bitterly cold winter of disease and starvation.[12] There were few bright signs of hope in the midst of that tragic winter. A bold band of young Zionists saved lives by forging documents and smuggling food into the ghetto. And it was in a Budapest all but bereft of hope that a small, informal network of diplomats from neutral nations wrote one of World War II's most heroic chapters through their tireless efforts to rescue as many Hungarian Jews as possible. Led by Switzerland's Charles Lütz and Sweden's legendary Raoul Wallenberg, the group—which also included diplomats from Portugal, Spain, and the Vatican—faced down German and Hungarian Nazi officials by issuing thousands of Jews *Schutzbriefe* and *Schutzpässe*—protective letters or passes as well as group passports and questionable Latin American identity cards. They also brazenly established what became known as "the international ghetto," a group of safe houses where Jews could live under the protection of neutral diplomats.

Other Budapest Jews, particularly children, owed their survival to representatives of several Christian organizations as well as the International Red Cross. But it was the righteous diplomats whose bravery still shines most brightly in those last weeks of Nazi control, as they carried on a desperate tug-of-war for the lives of Budapest's Jews. With the Axis armies crumbling, Adolf Eichmann and his allies among Hungary's Arrow Cross "dejudaizers" were working at lightning speed to fill trains and transport a maximum number of Jews to their deaths.

"Sometimes we literally pulled people from the death trains," recalled the late Jorge Perlasca, an Italian-born Spanish citizen who helped save untold thousands. "The Swede [Wallenberg] and I

---

[12] The ghetto lasted only from early December 1944 until the Soviet Army broke into Pest a month later, but conditions were so horrendous that more than 30,000 Jews had already died there.

Hans Biebow, the German administrative director of the Lodz ghetto in Poland, and an assistant inspect foreign currency confiscated from Lodz Jews deported to the Chelmno death camp. (*Yad Vashem Photo Archives, courtesy of USHMM Photo Archives*)

Nazi scrip issued for use in the Lodz ghetto. (*author's collection*)

A Yugoslavian Jew is forced to remove his gold wedding ring before being executed by Croatian Ustase troops. (*Jewish Historical Museum of Yugoslavia, courtesy of USHMM Photo Archives*)

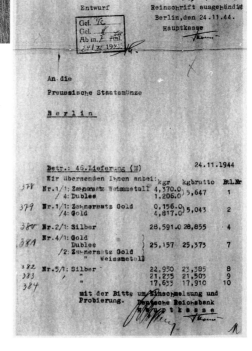

TOP: Polish Jewish women prisoners sort clothing confiscated from Jews deported to the Chelmno death camp. *(Beit Lochamei Hagetaot, courtesy of USHMM Photo Archives)*

CENTER: Barracks 12 at Auschwitz-Birkenau, where gold was sometimes removed from the teeth of corpses. *(Richard Chesnoff)*

RIGHT: A draft list prepared by the Reichsbank of the forty-sixth shipment to the Prussian State Mint of gold yanked from human teeth. *(National Archives, courtesy of USHMM Photo Archives)*

ABOVE: A 1938 photo of the Great Tlomackie Street reform synagogue in Warsaw, leveled by the Nazis after the Warsaw Ghetto Uprising of 1943. *(author's collection)*

LEFT: On its site today—and with no memorial placard—the Blue Tower, Warsaw's tallest commercial building. *(Richard Chesnoff)*

LEFT: Budapest Jews read a 1944 government notice instructing them to make an inventory of their possessions. *(Magyar Nemzeti Múzeum Torteneti Fenykeptar, courtesy of USHMM Photo Archives)*

BELOW: With permission of the authorities, Hungarian peasants plunder Jewish property after the liquidation of a small town ghetto. *(Jewish Museum of the Dohany Synagogue, courtesy of the USHMM Photo Archives)*

Pro-Nazi meeting in prewar Switzerland. *(Simon Wiesenthal Center)*

Argentinean First Lady Evita Perón dancing in Berne with Swiss Foreign Minister Max Petitpierre, 1947. *(Associated Press)*

Lisa Mikova in Prague with the note her father left in his Swiss safety deposit box. *(Richard Chesnoff)*

American banker Thomas McKittrick (center) poses in front of the Basel headquarters of the Bank for International Settlements with his closest BIS colleagues, among them Japan's Y. Yamamoto (third from left) and Nazi Germany's Paul Hechler (second from left), the Reichsbank man in Switzerland and McKittrick's deputy.

Bundles of looted currency, art, and other valuables discovered
in the Merkers salt mine by U.S. troops in 1945. (*National Archives,
courtesy of USHMM Photo Archives*)

Generals Dwight Eisenhower, Omar Bradley, and George Patton inspect
stolen art treasures in the Merkers salt mine, April 12, 1945. (*National
Archives, courtesy of USHMM Photo Archives*)

The World Jewish
Congress's Israel Singer,
Edgar Bronfman, and
Elan Steinberg.
(Andres Lacko)

U.S. Undersecretary of State
Stuart Eizenstat and British Foreign
Minister Robin Cook at the 1998
London Gold Conference
(Alastair Grant/Associated Press)

The embattled head of the Swiss Task Force on
Holocaust Assets, Thomas Borer. *(Andres Lacko)*

would go to the train station and bluff until we got Jews away by claiming they were our nationals."

Perlasca is one of the lesser known of Budapest's diplomatic angels, but among the most fascinating. A formerly fervent Italian Fascist who volunteered in 1937 to fight on Francisco Franco's side in the Spanish Civil War, Perlasca went on to work as an intermediary for Spanish and Italian companies, eventually becoming Budapest representative of a corporation that supplied canned meat to the Italian Navy. When Mussolini fell, Perlasca remained in Hungary, and in 1944 managed to acquire a Spanish passport, by then a safer bet than his Italian one. Soon after, Spain, sensing the coming Allied victory, withdrew its diplomats from Budapest. But not before the head of the mission gave the gregarious Perlasca a card identifying him as a Spanish consular official.

Many of Budapest's Jews were frantically begging to be placed under the protection Franco had offered Sephardic Jews who could trace their roots back to fifteenth-century Spain. Moved by their plight, Perlasca found a set of consular stamps and, without asking the permission of anyone in Madrid, began issuing his own "Spanish refugee cards" to Jews, Sephardic or not. He also took steps to personally protect the more than 3,000 Hungarian Jews who had already found shelter in Spanish-owned "safe houses" around the city. "The Nazis would come to take them away, and I would say, 'You must leave this place. I am here. Here is the Spanish flag.' "

Shortly before his death in 1993 at the age of eighty-two, Perlasca was interviewed for French author Marek Halter's prizewinning documentary film *Tzedek* ("The Righteous"). Asked by Halter why he had done what he had done, Perlasca replied, "These people were in danger, and I asked why must someone die because they are of another faith? I had a chance to do something. I couldn't refuse."

The savagery ended on February 13, 1945, when troops of the Red Army finally took all of Budapest. "The Russians were not very nice to Hungary," says Miriam Wekesivi, who survived the assault, "but at least they stopped the killing of Jews."

Not, however, before triggering one of the war's greatest remaining mysteries: the arrest and disappearance of one of the Jews' few saviors, Swedish diplomat Raoul Wallenberg. The maverick scion of Sweden's leading banking and industrial family had continued his heroic lifesaving efforts throughout the entire Soviet siege. Once they had advanced into Budapest, Wallenberg crossed through the battle zone in order to make rapid contact with the conquering Russians. It was his way, he said, to ensure the safety and welfare of the liberated Jews in his care. But the Soviets were already extremely suspicious of official Swedes, most of whom Stalin believed were still aiding the German war cause. On January 17, 1945, several witnesses recall seeing Wallenberg in Budapest in the apparent custody of Soviet troops. After that, he completely vanished from sight.

For more than a decade, Kremlin officials stubbornly claimed they had no knowledge of Wallenberg's fate. Then, in 1956, faced with the testimony of former German POWs who testified that they had met him in various Soviet prisons and work camps, Moscow finally acknowledged that, in fact, the Stalinist regime had taken the Swedish diplomat prisoner. Moreover, said Moscow, Wallenberg had died in captivity in 1947.

Many of Wallenberg's supporters, including his mother and most immediate family, refused to believe this new Soviet version of events. And based on a variety of testimonies and continued claims of Wallenberg sightings, many believe he actually survived in some gulag for many years after 1947. Even today, a few hold on to the fervent belief that Wallenberg may still be alive, old and infirm, but somewhere in the former Soviet Union.

That is doubtful. But the actual circumstances of his presumed death are still unknown.

There is another unanswered question: Why did the Russians arrest Wallenberg in the first place? Who gave the order for his detention and secret transfer to the Soviet Union? And why had the leading members of his prominent Swedish family made only minimal public attempts to locate him in the postwar years?

Recent research, especially reporting by Victoria Pope and Charles Fenyvesi in *U.S. News & World Report,* indicate that while Wallenberg's humanitarian efforts were genuine, the Swedish diplomat was also working as an American agent, supplying vital information on Soviet movements in Hungary to the Office of Strategic Services (OSS)—the precursor to the CIA.

That by itself might have been enough to tempt the Russians into the breach of diplomatic behavior that Wallenberg's arrest represented. But another theory involves the enormous quantities of loot Nazi officials amassed in Hungary and then transferred to neutral Sweden in the last months of the war. Wallenberg-family-controlled banks and institutions reportedly provided major portions of the laundering process. Had the Soviets hoped to gain access to either the loot or information about its whereabouts by taking Raoul Wallenberg prisoner? Had Wallenberg used his position and name to bribe German officers into turning Jews over to him?

Wallenberg expert Susan Mesinai, who has devoted ten years to researching the fate of the Swedish diplomat, does not rule out the theory. And Mesinai, who with unprecedented Russian cooperation and Swedish government support is currently combing and analyzing classified KGB files in Moscow in an attempt to finally determine what happened to Wallenberg, believes there were other reasons for his seizure as well. "Given the Wallenberg family's central role in Swedish industry—and in supplying the war efforts of both the Allies and the Germans—there was certainly some connection between his disappearance, industrial espionage, and industrial materials and know-how. The Soviets thought he either had information or could obtain it, and that he had vital connections that would be useful to them."

Mesinai also says that recently uncovered documents confirm

that Wallenberg's mission to save Jews had the blessings of both his powerful family and the Swedish authorities, as well as of the U.S. government's War Refugee Board. "But they all had precise goals," she says. "Raoul had been charged with saving a specific 654 Jews, people who had been preeminent in prewar Hungarian industry. I'm convinced that saving them may have well involved all sorts of under-the-table, strategic-material deals with the Germans. The Swedes, the Wallenberg family, and the U.S. government felt these 654 people were needed to rebuild postwar Hungary. That Raoul saved so many others as well was his own doing, out of his own sense of sheer humanity."

Mesinai also says that Wallenberg, who had been working on a plan for the reconstruction of Hungary, kept meticulous records regarding the next of kin of all his charges, as well as the location both of assets inside Hungary and of those that had been spirited out of Hungary and transferred to Sweden (anyone receiving a Swedish passport had the right to transfer material assets to Sweden). "When he disappeared with his Soviet captors, his records disappeared with him."

By this time, the German high command had fled, together with many of its most important Hungarian collaborators. They did not flee empty-handed. At least twenty-four rail cars packed with huge quantities of confiscated Jewish valuables—including 88 sacks of precious metals; 630 kilograms of "worn" gold objects; carloads of porcelain, silver, and watches; 2,700 carpets; 12 kilograms of diamonds of more than three carats each; 65 kilograms of "lesser" diamond jewelry; and large numbers of art objects (not to mention the Hungarian Minister of Finance and members of Hungary's princely families)—were supposedly part of the infamous "gold train" that departed Budapest for Germany in January 1945 under orders from Himmler. The forty-six-car train, whose true destination was rumored to be Switzerland, was continually delayed along the way, and several cars and many passengers were dropped off. Eventually what was left of the railroad caravan made it into Austria, where the twenty-four cars still loaded with much of the booty were discovered by Allied troops not far from Salzburg in late May 1945.[13]

With the liberation of Hungary, Jewish-communal property—including hundreds of synagogues, cemeteries, schools, yeshivas, hospitals, and others—was restored to the Central Council of Hungarian Jews. But the once giant community of Hungarian Jews had been more than halved. Faced with a decimated community, the council opted to sell off some of its many properties.

What was left was expropriated yet again when the Communist government, some of whose leading figures were Jewish-born, took power in the postwar years and seized any and all property belonging to Hungarian religious bodies. The confiscation was cloaked in Stalinist legal gibberish. "Formal agreements," says World Jewish Congress scholar Lawrence Weinbaum, "were concluded between the state and the religious communities, according to which the state would contribute to the maintenance of religious institutions and the clergy." And, in fact, some payments were made, often more as a means of controlling the religious communities than supporting them. For more than fifty years, Hungary's Jews lived under a particularly harsh shadow of surveillance. Ties to the world Jewish community were ordered to be severed, depriving Hungarian Jews of vital assistance and its Holocaust survivors of their major foreign source of welfare support—the American-based Joint Distribution Committee. "The Communists came in 1953 and told us we had to close down," says centenarian Hilda Barinkai, who had reopened the Joint's Budapest office on the day

[13] Much of the contents of the fabled train disappeared with some of its passengers. According to some reports, a number of the American officers and troops who discovered the train also helped themselves to parts of the treasure. The balance was auctioned off for refugee relief or returned to Hungary. In an interview with British author Adam Bower, the late Zionist official Gideon Rafael said that some $8 million of the train's value was later acquired by the Joint Distribution Committee and Jewish Agency in Jerusalem to help pay for refugee resettlement.

Soviet troops entered the city. "But even after they made us shut down," says Barinkai, "we managed to continue helping some of those in need with funds that were transferred to us from Switzerland."

When the Communists were finally swept from power in 1989, the new democratic Hungarian government quickly promulgated a freedom-of-religion law that effectively repealed all the "agreements" Hungarian religious communities had been coerced into signing by the Marxists.

But a special 1991 law on the ownership status of ecclesiastical real estate stipulated that it applied only to buildings and not to land expropriated after January 1, 1948. Its purpose, the law said, was to restore to religious communities only those properties needed to help them resume religious activities. "For a community from which so many had died or had emigrated," says Hungarian-Jewish communal leader Peter Feldmajer, "it meant that we could not claim buildings in places where there were no longer any Jews, where the communities had evaporated. It was very 'moral.'"

There was more than a question of morality. The law also stood in clear violation of Article 27.2 of the post–World War II peace treaty, to which Hungary was a signatory. In that agreement, points out the WJC's Weinbaum, Hungary pledged "to transfer heirless and unclaimed property of persecutees [including property of persecuted associations or communities] to organizations in Hungary representative of such persecutees."

In addition, Law XXV of the 1946 postwar Hungarian government specifically provided for the establishment of a special Jewish Rehabilitation Fund to collect and dispose of unclaimed and heirless assets of individual Jews. As of 1993, the fund had still not been established, a fact that caused the Constitutional Court of post-Communist Hungary to rule that Hungary remained in breach of its World War II peace-treaty obligations.

As elsewhere in Eastern Europe, other compensation laws left

Jews and the Jewish community at a distinct disadvantage. "The laws always specify properties expropriated or nationalized *after* June 8, 1949—the date of the first parliamentary session that came after the Communists took over," says Feldheimer.

Vast amounts of property were still involved in even this limited compensation equation. Among them: some 4 million hectares of agricultural land, more than 400,000 residential and commercial premises, and almost 400 large industrial and commercial enterprises. But under the law, only Jews whose properties were restored to them between the end of the war and the Communist takeover, or who had acquired any property during that period, had any right to make claims. The Hungarian government had jumped past a crucial period of history. "Clearly the lion's share of Jewish property could only be restored by repealing the expropriations dating back to the Horthy regime's anti-Jewish laws," explains Weinbaum.

Even those who did qualify for compensation found that many of the finer details of the law left them decidedly disadvantaged. General-inheritance laws, for example, were declared invalid, with only direct descendants or surviving spouses eligible to make claims. Citizens of countries with whom Hungary had signed compensation agreements were automatically ineligible; this included U.S. citizens, but not those of Israel. And since the law provided for partial compensation, not full restitution or indemnification, recipients received as little as 10 percent of the true value of their stolen property.[14]

At first Hungarian officials balked at the idea of modifying their hard-nosed restitution policies. "The general concept," says Deputy Finance Minister László Akar, "was that we are not in an economic position to be overly generous." Nor did the estimated

---

[14] The law made absolutely no provisions for property losses suffered by Hungarian citizens in areas of Romania and Slovakia that had been under Hungarian control during the war years.

100,000 Jews of Hungary,[15] by far the largest remnant community in Eastern Europe, feel either strong or safe enough to try to pressure the regime into what might be publicly perceived of as "Jewish demands." As communal leader Gustáu Zoltai puts it, "After what we have lived through these past sixty-five years, older people especially are too frightened to do anything else but be apathetic."

Eventually the Hungarian community enlisted the assistance of World Jewish Congress president Edgar Bronfman, as well as that of Ronald Lauder, former U.S. ambassador to Austria and a major investor in the new Hungary. With Hungary seeking NATO involvement—not to mention heavy Western economic aid—more sensitive and pragmatic Hungarian government thinking came to bear.

While many younger Hungarian Jews see great justice in restitution and hope that it will enable their community to be truly resuscitated, many in the older generation of Holocaust survivors express mixed emotions. Most have led tenuous, nearly poverty-stricken lives since the end of the Nazi terror. "Of course all of us can use some help," says ninety-nine-year-old Hilda Barinkai, who received an initial pension payment of $400 in 1998. "But nothing will compensate for the husband and daughter I lost. Nor," she says, pointing to the shabby, once bustling streets outside the Dohány Street Synagogue, "will it ever bring back all those others who gave such life to Budapest."

---

[15] Though increasingly active and boasting new Jewish schools, barely 20,000 Hungarian Jews have any contact with organized Jewish-communal life. Those who do are sharply divided between Orthodox, Liberal, and secular communities.

8

Switzerland

Neighbors Make Good Fences

Auschwitz was not in Switzerland.
  —Swiss President JEAN-PASCAL DELAMURAZ, defending his
  country's wartime policies toward Jews

Auschwitz was also in Switzerland.
  —Swiss novelist ADOLF MUSCHG on his country's wartime
  policies toward Jews

The Swiss were the biggest bastards of all.
  —EDGAR BRONFMAN, president, World Jewish Congress

Edek Szach stepped off the night train from Warsaw, and while no
one knows for certain, chances are he heaved an audible sigh of
relief before disappearing into the crowd that filled the platform of
Zurich's cavernous Hauptbahnhof. It had been a long, sleepless
trip. This was the summer of 1939, and the thirty-seven-year-old

Szach would have feared less for his personal safety than he did for that of the large black leather briefcase he carried with him. Even now, rather than check into a hotel and rest, it is likely he chose to cross the tram tracks outside the station and, after asking directions, walked straight in the direction of Paradeplatz, heart of the city's burgeoning banking industry.

Szach would easily have found the particular bank he sought and asked to see the deputy manager, whose name he'd been given by a business contact in Kraków. Within minutes, he would have been ushered into a small brown office whose heavy double doors were inevitably leather-padded to prevent eavesdropping. The middle-aged Swiss who greeted him would have smiled broadly, shaken his hand, and asked for perfunctory identification. "Another Jew," he probably thought as he inspected Szach's Polish passport. Was he the twentieth that week? The fiftieth?

Less than half an hour later, Szach's mission would have been over. After opening his carefully guarded briefcase, he would have turned over the small fortune in U.S. dollars, pounds sterling, bearer bonds, and small gold ingots that his grandfather, father, and uncles had entrusted to him. His name and that of his father would have been recorded on documents that he was told only senior bank officials would ever see. Then a code number would have been designated for his family's now untraceable secret account. "Do not worry, Herr Szach, we shall take good care of your family's money," the banker would undoubtedly have said as he shook Szach's hand enthusiastically and ushered him out toward the sunny Bahnhofstrasse.

It would be the last time Szach, or any other member of his extended family, would ever see the banker or their family fortune again. Within two years of the Nazi invasion of Poland, Szach, his father, and grandfather had been slaughtered by the Nazis. A year later, it became the turn of Gusta Weitzner, the widow of Szach's cousin, and her twelve-year-old daughter Lea Weitzner. It was September 5, 1942, and like the other Jews of her region, Lea, her mother, and her grandmother, Helena Feldman, had been arrested by SS troops, then dragged from their comfortable home to the local train station and herded aboard a sealed cattle car with more than a hundred other frightened Jews.

Their destination, they were told, was "a work camp" in Russia. As the overcrowded transport train neared Belžec, where SS units had already begun to murder and incinerate tens of thousands of Jews, the putrid smells of death and decaying flesh invaded their nostrils and told them the truth. "People grew panic-stricken, they began to scream and cry, because they knew we were being sent to our deaths."

At that moment, says Lea, who had clung to her mother as the train rolled through the Polish countryside, her mother drew her even closer. "She had told me once right after the war broke out that if something happened to everyone and somehow I would survive, I should remember that my father's cousin Edward Szach, 'Edek' as we called him, had deposited large amounts of family money in Switzerland before the war."

Now Gusta Weitzner repeated her admonition. "Look for it, Lea. If you survive and you are alone, you will need it." Then she added, "Listen, I gave birth to you, and now I must do something that may kill you. But if there's a miracle and you live, don't speak too much of this. Say that in that time, mothers had to make terrible choices."

With that, a group of other prisoners helped Gusta Weitzner construct a "ladder" from the bodies of those who'd already died aboard the cattle car. Quickly they hoisted the now-screaming Lea to the top of the pile and managed to push her through a tiny high window—the only air opening in the cattle car—and off the train. Landing in a pile of soft shrubs, Lea miraculously rolled safely down an embankment and watched in shock as the transport of Jews with her mother and grandmother continued its one-way journey to Belžec.

During the next two years, Lea posed as a Catholic and stayed protected by a sympathetic farming family. When the war ended and she discovered that none of her immediate family had survived, she made her way at the age of fourteen to a DP camp in Germany. There she joined a group of other orphans headed for Palestine aboard a ship of illegal immigrants. Intercepted by the British Royal Navy, the orphans were sent to a detention center in Cyprus.

Eventually she reached Israel, married Polish-born kibbutznik Efrayim Paz, who had himself survived a German prison camp during the war, and became a kindergarten teacher. "I never forgot what my mother had told me about my cousin Edek," says Lea, now retired and living near Tel Aviv. "But I had no idea in which bank the money was left. So one day we sat down and wrote letters to all the big banks in Switzerland. Some of them just didn't answer; those that did sent cold form letters, asked for a lot of money to conduct a search, and said they doubted they could find anything. So I gave up."

Others, like aging New Yorker Estelle Sapir, found that even having details and receipts from the account her Auschwitz-murdered banker father had opened in Switzerland was not enough. "In 1946 I went to Switzerland, to Geneva," recalled the tiny, bird-like Sapir. "I went to Crédit Suisse, where my father had an account, [and after I told my story] a woman came with a whole chart in her hand. And I saw it said 'J. Sapir,' Josef Sapir. Then a man came and asked, 'Can you prove you are his daughter?' and I said, 'Sure.' 'You have a death certificate from your father?' he asked. 'No one got a death certificate in Auschwitz,' I said."

Sapir received the same reply on another visit to Crédit Suisse in 1954. " 'We can do nothing for you until you give us a death certificate,' they said. And I said, 'What do you want me to do, wake up Himmler? Hitler? Eichmann? Mengele? I cannot find them.' . . . So I ran out. I was crying with anger and frustration. I could not stop. I was screaming, and some people were kind and stopped. But this man in the bank, he had no heart. For me, he was a Nazi."

It was the antithesis of the hope that Switzerland once held out for those who would become the Holocaust's victims. For most European Jews, visas to safe havens were unavailable. But to the many desperate Jews who journeyed there in Europe's fading prewar years, Switzerland represented a real hope of securing family savings for the future and from the nightmare threat of Nazi conquest and confiscation.

The Swiss had been quick to recognize the potential profit the Nazi threat represented for a relatively small economy. In a cunning move aimed at cashing in on Germany's seizure of Jewish-owned property, the Swiss banking industry (with government approval) devised the system of numbered accounts that became the foundation of Switzerland's banking power. From 1935, Jews—and anyone else fearing Nazi confiscations—could transfer their assets to Swiss banks. Only top officials would know the true identity of the account owner. "This was our way of helping people in those years," insists Robert Studer, the former head of Switzerland's Union Bank—the same Union Bank that was discovered burning Holocaust-period bank records in late 1996.

"We would become the innkeepers for people's money," says Zurich attorney Marc Richter, "and we could make a profit in the process."

It was a successful gambit. The worse the Hitler threat grew, the more funds flowed into Swiss banks, either for deposit in Alpine vaults or for transfer to branch banks in Britain and North America. Just in August 1939, there were more than 17,000 transfers of funds from Poland to Switzerland.

Not all the accounts were large. Many consisted of relatively small amounts. But there were tens of thousands of them. Some Jews employed couriers to transfer their assets to Switzerland, and some of the couriers simply disappeared with the funds entrusted to them. Most depositors, however, made the sometimes dangerous trip themselves. Arriving aboard overnight trains from Amsterdam, Paris, and Brussels, from Bucharest, Budapest, Prague, Zagreb, and dozens of other European locations, they would disembark at the central stations in Lugano, Zurich, Basel, and Bern carrying parcels of cash and bearer bonds often smuggled past the restrictive rules of their own home countries.

While many went to banks and bankers to whom they had been recommended, some walked in cold off the street. Others consulted attorneys and *Treuhänder*—fiduciary agents who acted in their stead. "Not all of these fiduciaries were honest," says Rolf Bloch, chairman of the Swiss Jewish Community. "When someone did not return at the end of the war, there were those—like there were in the banks—who took advantage and took what they could. Some of their families have lived quite well ever since."

But while the Swiss welcomed the Jews' money, they were far less enthusiastic about welcoming Jews. Though small numbers of Jewish farmers and tradesmen had lived there since the Middle Ages, Switzerland was one of the last countries in Western Europe to fully emancipate the Jews.[1] On the eve of World War II, the tiny Schweizerischer Israelitischer Gemeindebund (Swiss Jewish Community) numbered fewer than 18,000 souls, or .04 percent of the national population.

Fearing a major flow of Jewish refugees, the Swiss took steps to weed out "undesirables." In an initiative directed by Swiss Chief of Police Heinrich Rothmund, who worried publicly about *Über-fremdung*—ethnic contamination—Bern suggested to Berlin that the Reich's Ministry of the Interior stamp the passports of German and Austrian Jews with a bright red J for *Jude*. In this way, said the Swiss, German and Austrian Jews could not enter Switzerland as tourists. It was not a practice entirely unknown in Switzerland. According to historian Jacques Picard, Swiss officials had been marking the citizenship applications of Jews with the letter J or with red-stamped Stars of David for decades.

---

[1] Until 1874, Jews were allowed to live only in restricted areas of the country.

The Reich was more than willing to comply with the Swiss suggestion.² On October 5, 1938, a decree was published ordering Jews to turn in their passports for J-stamping. Thanks to the odious Swiss initiative, other European countries were also able to turn away Jews seeking refuge.

"Of course, there was considerable anti-Semitism here [even before the war]," says Hans Bär, former head of the family-owned Bank Julius Bär, one of the few Jewish-owned banks in Switzerland to continue operating during the war. "I think it's a matter of record that my uncle Jacob, who was chairman of the Zurich Stock Exchange, was forced out for being Jewish."³

Children were no exception. "I remember being uninvited for an after-school visit by a classmate whose mother told her not to bring a Jew home," recalls Czech-born Kitty La Perrière, who'd been left with her Swiss grandparents just before the Nazis took Prague. "In school, Dr. Matzig, our philosophy teacher, often wondered out loud how long I would be allowed to stay in Switzerland," says La Perrière, today a New York psychotherapist. " 'Here you sit safely in class,' he would say, 'while our German brethren are being slaughtered by the Asiatic hordes.' "

And there were Swiss Nazi sympathizers and Fascist political parties, some of them financed by contributions from Switzerland's largest and most prestigious corporations. Among them: the Nestlé Company, which subsequently won the lucrative wartime contract to supply the Wehrmacht with chocolate.

The Swiss would argue in later years that their position as a tiny island of neutrality surrounded by the Facist-Nazi sea of Italy, occupied France, and the Third Reich necessitated their coopera-

² The Reich demanded that the Swiss reciprocate with J's in the passports of Swiss Jews, a demand that was met by the Swiss government but never implemented, largely, says Jewish journalist Gila Blair, because "no Swiss Jew wanted to travel to Nazi Germany."

³ Ironically, it was Bär whom the Swiss Bankers Association chose as its initial spokesman when the scandals involving dormant Holocaust accounts resurfaced in 1996.

tion with the Nazis. "We were in a very, very difficult situation during the war years," says Thomas Borer, Switzerland's spokesman on Holocaust-era issues. "The Nazis had on several occasions plans to attack Switzerland. They threatened us very often. Therefore we had on certain occasions to deal with the Nazis."

That same isolation, the Swiss argued, also meant limited resources and food for its own population and little room for the more than 300,000 refugees the Swiss did accept within their borders—among them some 22,000 Jews.

But more than 30,000 Jews were cruelly turned back at the borders—or even turned over to waiting Nazis—sometimes after having successfully traversed mountain borders by foot. Most of those turned away would eventually perish in the death camps of Eastern Europe.

Any Swiss caught trying to help illegal Jewish refugees was subject to criminal charges. Swiss authorities were particularly harsh on conscience-stricken officials who did so. The noble police commandant Paul Gruninger in the canton of St. Gall near Lake Constance, who is believed to have assisted more than 3,600 Jews cross illegally from Austria into Switzerland, was summarily dismissed from his job when his "disloyalty" was discovered with the help of a tip from the German embassy. Drummed out of the Swiss police, denied his pension, and largely ostracized, he was only posthumously exonerated in recent years.

Many of those Jews who were allowed into Switzerland ended up incarcerated in a network of sixty-two work camps that the Swiss built around the country. According to a report prepared for the Simon Wiesenthal Center by historian Alan Morris Schom, most of the cost for their upkeep was paid by funds "contributed" by the tiny Swiss-Jewish community, grants from international Jewish-welfare groups, and a special "Jew tax" imposed on the wealthier refugees.

Some surviving veterans of those camps recall the experience somewhat kindly—especially considering that the alternative was to be turned back and abandoned to their fate at the hands of the Nazis. Some, like Budapest-born Canadian investor Peter Munk, who arrived in Switzerland as a boy on the Kasztner train together with fourteen members of his family in the summer of 1944, have nothing but praise for the Swiss. "There were no Jews in Europe then who would not have given up everything to be in our place in Swiss labor camps. They were . . . heaven on earth."

Others remember the experience as unkind, even brutal. Walter Fisher, eighty-two, of France, spent three years in Swiss camps and remembers hunger and threats. The Swiss, he told a *Time* magazine reporter, "exploited us and they have blood on their hands." And sixty-eight-year-old Betty Bloom, who escaped across the border from a home for Jewish refugee children in France when she was thirteen, recalls six months in various Swiss camps "without proper food, medical attention, or even a change of underwear. . . . There were armed guards. We were treated like animals."

For some, the results were tragic. The fate of the brilliant Romanian-born operatic tenor Josef Schmidt is a case in point. A star of German radio in the years before the Nazis, Schmidt, who had received cantorial training as a youth, was banned from the airwaves by the Nazis. He fled to Vienna and was then forced to flee again after the Anschluss. Despite the fame he enjoyed in the United States, where he had received rave reviews for his smash-hit concert tours in the mid-thirties, Schmidt was unable to obtain an American visa. At first he hid in Belgium and France. But as the Nazi advance continued, he made a desperate race to Switzerland with the help of a refugee smuggler. He crossed the border penniless.

Swiss friends and fans offered to give Schmidt a home. But the Swiss authorities ordered him into the cold and damp Gyrenbad internment camp, where he was given a straw mattress, handed a pickax, and told to cut trees. Schmidt soon complained of chest pains. Removed to a hospital, he was quickly discharged by a Swiss government doctor who insisted that, save for a sore throat, he was not really ill, merely faking. The Swiss police sent him back to the camp, where two days later, on November 16, 1942, he suffered a massive heart attack and died, age thirty-eight. The Swiss allowed Schmidt to be buried among them. His tombstone in a Zurich cemetery bears the title of one of his films: *Ein Stern fällt*—"A Star Falls."

Swiss financial policy toward refugees "began to look scandalous," says Swiss-Jewish historian Jacques Picard. In the decade between 1933 and 1943, the Swiss had allocated only SFr428,000— barely $100,000—for Jewish refugees, "and this only in the form of contributions toward the cost of sending them out of the country to travel to third countries." The contributions were increased to SFr9.2 million between 1944 and 1952, but Swiss and foreign Jews were still bearing the bulk of the financial burden, especially in the postwar era.

At the war's end, an estimated 3 million European Jews (one out of three of the prewar population) had outlived the Nazi organized slaughter that had taken place in the ghettos and countryside—some in hiding, others as Resistance fighters, the luckiest in the safety of neutral countries. Fewer than 100,000 survived the death camps.

Some of those who did survive remember the look of sheer horror on the faces of the Allied troops who liberated them. "I shall never forget this black sergeant," recounts former Buchenwald prisoner Elie Wiesel. "Giant and full of humanity, he shed tears of helpless anger and shame—shame for the human species to which we all belong."

The Nobel Prize laureate and Holocaust chronicler also remembers that he and the others that the GIs set free that day were so weak "we could not even cheer our liberators," so drained they could not celebrate their own salvation. "It is a day I remember as an empty day—empty of hope."

Eventually some of those survivors came to Switzerland seeking restitution from Swiss banks either for their own assets or for those they knew or believed had been deposited by murdered family members. Some received their money immediately. But the first refusals also began immediately.[4]

It soon became evident that large numbers of prewar accounts had somehow disappeared into the ledgers of the Swiss banks they had been entrusted to. Many of the accounts had been transformed into fiduciary accounts by bank managers who had been granted power of attorney.

According to testimony from French-born Michel Etlin, a Brazilian banker, one French Jew of his acquaintance arrived in Geneva soon after the Liberation to claim the contents of his numbered prewar account. "After presenting the necessary identification papers," Etlin told the WJC's Sidney Gruber, "the man was told that the account—which had some $400,000 in it when the war broke out, now had a zero balance."

Visibly upset, the Frenchman was taken to see the bank manager, who greeted him warmly and expressed his joy at seeing his old client alive. His account, the manager told him, had been transformed into a fiduciary account "to protect it from the Gestapo." It was now worth $500,000, he proudly informed his French client.

Others did not fare as well. Czech survivor Lisa Mikova had been at her father's side in 1938 when, she says, he rented a safety deposit box in the St Gallens' branch of the Crédit Suisse bank. Inside, says Mikova, he placed a large quantity of jewels and pre-

---

[4] The Swiss were not alone in making it difficult to reclaim assets that had been deposited with them. Britain, for example, had frozen all accounts in British banks that belonged to "enemy aliens"—whether Jews or gentiles. In the case of Hungarian-born Péter Csángó, for example, the monies his Jewish father had deposited with the Swiss Bank Corporation had been transferred to that bank's London branch. When Hungary's wartime Fascist government grew too close to the Nazis, the British government's Custodian for Enemy Property confiscated the Csángó account. Csángó's postwar claim that the money belonged to victims of Nazism, not collaborators, fell on deaf ears.

cious stones, together with a handwritten card. "I didn't know what he had written on it, nor did I hear what he said to the bank manager. But my father told me that he had paid ten years rent in advance and that I must always remember the branch and the name of the manager, Mr. Boepsci."

Eight years later, Mikova—whose parents died in Auschwitz—returned to Switzerland together with her husband, who had won a study grant there. "We soon went to the St Gallen's bank and I asked for the manager who remembered both my father and me and said he'd always wondered what happened to us. I had no key for the box, but he kindly obtained formal permission to open it."

Inside were both the jewels and her father's handwritten note. It read: "It is the year 1938. Major things are happening and I am afraid of Germany. There will possibly be a war. If so, I am not certain that either I or my wife will survive. But our only daughter, Lisa, has chances to live. In such a case, all belongings in this safe are hers. (signed) Josef Lichtenstern."

"The manager told me to take only one or two pieces of jewelry," says Mikova, "that it would be safer to leave the rest in the bank. So we opened another box in my name and returned to Zurich, where my husband and I were staying. I said I would come back to fetch some more pieces to sell."

Mikova returned the next day with a bouquet of flowers for the manager's wife "to show my gratitude. But the manager stood there white as the wall. 'Something has happened,' he said. 'Because you are from Czechoslovakia the Swiss government has put an embargo on the contents of your safety box. You cannot take the jewelry.' "[5]

Instead, bank officials suggested that they dispose of the jewelry for Mikova, open a savings account in her name with the

[5] Assets of anyone from Germany, Austria, or Nazi-controlled Czechoslovakia had been frozen immediately after the war and been released only three years later.

proceeds, and arrange for her to draw a small monthly allowance from it.

"I was shocked," remembers Mikova, "especially when they insisted that I wouldn't get very much for the jewelry because, they said, so many emigrants had been selling jewelry during the war. They knew I couldn't go to the Czech Embassy to complain—the Communists would have taken everything anyway. In the end, they came up with a list of proceeds that amounted to next to nothing and during all these years they have refused to make any amends. I eventually received a ring that had been in the box, and, of course, I still have my father's note. But nothing else. The Swiss were not nice."

The unanswered question remains, How many safety boxes and accounts of those who did not survive disappeared in similar ways or were never acknowledged?

The Swiss banks were not eager to provide the information. Both the World Jewish Congress and the Swiss Jewish Communities Association (SIG) had asked Bern as early as 1946 to release heirless assets, which SIG estimated in 1947 to be "several million Swiss francs," to help in relief work for the survivors. Historian Picard says an example was cited of a Swiss shoe manufacturer whose Jewish representatives and distributors in the rest of Europe had not been heard from at the war's end—but whose seventy-five Swiss bank accounts still existed.

In June 1947, the International Refugee Organization (IRO) passed Resolution Number 37, which called on the Allied powers to begin negotiations with the neutral states. The IRO, says Picard, "considered the lifting of banking secrecy as imperative."

The Swiss considered it imperative *not* to do so—at least when it concerned the welfare of Holocaust survivors and their heirs. "We had our bureaucratic rules," says Thomas Borer, the head of the Swiss government's task force on the assets of Nazi victims.

The Swiss refused to budge beyond pittance releases for refugee relief. After all, they argued shamelessly, had not the entire system of numbered accounts been designed to help Jews hide their assets from the Nazis? "Professional secrecy," as the Swiss called banking secrecy, was sacrosanct—no matter what the IRO said.

But the Swiss felt no compunction about tearing large holes in their blanket of "professional secrecy" the moment their own national interests were at stake. Eager to cement postwar ties with Eastern Europe's new regimes to protect some 53 million francs' worth of Swiss-owned businesses, bank accounts, agricultural properties, and other assets in Poland, the Bern government began negotiating in 1947 for the transfer of dormant Polish assets in Swiss banks to the coffers of the Communist regime in Warsaw.

The assets, which the Swiss were both able and prepared to pinpoint albeit with "professional secrecy," had to have belonged to any Polish citizen resident in Poland on September 1, 1939. The only other condition: "Since May 9, 1945, there had been no sign that this person was still alive." Any heirs these depositors might have had were effectively disinherited by the Swiss through administrative regulations.

With 90 percent of Poland's 3.25 million Jews among the victims of the Holocaust, it was clear just who most of the "persons" were.

Both the World Jewish Congress and SIG loudly objected. "Aside from everything else," recalls Gerhart M. Riegner, the WJC's wartime representative in Geneva and among the first to inform the West of details of the Holocaust, "we pointed to the injustice of turning over the money of victims to a nation with a wartime record of anti-Semitism, and where those attitudes continued after the war."

Undaunted, the Swiss began similar negotiations with the new Communist government of Hungary. The bilateral agreements became bogged down in parliamentary debate in Bern. Nonetheless, despite further objections from both the public and some members of the Swiss federal parliament, the agreements eventually passed into law—with parts of their protocol kept secret.

In 1949, Switzerland discreetly made use of these "quiet arrangements" to take care of their own. With little fanfare, a group of Swiss businessmen whose property assets in Poland had been seized by the Communists were reimbursed by the Bern government for their losses. The funds used came from dormant Swiss bank accounts that had been identified by the Swiss as having belonged to Poles. Almost all were Holocaust victims. The monies were deposited into a specially designated Polish-government Swiss account. "Suddenly the Swiss had no trouble at all identifying who owned numbered accounts," says the WJC's Israel Singer. "No problem locating records. Nor was anyone losing any sleep about breaking the rules of 'professional secrecy.' They simply produced an appropriate list of accounts."

Most shocking, the confiscated accounts included those where records on file clearly gave the names and addresses of relatives in the West who had survived the war and were certainly more entitled to the assets of their slaughtered relatives than were Swiss businessmen.

"It's very clear," says Israel Singer, "that when the Swiss say they have no records, they're not telling the truth. They found money. And they knew exactly who was dead and who was alive, and they only gave money from the accounts of dead people."

In the more than half a century that passed since the end of the war, inquiries into the fate of Swiss bank accounts by Holocaust survivors and by Jewish organizations in Switzerland, Israel, and the United States were met mostly by half responses, if not stony silence. Only small amounts were ever returned to the claimants.

"It was impossible to ever get a clear accounting as to how much money was placed in their vaults by Jews," says Singer. "In 1946, Swiss banks said they found 248,000 Swiss francs in dormant accounts. In 1949, they found 309,000 Swiss francs in dormant accounts. And in 1962, they found 2 million Swiss francs. Those figures should make the lack of sincerity of their methodology very clear."

In fact, the Swiss were being stonewalled by their own banks. A 1962 bill by Swiss parliamentarian Heinrich Huber called on Swiss banks to report dormant-account figures to the government. "Very few," recalls Huber, "even bothered responding."

The Swiss government, however, was even less forthcoming in accounting for the mountainous quantities of looted gold the Swiss had obtained during the war from the Germans. "We became the Nazis' primary bankers," says Zurich attorney Marc Richter. "And this country grew fat on stolen gold—both monetary gold the Nazis looted from governments and victim gold stolen from individuals in the most horrible manner. It bears little resemblance to the myth of brave little Switzerland that we all grew up with."

The late Swiss author Friedrich Dürrenmatt put it more bluntly. "Switzerland wanted to emerge guiltless from the war," he wrote. To do that it concocted the myth of "a country inflated to heroic proportions."

"Dürrenmatt likened Switzerland to a girl who works in a brothel but wants to remain a virgin," says gadfly Swiss parliamentarian Jean Ziegler, one of the harshest current critics of Switzerland's wartime role.

In fact, the Swiss lost their virginity the moment they accepted the stolen gold that was used to enable the Germans to buy the tungsten, manganese, and other minerals and chemicals they needed for their war effort. While some commercial banks were involved, the primary mechanism for the Swiss purchase of Nazi gold was the Swiss National Bank. And it made its purchases with the help of one of Europe's strangest wartime operations: the Basel-based Bank for International Settlements.

Formed in 1930 by the United States, Britain, Belgium, France, Japan, and Italy as a precursor to the World Bank, the BIS initially functioned in large measure to facilitate the repayment of the reparations debt imposed on Germany after World War I. The BIS, says its current general manager, Andrew Crockett, had hopes of becoming "some kind of international manager of the international financial system." Working out of an unpretentious building, conveniently located across the road from the Basel Central railway station, the BIS became known as "the central bank for central bankers," an exclusive club of financiers and national money managers who crossed both political and geographical borders in the pursuit of profits. But its biggest role came during the war, when its key clients were the German Reichsbank and the Swiss National Bank, for whom it served as a funnel to launder stolen gold.

"The BIS," says Princeton University historian Harold James, "was a central transmission place where deals were struck, where the Portuguese representatives would meet Reichsbank representatives."

Oddly enough, though the United States did not become an official member of the BIS, the man who headed the BIS in those war years was American banker Thomas Harrington McKittrick. A well-connected Harvard man from St. Louis, the pink-cheeked McKittrick was once described as "a perfect front man for the [international financial] Fraternity, an associate of the Morgans and an able member of the Wall Street establishment." No opponent of Nazism, he traveled to Berlin in early 1940 for a meeting at the Reichsbank with Baron Kurt von Schroeder, head of the J. H. Stein Bank of Cologne and the leading financier of the Gestapo. The purpose of their meeting, according to writer Charles Higham, author of *Trading with the Enemy,* was how to continue "doing business with each other's countries if war between them should come."

McKittrick himself once described the BIS as "a sort of club"—an institutional world all but oblivious to the horrifying war for survival that raged around it, a place where the BIS bankers could maintain an "old-boy camaraderie of cigars and bar talk and walks along the quiet cobblestoned streets of Basel." It was also a world where McKittrick could maintain a warm business-as-usual relationship with his German counterpart, Emil Puhl—the Reichsbank's vice president and de facto foreign minister—as well as with the Germans who made up much of both his wartime BIS board and staff and basically controlled both.

One of McKittrick's closest associates, assistant general manager Paul Hechler, was in charge of the BIS's banking sector. Hechler was both an active member of the Nazi Party and, in effect, the representative of the Reichsbank, the central German bank that became the Holocaust's paymaster.

Amazingly, as late as the spring of 1943, McKittrick himself was traveling to Berlin with an Italian diplomatic visa in his American passport, hobnobbing not only with such BIS board friends as Puhl and his boss, Reichsbank president Walter Funk, but with other major Nazi financial figures, to whom, according to Arthur Smith—author of *Hitler's Gold*, one of the earliest studies of wartime Nazi looting—he imparted crucial intelligence information on U.S. financial problems. The trip had been authorized by Himmler himself.

McKittrick could have saved himself the travel. Both Puhl and other Reichsbank figures spent much of their time in Switzerland throughout the entire war. "In the documents you find where [Puhl] remarks on how nice it was to be a guest of the Swiss bankers and what 'old friends' they were," says Arthur Smith.

The U.S. government was well aware of both McKittrick's and the BIS's activities in laundering the Nazi gold into acceptable foreign currencies, even into U.S. dollars. In one of the war's most remarkable espionage operations, U.S. intelligence forces had established a Bern-based network they called "Safehaven." Directed by the legendary "Wild Bill" Donovan—head of the wartime Office of Strategic Services, the precursor of today's Central Intelligence Agency—Safehaven was charged with tracking the flow of contraband Nazi money into Switzerland and other neutral countries. The head of its Swiss end was Allen Dulles.

The reports of the activities of both McKittrick and the BIS particularly irked Franklin Roosevelt's squeaky-clean Secretary of the Treasury, Henry Morgenthau, Jr. A fervent anti-Nazi, and an active member of the American Jewish community, Morgenthau was outraged when McKittrick, whose job as chairman of the BIS had been enthusiastically approved by the Reichsbank and the German and Italian governments almost two months after Pearl Harbor, returned the favor by arranging a loan of several million gold-backed francs to the Nazi government of occupied Poland as well as to the Fascist Horthy regime in Hungary.

"My father considered these actions as traitorous," says Robert Morgenthau, the New York City District Attorney. But the elder Morgenthau and other U.S. critics of both the BIS and McKittrick's wartime performances were silenced. At the war's end, Henry Morgenthau was pushed out of office by the Truman administration that succeeded Roosevelt. McKittrick returned to America, where he became senior vice president and a much honored director of the Chase National Bank. McKittrick retired in 1954 without ever being forced to give an accounting of his scandalous behavior. When he died in 1970, his obituary in the *New York Times* carried only praise for his work and glossed over his wartime role. Nor did it mention that barely five years after the war, the Reichsbank's Emil Puhl had visited the United States as the guest of his BIS buddy Thomas Harrington McKittrick.

The Swiss later claimed that Puhl constantly assured the Swiss National Bank and the BIS that the German gold they so eagerly took in was not looted. "They were more than eager to take his word for it," says Bronfman, "even though they probably didn't believe it."

It was a case of what Swiss parliamentarian Jean Ziegler calls "willful ignorance." For even the most basic arithmetic calculation made it clear to both the Swiss and McKittrick that the volume of Nazi gold Puhl transferred through Switzerland was far in excess of what rightfully belonged to the Third Reich. On the eve of the war, the worth of Germany's gold reserves totaled less than $100 million ($1 billion by today's standards). By the end of the war, the Germans had sold more than $700 million ($7 billion by today's standards)—at least $400 million ($4 billion) of it through Switzerland and the BIS.

Where had the gold come from? In largest measure, straight out of the treasuries of the nations Hitler conquered, most notably Holland, Belgium, and Czechoslovakia. The story of Belgium's gold is typical. In 1940, just weeks before the Nazis overran the Low Countries, the frantic Brussels government shipped its more than $100 million worth of gold reserves to France for safekeeping. Thinking it would be even more secure outside Europe, the French government then transferred Belgium's gold reserves to its West African colony of Senegal.

Soon after France fell to the Germans, the collaborationist Vichy government ordered the gold moved back from Africa, across the Sahara. "It was quite an adventurous route, with camels as well as aircraft," says Harold James. But once in German-controlled Europe, Belgium's gold became prey for the Nazis.

At the end of 1942, say intelligence documents, the Belgian gold was shipped from Paris to Berlin. There, according to James and other experts, the Reichsbank had it melted down and carefully shaped into new gold bars all decorated with the Nazi swastika and phony prewar dates. "They provided certificates and [false] documentation that this was gold that had been minted in this way in 1935 or 1936. In other words, from prewar days."

The same was done with gold stolen from Holocaust victims. Every one of Germany's extermination camps—and even ordinary concentration camps such as Dachau—had special facilities for the removal of dental gold from bodies. "It was melted down like everything else and recast in gold bars with swastika symbols," says the WJC's Elan Steinberg. The Swiss would claim they had no knowledge of these bars' origins. But they did know details of the Holocaust long before almost anyone else. In addition to Riegner's report, news of the Nazi slaughter was brought back to Switzerland in 1942 by a team of Swiss doctors who had volunteered for a Red Cross unit serving the Wehrmacht. When one of them returned home and tried to sound a public alarm, he was silenced by his government and through the intervention of the Swiss president of the International Red Cross, Dr. Max Huber, whose family reportedly had lucrative contracts with the German war machine.

Not every European neutral was ready for this degree of financial fornication with the Germans—at least not all the time. The Swedish government, which actively traded with the Nazis throughout most of the war, ultimately bent to Allied pressure and drew the line when it came to the looted gold; Stockholm simply refused to take any more. But the Swiss, says former U.S. Senator Alphonse D'Amato, whose Senate Banking Committee carried out extensive investigation of Switzerland's wartime role, "had no such compunctions. Even though they were put on notice by seventeen nations [that Germany was selling stolen gold], they continued to readily launder it anyway—in the case of Belgium, what was then worth $123 million and what today would be valued at well over a billion dollars."

Between 1940 and even as late as 1945, Switzerland continued earning immense commissions shipping gold for the Reichsbank to neutral nations, to be exchanged for essential strategic goods. These activities were carefully detailed in the Safehaven reports sent back to Washington. One recently declassified Safehaven cable was sent by an Allied spy code-named "The Saint":

HAVE CONTACTED HIGH-LEVEL SWISS WHO UNCOVERED A TRAIL OF 280 TRUCKLOADS OF GERMAN GOLD BARS SENT FROM SWITZERLAND TO SPAIN AND PORTUGAL BETWEEN MAY 1943 AND FEBRUARY 1944. TOTAL VALUE ESTIMATED BETWEEN 1 BILLION AND 2 BILLION SWISS FRANCS [$666 MILLION TO $1.3 BILLION AT CONTEMPORARY VALUES]. GOLD WAS SHIPPED FROM AC-

COUNT OF REICHSBANK AND TAKEN FROM VAULTS OF THE
SWISS NATIONAL BANK. SWISS NATIONAL EMBLEM APPEARED
ON EVERY TRUCK.

When the document was released during the 1997–98 U.S.
Senate's investigation of Switzerland's wartime role as Hitler's financier, Swiss officials initially reacted with outrage. " 'No!' they
said," recalled Senator D'Amato. "Then, several days later, they
said, 'Well, it wasn't two hundred and eighty truckloads. It was
only seventy truckloads of gold.' "

Good bankers that they are, the Swiss also found it expedient
to extend more than a billion dollars' worth of credit to the Third
Reich. "When the Swiss National Bank wanted payment on this
debt, and Hitler ran short on gold—even looted gold," says Gaylen
Ross, producer of the prizewinning documentary film *Blood
Money,* "the Swiss would just tell him where to find it."

In one notorious instance, shortly after Germany occupied Italy, Swiss bankers ordered the Reichsbank to take $12 million of
stolen gold from Italy's national vault and ship it on trains back to
Switzerland to repay a debt they claimed Italy owed them. According to period records, Germany graciously obliged its bankers.

Large numbers of Nazi officials, including the Führer himself,
had their own personal Swiss bank accounts. And as defeat of the
Reich seemed more and more inevitable, the flow into Switzerland
of private Nazi loot increased in tempo.

Germans living outside the war zone also began to ship their
own monies to Switzerland and other neutral countries. They were
not above seeking the shelter of financial institutions controlled by
Jews, the very people they had so hated and persecuted. A
Safehaven report dated April 30, 1945, just a week before V-E
Day, cites a British-embassy memo from Istanbul reporting "from
a reliable source" that "German subjects in Turkey were known to
have transferred money from Istanbul in the following two ways.

"First, many transfers by letter and cable in favor of local

Germans have been made by black market operators in Istanbul to Julius Bär & Co., Zurich, Switzerland. It is probable that many Nazi Germans now interned in Turkey have in their possession letters of credit to the above mentioned firm signed by local black market operators."

The second transfer system, according to the British source, involved Bulgarian government officials. "Many Germans are bearers of checks drawn on Union de Banques Suisses, Zurich, as indicated below. These checks have been put on the black market by Bulgarian government employees in Turkey. A large number of them bear the signature of Bimeroy, a former Bulgarian consul in Istanbul [during the wartime pro-Axis Bulgarian regime]. These checks have also been used by German banks in Istanbul to replenish their foreign exchange holdings in Switzerland."

Allied attempts to get a clear bookkeeping record of how much stolen gold and Nazi deposits the Swiss still possessed after the war was met with systematic stalling and blatant lying on the part of the Bern government. In a February 1, 1946, letter from the Office of Political Affairs of the U.S. Military Government to its Finance Division, U.S. officials said there was "a strong argument in our opinion against the Swiss bona fides. . . . It was known to monetary statisticians everywhere that at the start of the war, the Germans possessed monetary gold reserves of about $70 million[6] in gold which had been spent by Germany at the latest by 1943 in her war effort. If the Swiss accepted the 100 tons of gold offered them by the Germans in 1943 which was worth $123,000,000, how can it be conceded to the Swiss that they acted in good faith?"

Yet it was conceded—and with the enthusiastic cooperation of American, British, and French officials.

In 1946, the Allies and the Swiss negotiated the Washington Agreement, which entailed an "equitable" settlement of claims

---

[6] Further research proved the Reich had had $100 million in gold reserves; the Reichsbank itself acknowledged only $29 million.

against Switzerland's Nazi-gold holdings. The Swiss were represented by a delegation led by hard-nosed Bern functionary Walter Stucki, a master at stonewalling.

In point of fact, the Swiss were against a wall; they were short of raw materials and desperately needed those of their assets that had been frozen by the United States during the war. Nonetheless, the Allies lost the poker game to tiny Switzerland. Eager not to push the Swiss toward the postwar Soviet camp, the Allies—with strong French urging—finally agreed to a sweetheart deal under which Switzerland would turn over about $58 million in gold bullion to a Tripartite Gold Commission. When questions were raised by members of the U.S. Senate and the House of Representatives about the smallness of the amount, Acting Secretary of State Dean Acheson—one of whose senior aides, Seymour Rubin, had helped establish Safehaven and knew better—responded with a confidential letter asserting that there was no "reasonable evidence that Switzerland" had acquired any more.

Acheson and his staff lied. The total worth of looted gold the Swiss acquired from Germany was closer to $400 million—approximately $4 billion by today's standards.

Nor did Washington, London, or Paris make any mention or act with any concern for Holocaust victims' assets still in Swiss banks or elsewhere. To the chilling contrary; a draft letter from President Harry S. Truman to Edwin Pauley, the U.S. representative to the Allied Reparations Commission, instructed the ARC to "take account of the reparation claims of the Jewish people."

Truman approved the letter on August 12, 1947, and signed another one to the Secretary of State saying he had "been giving serious consideration to the question of finding some way to do justice to those people who were robbed and murdered by the Nazis. . . .

"I should appreciate it if you would see to it that the responsible officials in the State Department are acquainted with my aims in this respect so that everything may be done to facilitate the implementation of this policy in our negotiations with other Allied countries."

Fearful that any sizable amounts of relief funds sent to the Jews would enrage the Arab world, the State Department spiked Truman's letter. It was never sent. The State Department, which had worked so strenuously to stop the immigration of Jews both before and during the Holocaust, now blocked compensation to its survivors.

For the next fifty years, Nazi looted gold recouped from the Swiss would sit in the vaults of the U.S. Federal Reserve bank. Switzerland, whose trade with the Nazis might have prolonged World War II by as much as two years, would grow wealthier, and Estelle Sapir and many other survivors would live on in near-poverty.

9

The Other Neutrals

The line between profiteering and neutrality is always and everywhere blurred.
—AMOS ELON, Israeli author, 1998

Spain and Portugal: Playing Both Sides

I stand ready by your side today.
—FRANCISCO FRANCO, letter to Adolf Hitler, 1941

If Switzerland was the favorite first stop on the Reich's gold-laundering route, then the two nations of the Iberian Peninsula were undoubtedly the preferred seconds. Though officially neutral, the Fascist leadership of both Spain and Portugal tilted ideologically, if in varying degrees, toward Nazi Germany. The tilt was heaviest in Spain, where Francisco Franco's most ardent followers dispatched the División Azul—The Blue Division, a largely volunteer regiment of 50,000 fanatic anti-Communists—to fight alongside the Wehrmacht on the eastern front.

Still, Iberian sympathy for the Axis did not prevent both Spain and Portugal from resisting Nazi pressures to turn over refugee Jews to German authorities. Neither country ever allowed vast numbers of Jewish refugees into its territory, but both generally allowed those who made it across the borders to use Spain and Portugal for "transit."[1]

That sympathy did not extend to the stolen assets of either Jewish refugees or any of the nations conquered by the Nazis. Both Spain and Portugal readily provided the Germans and their Swiss fiscal agents with a conveniently accessible system of central banks for stashing and then trading looted gold bullion. After being initially laundered by the Swiss National Bank, the Reich's looted gold—most of it stolen from the national treasuries of occupied countries, but much of it "victim" gold plundered from individuals—was easily transported across the Swiss border and then by air, train, or truck through Nazi-controlled France. Once in Spain and Portugal, it could be transformed into currencies that, unlike the Reichsmark, were accepted by the rest of the world.

In many cases, the laundering was done only on paper. In his 1997 monograph "Movements of Nazi Gold," American historian/researcher Sidney Zabludoff reports that when "Germany wanted to transfer funds to Spain, the Reichsbank instructed the SNB [Swiss National Bank] by telegram to reduce its 'giro' account by so many Swiss francs and add the same amount to the giro account of the Banco de España at the SNB. The Spanish bank could then spend these Swiss francs anywhere or it could ask the SNB to con-

---

[1] Spain and Portugal also facilitated the wartime operation on their territories of Jewish refugee-welfare organizations such as the Joint Distribution Committee. In addition, General Francisco Franco himself gave the order that entitled Jews of Sephardic background to acquire Spanish travel papers, a move that in Hungary alone saved the lives of some 23,000 Jews.

vert the Swiss francs into pesetas and deposit them in the Banco de España in Madrid."

Safehaven records, mentioned in the previous chapter, indicate that just by using SNB giro-account transfers, Spain and Portugal acquired nearly $100 million from the Reichsbank.

Though much of the laundering exercise was intended to camouflage the source of the stolen gold, its most immediate purpose was to allow Germany to purchase the resources it desperately needed to sustain the Nazi war effort. The reason was simple: Under pressure from the Allies—and because they did not trust the Germans—most neutral nations would not trade in Reichsmark.

Both the Portuguese and Spanish banks fully exploited that German dependence on their fiscal services. In addition to acting as middleman for the purchase of raw materials from Asia and Latin America, Iberia—according to U.S. intelligence reports—provided Germany with many natural resources that it was unable to provide itself, including almost 100 percent of Germany's wartime supply of vital wolfram, "the essential mineral in processing tungsten for steel alloys used in machine tools and armaments, especially armor piercing shells."[2]

American and British agents worked frantically to try to block this trade, often by outbidding the Germans for supplies. And taking advantage of Allied efforts to block Nazi trade, Spain and Portugal profited from heated competition between the warring nations. According to a recent U.S. government report, the Portuguese were "the biggest winners." Yet even Spain profited enough from its wartime trade to completely pay off its Spanish Civil War debt and to provide the Franco regime's gold reserve with sufficient bullion to last Spain through 1958.

To assuage Allied anger at their economic complicity with the Nazis, both Spain and Portugal tried to employ the Swiss excuse:

[2] The U.S. government believed that "if Germany were deprived of wolfram, its machine-tool industry would virtually shut down within three months, severely diminishing Germany's capacity to continue the war."

Their failure to cooperate with the Germans, they argued, would provoke an invasion by the Wehrmacht.

In fact, the Germans did not invade Spain and Portugal for much the same reason they chose not to gobble up Switzerland: At this stage in their world conquest, the Nazis desperately needed a number of neutral nations for banking and trading purposes. Moreover, even after it became clear that Germany was losing the war, both Spain and Portugal continued to accept Nazi gold—despite Allied warnings that most of the gold had been stolen from other Europeans.

The trade continued almost to the very last day of the war. By then, according to records discovered in the Safehaven files and reconfirmed in the State Department's 1998 Eizenstat Report, German imports from Spain and Portugal had been financed with a total of "as much as $204 million [$2.4 billion by the standards of 1999] in looted gold."

Gold was only part of the loot that Portugal and Spain helped Germany fence. Hundreds of millions of dollars in diamonds had been stolen in Belgium and the Netherlands from the largely Jewish diamond industries. Most, according to Max Pardes of the Belgian-Jewish community leadership, were never found or returned. "We were told the stones had disappeared."

But while most of the gems were never found, carefully kept German records of the goods they had confiscated from Jewish diamond traders of Amsterdam and Antwerp, as well as from those among them who had tried to flee south to France, were found. Many of the German records, especially of the Antwerp seizures, were recovered by U.S. military authorities in the years immediately after the war. One 1948 Army report, based on interrogations of former Nazi officials, indicates that the plunder of cut diamonds had been placed in the hands of a Nazi functionary named Frensel. The liquidation of industrial diamonds was given to a Johannes Urbaneck of Frankfurt. Urbaneck's operatives had confiscated more than 940,000 carats of rough industrial diamonds in

Belgium, with a 1940 value of $10.5 million (more than $1.5 billion by current standards). Another 290,000 carats of Congo diamonds were seized aboard Belgian ships in 1940, an action that won Urbaneck "special congratulations" from Berlin.

Many of the stolen diamonds—both jewel-quality and industrial—were later smuggled by German agents into Spain and Portugal, sometimes with the complicity of local officials and certainly always with the knowledge and instruction of Nazi authorities in Berlin. Both Madrid and Lisbon, already wartime centers of intrigue, became major centers for the wartime and postwar fencing of stolen diamonds.

Spain also became a major postwar center for the clandestine smuggling of Nazi war criminals to asylum in Latin America and some Arab countries. A prime role in this criminal exodus was played by former SS Colonel Otto Skorzeny, who married a niece of Hitler Economics Minister Hjalmar Schacht and until his death at his home in Spain in 1975 ran a mysteriously but well financed Nazi underground-railroad network known to intelligence operatives as *Die Spinne*—the Spider.

Sweden: All in the Family

Cloaking is the art of hiding ownership.
—GERALD AALDERS and CEES WIEBES, 1996

During the bitter winter of 1944, while Swedish diplomat Raoul Wallenberg was heroically struggling to save the Jews of Budapest from being shipped to Nazi death camps, his banker/industrialist uncles Jacob and Marcus Wallenberg were safely back home in Stockholm busily trading gold with the Reichsbank, selling military resources to the German military machine, and earning income for their Stockholms Enskilda Bank with stocks and bonds stolen from the Jews of the Netherlands.

The wealthy Wallenbergs—whose holding company is today said to control more than 40 percent of the value of the entire Swedish stock exchange—were not the only Swedes to profit from Hitler's war. In keeping with its modern tradition, Sweden had declared its neutrality. To bolster that stance, Swedish authorities pleaded that the proximity of German troops in neighboring Denmark and Norway made anything else a suicide option.

There were many outstanding wartime instances of Swedish compassion and courage. As many as 7,000 Jews from occupied Denmark were saved from being shipped to Nazi death camps when, with Swedish agreement, the Danish Resistance clandestinely ferried them across the Kattegat in a dramatic convoy of tiny fishing boats and landed them on Swedish shores. In Berlin, Swedish church workers miraculously managed to hide a few Jews in the very heart of the beast. And it was the Swedish government that gave Raoul Wallenberg the diplomatic cover he needed for his American-funded rescue mission in Hungary.

Though many in Sweden sympathized with the German cause, there was also a degree of covert Swedish cooperation with the Allies, including the occasional repatriation of Allied Air Force personnel downed over Sweden and Norway and the transmission of some vital intelligence information by individual anti-Nazi Swedes.

For the most part, however, Sweden's World War II record was less than noble. "Sweden was clearly among the most helpful of the neutral countries to the German war effort," says U.S. Undersecretary of State Stuart Eizenstat. "Not only did it supply Germany with critical war supplies (iron ore and ball bearings) and receive substantial amounts of looted gold, but it gave the Germans significant transit rights across its territory to reach Finland in order to fight against Soviet occupation forces, as well as to facilitate the occupation of Norway."

German troop traffic through Sweden was especially heavy. By the time the Allies finally prevailed on Swedish authorities to halt German troop trains in August 1943, Stockholm authorities had authorized more than 250,000 trips by German troops across their neutral land, albeit in sealed rail cars. In addition, throughout almost the entire war, the Swedish Navy actively escorted Nazi convoys in the Baltic Sea. Swedish industrial giants traded with both sides, supplying the Germans with parts of the engines used in the deadly V-2 rockets that blitzed Allied ships and cities[3] and the Allies with ball bearings flown out of Sweden in the RAF's high-performance Mosquito aircraft.

"Every time there was an issue, the Swedish government would say, 'Remember the Wehrmacht is in striking distance,' notes Arne Ruth, editor in chief of Stockholm's daily newspaper *Dagens Nyheter* and one of the first Swedes to expose details of his country's pro-Nazi wartime activities. "The Allies tried to be understanding of these pressures on Sweden."

Washington and London were less understanding when they began to realize the quantity of essential goods Sweden was exporting to the Reich. "It was a generally held view among Allied economic warfare experts early in the war," concludes the U.S. government's 1998 Eizenstat Report, "that the German war effort depended on iron ore from Sweden and oil from the Soviet Union and that without these materials, the war would come to a halt."

So crucial was Swedish iron ore, in fact, that British experts were convinced both during and after the war that Swedish exports to Germany—which as late as 1943 still totaled 9.5 million tons of ore a year—were the most valuable of all the contributions neutral nations made to the Nazi war effort. That Swedish contribution was made extra sweet for the Nazis when the Swedes agreed to transport the ore to German ports aboard Swedish freighters, a move that relieved pressures on Hitler's already overstretched merchant fleet.

It was only after heavy pressure from the Roosevelt adminis-

[3] Bomb shards discovered at Antwerp harbor in 1944, for example, carried "Made in Sweden" labels.

tration—and some not so veiled threats from the Kremlin—that the Swedes finally agreed to cut back, though not completely halt, their wartime exports to the Reich, and then only during the last eighteen months of the war. In 1944, steel-ore shipments to Germany were reduced to 7 million tons and finally cut completely in November of that same year. The Swedes also belatedly agreed to cease their export to Germany of ball bearings and ball-bearing steel. While some 90 percent of the 100 million antifriction ball bearings used by the Nazi forces each year were made in Germany, 60 percent of them were produced at a German subsidiary of the Svenska Kullagerfabriken [SKF], which was owned by Stockholms Enskilda Bank—which in turn was under the control of the Wallenberg family. When the German plant was destroyed by U.S. air raids, thanks in part to information passed on to the OSS by two anti-Nazi officials of SKF, the Wallenbergs increased the export to Germany of finished Swedish-made ball bearings.

The banking Wallenbergs, who were reportedly on less than warm terms with their altruistic diplomat nephew Raoul, had begun cultivating close fiscal ties with the Nazis even before Hitler invaded Poland. Their lucrative connections with Berlin increased with the spread of the Nazi onslaught. Among the most notorious Wallenberg-Nazi deals: the "purchase" by Stockholms Enskilda Bank in 1940 of the American Bosch Corporation (ABC), the U.S. subsidiary of the Nazi German firm Robert Bosch, GmbH. According to Justice Department reports, the Stockholms Enskilda Bank purchase was no more than a cloaking deal. The Wallenbergs had quietly agreed that they would return ABC to the Nazis when the war ended—ostensibly with a German victory. Part of the payment they received in return: the deposit of 1,150 kilograms of Reichsbank gold into a special Swiss account on behalf of Stockholms Enskilda Bank.

The Reichsbank, according to Dutch investigative historians Gerard Aalders and Cees Wiebes, also had the determined if surreptitious assistance of the Wallenbergs and their banking institutions in bypassing American embargos on trade with Nazi Germany. One of their slickest moves was aimed at buying up stocks and bonds on the New York financial markets. One purchase of German debenture bonds was carried out in New York through Brown Brothers Harriman & Company by Marcus Wallenberg himself. He arrived in New York from Lisbon aboard the S.S. *Exorchorda* just a few months after Nazi troops had overrun Europe. The FBI agents who quietly tailed Wallenberg from the moment he disembarked at New York docks later learned that after purchasing $2.7 million in German bonds, assets, and securities through Brown, he arranged to have them shipped to the Banco Hispano Americano in Madrid. They were then transferred to a Rome bank, from where they were soon sent to Berlin.

More direct Enskilda's involvement in Hitler's war effort included the financing of a wide variety of other German enterprises, including, says the U.S. State Department, an arrangement with the Reich's War Ministry by which German naval ships were built in Sweden but officially described only as "fishing boats." A February 1945 memo from Treasury Secretary Morgenthau complained that "as late as 1943, Stockholms Enskilda Bank made substantial loans to the German-controlled Norsk-Hydro (the central figure in the old nitrogen cartel[4]) without receiving any collateral" other than reliance on German control of all Norwegian industry.

The Wallenbergs, as well as several other Swedish financiers, were also deeply involved in the laundering of Nazi-confiscated foreign currency and looted securities, including large quantities of the stocks and bonds the Nazis stole from Jews in the Netherlands and other Nazi-occupied European nations. Interrogated at the end of the war, Reichsbank vice president Emil Puhl himself told Allied investigators that Enskilda Bank had been among Germany's "prime correspondents" in the sale of looted Jewish securities.

There were few lines separating the Wallenbergs and the Swed-

---

[4] Nitrogen is vital in nuclear research.

ish government. So vast was the family's holdings, and so far-flung was their influence, that the Swedish government appointed Jacob to be in charge of trade relations with the Axis and Marcus to be in charge of commercial ties to the Allies.

It was also the Wallenbergs who urged the Swedish government to purchase the gold that the Swedish National Bank obtained from the Nazis. Swedish purchases, U.S. State Department experts calculated, included more than $31 million in gold bullion, much of it stolen from Belgium and the Netherlands—a fact that might well have been known to both brothers. It certainly was suspected in Sweden, where details of Nazi atrocities, including the Holocaust, were known early on. The government policy, says Arne Ruth, was "don't ask—just buy it."

Nonetheless, according to little-noticed research published in 1997 by historians Gerard Aalders and Susanne Berger, a German memo dated December 1943 and recently released by the U.S. National Archives reveals that Jacob Wallenberg himself, fearful of possible Allied retribution, raised the issue of the gold's possibly contaminated origins when he received further payments from the Germans for his Bosch cloaking.

"Wallenberg," the memo said, "asked where the gold actually came from and suggested that its origins be investigated. If its origins proved objectionable, Wallenberg recommended that the gold be sold and Swiss or Swedish securities purchased in its place."

That, say Aalders and Berger, "is exactly what subsequentally happened." In May 1944, the Germans delivered the gold to the Swiss National Bank. A large packet of Swiss securities was purchased for its value and placed in a safety-deposit box.

"This was a time of German conquests and of the final liquidation of the Jews," the U.S. report goes on to say. The gold was made available by the previously gold-short Reichsbank, it notes, "at precisely the time [the Nazis] gained access to substantial quantities by means of expropriations and extermination camps."

Toward the end of the war, Sweden also became another major destination for the loot of individual Nazis—especially from Hungary, where Raoul Wallenberg carried out his rescue work before his mysterious disappearance. Despite the chasm of differences in their political approaches, the banking Wallenbergs had been among those that helped finance Raoul's mission, largely, it is believed, because they were using him to track and protect the assets of wealthy Hungarian Jews whose industries they wished to exploit in the war's aftermath.

At the end of the war, and only after lengthy negotiations and foot dragging, the Swedish government agreed to return some 14 tons of the stolen gold to the Dutch and Belgian treasuries and to transfer three-quarters of the more than $90 million in German assets in Sweden to international organizations for postwar relief efforts. But another 7.5 tons of "suspect" gold the Swedes had purchased from the Nazis were simply hidden away in the Swedish treasury.

For their part, the Wallenbergs, who were blacklisted during the war by the Allied governments, were soon back in those governments' good graces. They refused to return the Dutch securities and other stolen assets they had acquired, arguing that none were "looted property" and all had been purchased "in the ordinary course of business." They have also never built a family memorial to their noble nephew Raoul.

But even the war did not end Swedish cloaking and fencing. A recently declassified Safehaven report indicates that in 1946, some personnel attached to the Swedish Red Cross had been discovered using their humanitarian cover to smuggle in silver, gold, documents, paintings, and other art objects from the ruined Reich to still, ever-neutral Sweden.

Argentina: Latin Safehaven

Switzerland is the country . . . where all the bandits come together (and) hide everything they rob from the others.
—JUAN PERÓN, 1960

A photograph taken in Bern during Eva Perón's notorious 1947 "Rainbow Tour" of Europe depicts the glamorous Argentine First Lady, bejeweled and elegantly garbed in a Paris gown, gaily waltzing with Switzerland's dashing Foreign Minister, Max Petitpierre.

Historians believe that Señora Perón's first and only visit to Switzerland was tied more to the Peróns' Swiss bank accounts— and most specifically to a personal account that "Evita" opened while in Bern[5]—than it was to foreign affairs. A March 23, 1972, Central Intelligence Agency file alludes to "millions of dollars" deposited in Switzerland by Evita during that summer 1947 jaunt, much of it reportedly carried in sacks of cash and gold aboard the chartered Iberian aircraft she traveled on. At least part of the money is believed to have come from the sale of Argentine residency permits to Nazis fleeing Europe, sales Juan Perón made during his tenure as Argentine Minister of War. According to some reports, during the last days of the war, Perón supplied the German embassy in Buenos Aires with as many as 8,000 Argentine passports.[6]

Of course, Argentina's dynamic duo was neither the first nor the last of the world's dictators to take full advantage of Swiss banking secrecy. Moreover, the evidence shows that during World

[5] After Evita's death in 1952, Perón sent envoys to Switzerland, where they discovered a Crédit Suisse safety box in Bern, registered in the name of Evita's brother, Juan Duarte, the coordinator of her European tour.

[6] Among the leading war criminals and thousands of other Nazis who took refuge in Argentina: Adolf Eichmann, Auschwitz doctor Josef Mengele, and Erich Priebke, the SS captain who ordered the murders at the Andreatine Caves outside Rome—and was only recently extradited to Italy.

War II and in the years immediately following the defeat of the Third Reich, Argentina and Switzerland waltzed together even more closely than Evita and Foreign Minister Petitpierre had at the diplomatic ball in Bern.

Between 1942 and 1944, more than two hundred German companies established major offices in Argentina and, until 1945, operated without any Argentine financial controls. The transfers of their capital and assets from Europe—much of it stolen from Jewish "enemies of the Reich"—were easily executed through Argentine branches of German banks, including the Deutsche Bank and the Banco Alemán del Río de la Plata. These and other Argentine banks were also believed to have been the destination of other monies dispatched during and immediately after the war to Argentina for use in helping transport and harbor Nazi war criminals fleeing to Argentina and elsewhere in Latin America.

The constant flow of Nazi gold and other assets into Argentina became so heavy toward the end of the war that it set off loud alarm bells in the offices of U.S. Secretary of the Treasury, Henry Morgenthau, Jr. According to a recently declassified National Archives document, Morgenthau personally wrote in February 1945 to Acting Secretary of State Joseph C. Grew suggesting that Treasury Department sleuths be dispatched to Argentina to undertake a Safehaven-style investigation of Nazi assets there. "Argentina is not only a likely refuge for Nazi criminals," the feisty Morgenthau warned, "but also has been and still is the focal point of Nazi financial and economic activity in this hemisphere."

The State Department, however, had another agenda. Citing "political considerations," Grew rejected Morgenthau's suggestion (there were already enough American representatives in Buenos Aires, he said.)

At the Inter-American Conference on War and Peace (known as the Chapultepec Conference) held in Mexico City between February 21 and March 8, 1945, delegates drafted a resolution backing the Bretton Woods Resolution of July 1944 that called upon all neutral states to prevent the transfer of Nazi assets to their territory. All well and good, except that the wording of the resolution also effectively absolved the nations of the Americas from maintaining control mechanisms that would force them to report such transfers. It also granted all North and South American states—including the United States—permission to hold on to German assets within their own respective jurisdictions.

"Neutral" though hitherto Nazi-leaning Argentina became a partner to the agreement only when it officially—if belatedly, like another neutral, Turkey—declared war on the Axis in March 1945. (Turkey had declared war on Germany the previous month.) Despite a variety of subsequent attempts to track Nazi assets in Argentina, no thorough accounting was ever provided by the Argentine government. The United States did eventually begin gathering investigative material on Argentina's ties to the Nazis during the immediate postwar period, and a report dubbed "The Argentine Blue Book" was delivered to the Argentinean government and those of the rest of Latin America in 1946. The focus was Argentina's potential as a breeding ground for a Nazi political revival—and it was a clear attempt to discredit Perón. But it also provided fascinating details on German financial workings in Argentina.

Almost unhindered, Nazi Germany had transmitted more than $4.1 million to its embassy in Buenos Aires between 1939 and 1945, much of it earmarked for espionage and resource acquisition. The report confirmed that in addition to the absence of any meaningful Argentine controls over German companies, two German banks continued operation in Argentina as late as June of 1945, providing adequate time for financial transfers from the crumbling Reich. Moreover, according to Blue Book data, even after it agreed to the Chapultepec resolution, the Argentine government, as U.S. Undersecretary of State Stuart Eizenstat puts it, "delayed action [on German companies] so long that the managers of these firms had ample time to distribute or dissipate their assets."

That notwithstanding, the Perón government was eventually able to use the inter-American accord as the basis for which to lay claim to some 680 million pesos ($200 million) in German "enemy" assets in Argentina. "That's the amount that didn't get away—or didn't go into the Peróns' personal accounts," according to Argentine journalist Pedro Tomarkin.

How much all the extracurricular German loot amounted to, no one knows for sure. The Argentineans have yet to provide a full accounting of their wartime and postwar financial dealings with the Nazis. As a result, tales still abound of vast amounts of Nazi looted gold eventually reaching Argentina. Among the more popular ones is a report that two German U-boats carrying a Reichsbank trove of 2,511 kilograms of gold bullion, 4,638 karats of diamonds, piles of jewels, works of art, and tens of millions of dollars' worth of a variety of currencies were dispatched to Argentina by Hermann Göring in the spring of 1945. No substantive proof has ever been discovered of any such golden submarines. But there were Allied intelligence sightings of German subs in Argentine waters all throughout the war, and even after. During the late summer of 1945, months after the fall of Berlin, two mysterious U-boats steamed into Mar del Plata. A 1945 State Department study lists the reported assets in Argentina of several leading Nazis. Among them: Reichsmarschall Hermann Göring, $20 million sent via the Swiss Bank of Geneva; Propaganda Minister Josef Goebbels, $1.8 million in a safety-deposit box at a German-controlled bank in Buenos Aires; Foreign Minister Joachim von Ribbentrop, $500,000 in another such box.

In addition, paintings looted by the Nazis from European Jews have shown up from time to time in Buenos Aires galleries; among them, several by eighteenth-century Italian master Antonio Canaletto believed to have once been owned by an Austrian-Jewish collector.

A Safehaven investigative team was finally sent to Argentina in

1946. It predictably received little if any cooperation from the Perón government (it was unable, for example, to review the records of the Argentine Central Bank). Safehaven's report of May that year indicates no evidence of any major amounts of new Nazi loot in Argentina. But, as the Eizenstat Report would state more than fifty years later, "the fact that looted gold was not discovered in Argentina's German banks still leaves open the possibility that it was concealed in other Argentine financial institutions."

Indeed it was. According to new evidence discovered by Argentine government researchers in May 1999, Juan Perón's government issued a direct order in 1946 that the Argentine Central Bank accept Nazi gold for deposit.

In 1947, Argentina shipped $320 million in gold to New York for deposit into its national account at the Federal Reserve Bank. Part of the gold had been acquired from the Swiss National Bank between 1940 and 1947. The Argentineans gave the United States written assurances that not one gram of the gold it had acquired in trades with Switzerland had come from the Reichsbank or been German-owned. At the time, Undersecretary of State Robert Lovett demanded that Argentina provide bar numbers, mint marks, and other identifying numbers as proof of provenance. The Buenos Aires government never sent them. And as the State Department recently admitted, "the matter appears not to have been pursued further."

Turkey: Booty Bazaar

I was becoming resigned to Turkish neutrality.
—WINSTON CHURCHILL, *Triumph and Tragedy*, 1948

Like most of the neutrals, Turkey profited heavily during World War II from robust commerce with both Allies and Axis. As a result—and because Istanbul continued to serve as a major gold-trading center during the war—Turkey's prewar gold reserve of just under 27 tons grew by 1945 to 216 tons.

Turkey's most important sales to the Germans, like those of Portugal and Spain, were of raw materials, especially Turkish-produced chromite ore, an essential ingredient in the manufacture of stainless steel and thence of artillery. Indeed, in his memoirs, the Reich's Armaments Minister, Albert Speer, writes that he informed Hitler himself in November 1943 that "should supplies from Turkey be cut off, the stockpile of chromium is sufficient for only five to six months. The manufacture of planes, tanks, motor vehicles, tank shells, U-boats, almost the entire gamut of artillery would have to cease from one to three months after this deadline."

This Turkish-German trade, which involved German ships having access to the Bosporus, continued until July 1944, when the Turks—who because of their strategic location probably had more reason to fear a German invasion than most of the other neutrals—received a stern American warning that they faced an Allied blockade unless they ceased all trading with Berlin. Finally seeing the writing on the wall, the Turkish parliament voted to sever all economic and diplomatic relations with Germany. On February 23, 1945—just five days before the deadline to qualify for participation in the founding conference of the United Nations in San Francisco, and just slightly more than two months before V-E Day—Turkey declared war on the Axis.

Turkey's late-in-the-game decision to change status and become a belligerent also enabled it to demand not to be treated as a neutral in questions regarding the postwar repatriation of stolen gold. In fact, the Turks have never given a clear accounting.

No one knows for certain just how much looted gold Turkey absorbed during the war. While the government purchased and stored the Nazi gold in its financial institutions, a great deal of gold was exchanged in "private transactions" on Turkey's thriving open market. That notwithstanding, most postwar experts concluded that more than one-third of the close to $10 million in gold that Germany officially sold to Turkey was in fact looted gold—most of it from Belgium, but some of it from individual victims.[7]

But the end of the war did not end Turkey's dealings in stolen German gold. According to the U.S. government's Eizenstat Report of June 1998, at least $400,000 ($4 million in today's values) in gold ingots and assorted coins are known to have been transferred to the Turkish authorities in September 1945 from accounts and safety vaults belonging to the German Dresdener Bank's Ankara branch. U.S. officials later determined that the accounts had belonged to Nazi Foreign Minister Joachim von Ribbentrop. The handover to the Turks was made by the Ankara diplomatic legation managing affairs for the defeated Third Reich—the Swiss.

The Vatican: See No Evil

The ancient principle of Catholic moral theology applied then, as it does today: silence presumes consent.
—FATHER ANDREW GREELY, University of Chicago, 1999

When Francis Osborne D'Arcy, envoy of the Court of St. James's, had an hourlong private audience with Pope Pius XII at the Vatican on November 1, 1943, the Pontiff insisted that he had no complaints about the Nazi occupation of Rome. On the other hand, Pius did voice concern to the British diplomat about troubles the Eternal City might well face in the interlude when the Germans left and the Allies moved in.

Somewhat taken aback, Osborne D'Arcy detailed a list of some of the blatant abuses the German Army and Gestapo had

---

[7] Records from the Reichsbank and Prussian Mint found in 1947 indicated that 249 bars of Belgian monetary gold had been resmelted by the Germans and sent to the Turkish National Bank in March 1943.

already visited on the city. "I said . . . the open city was a farce," he wrote in a secret report forwarded to Washington by the British High Command. "[Rome] was wide open to the Germans who were systematically stripping it of all supplies, transport and labour, were arresting Italian officers, *Carabinieri* and youth and were applying their usual merciless methods of persecution of the Jews. Rome was suffering the fate of all cities occupied by the Germans."

Osborne D'Arcy's memo, which became declassified only in December 1998, indicates no response from Pius XII to his rejoinder. That and the tone of the remainder of the conversation underscore the somewhat strange, often ambivalent neutral role the Pontiff charted for the Vatican during World War II.

Evidently far more concerned about the threat he believed godless communism posed to the Church than he was about the horrors fascism was perpetuating on the world, the Pope appears to have decided early on that the Vatican's wartime priority was to perform a balancing act whose primary role was to keep the Nazis at bay and safely away from the doors of the Vatican. Accordingly, the Pope, who as Eugenio Pacelli had served as a papal diplomat in Germany, scrupulously refrained from any overt denunciations of Hitler's war of aggression. Above all, despite the fact that the Vatican knew details of the Holocaust as early as 1942,[8] he consistently avoided any explicit condemnation of Nazi persecution of the Jews.

Even after the Germans occupied Rome in September 1943, the Pope tragically delayed coming to the defense of the city's two-thousand-year-old Jewish community. When German troops encircled Rome's ancient ghetto on October 16, 1943, and arrested more than a thousand Italian Jews, appeals for papal intervention went unanswered. Within two days, the arrested men all had been

---

[8] Details of Gerhart Riegner's autumn-1942 memo on the Final Solution had been passed to the Vatican by U.S. Undersecretary of State Sumner Welles.

shipped to Auschwitz. Only fifteen of the Pope's deported neighbors ever returned.[9]

Many historians, both Jewish and gentile, have been sharply critical of this and other examples of the Vatican's wartime silence in the face of the Holocaust. At the very best, some see the Pope's inaction as an enormous sin of omission. "The historical responsibility of the Church," says French historian and scholar Zeev Sternhell, "consists of its refusal to see in Nazism absolute evil."

Others have been harsher in their judgment, defining the Pope's inaction as a massive moral failure. "Despite numerous appeals," writes historian Michael Marrus, "the Pope refused to issue explicit denunciations of the murder of the Jews or call upon the Nazis directly to stop the killings. Pius determinedly maintained his posture of neutrality and declined to associate himself with Allied declarations against Nazi war crimes. The most the Pope would do was to encourage humanitarian aid by subordinates within the Church, issue vague appeals against the oppression of unnamed racial and religious groups, and try to ease the lot of Catholics of Jewish origin caught up in the Nazis' net of persecution. And with distinguished exceptions, the corps of Vatican diplomats did no better."

Church defenders claim that criticism of the wartime Pope and his Vatican foreign policy is disingenuous, if not malevolent. "Persons very dear to the Catholic faithful have been condemned without proof," declared Edward, Cardinal Cassidy, the American president of the Vatican's Commission for Religious Relations with the Jews. Had Pius XII candidly condemned the Nazis from his pulpit or openly organized Catholic succor for Europe's Jews, Cassidy and others argue, not only would it have placed the church, its clergy, and believers in occupied Europe in peril, it would have provoked Hitler into greater persecution of all his victims, espe-

---

[9] After that, thousands of Rome's Jews went into hiding, many of them finding refuge in Catholic-run institutions.

cially the Jews. "Pius felt that discretion was wiser, that working behind the scenes would be far more effective," says Baltimore's William, Cardinal Keeler. And, adds Rabbi Barry Friedman, "what we tend to forget is that Pius was the Pope of the Catholics, not the Jews."

"The Pope's crime—if that is what it is" says veteran *Newsweek* religious-affairs editor Kenneth Woodward, "is that he chose the role of diplomatic peacemaker rather than martyr for the cause."

Yet in the face of unending criticism, there have been increasing claims that Pius XII and the Vatican in fact were *not* silent and actually took effective action to save Jews. The Vatican's March 1998 mea culpa document, "We Remember: A Reflection on the Shoah," speaks about "what Pope Pius XII did personally or through his representatives to save hundreds of thousands of Jewish lives."

Woodward, in a 1998 essay criticizing those who criticize the wartime Pope, goes even further, speaking of "an estimated 700,000 Jews [the Vatican saved] from the Nazi death camps— mainly by issuing false baptismal certificates to Jews, disguising some in cassocks and hiding others in cloistered monasteries and convents."

Neither document gives additional details about the "hundreds of thousands." Nor does either point out that most of those Jews saved by Church intervention were helped not because of papal action but through the individual deeds of courageous priests and nuns such as Father Jacques Lucien Bunel, whom the Nazis sent to Mauthausen concentration camp for the crime of sheltering French-Jewish children.

The Pope's defenders also fail to mention that the active collaboration in the Holocaust by such antiheroes as pro-Nazi priest/politician Jozef Tiso in Slovakia passed with minimal criticism and virtually no disavowal from either the Vatican or Pius XII.

Much of the problem lies in the Vatican's ongoing refusal to fully declassify its period archives. While most states maintain a fifty-year period of silence on classified material, the Vatican insists on at least seventy-five years, and then only selectively releases material.

This overly cautious release of data has also left a nagging and growing slate of unanswered questions regarding accusations that the Vatican too dealt in Nazi gold and stolen Holocaust assets, especially in the chaotic years that followed the war.

One of the prime charges relates to loot stolen from Yugoslavian Jews and Gypsies by the Ustasha, the Croatian Fascist movement that ran the wartime puppet state the Nazis established in "independent" Croatia. The plunder, mostly in gold coins, disappeared when the Ustasha were driven from power in 1944 and was believed to have been used in Western Europe and South America to set up a postwar power base by exiled Ustasha leader Ante Pavelić.

In 1997, a research team working on the American television documentary *Blood Money* uncovered a previously classified 1946 report by Emerson Bigelow, a U.S. Treasury expert in illicit funds. In a memo to Harold Glasser, the U.S. Treasury Department's director of Monetary Research, Bigelow claims that the gold, valued at SFr 350 million ($295 million in today's values) went in two directions: to the Bank of England's gold pool and to the Vatican.

"Of the funds brought from the former independent Croat state where Jews and Serbs were plundered to support the Ustasha organization in exile, an estimated 150 million Swiss francs were impounded by British authorities at the Austro-Swiss frontier; the balance of approximately 200 million Swiss francs was originally held in the Vatican for safekeeping. According to rumor, a considerable portion of this latter amount has been sent to Spain and Argentina through the Vatican's 'pipeline,' but is quite possible that it is merely a smoke screen to cover the fact that the treasure remains in its original repository."

Discovery of the document prompted a new and as yet unfinished investigation by U.S. authorities. It also evoked adamant denials by Vatican spokesmen—and a fresh refusal by the Holy See to release any documents of the relevant period.

What is known is that after the defeat of the Nazis and the Communist conquest of Yugoslavia, the Vatican maintained close ties with the Ustasha whose anti-communism was of far greater importance to the Holy See than their Nazi past. The primary connector was Father Krunoslaw Dragonovic of the pontifical college of San Girolamo, a Vatican center for Croatian clerics. Dragonovic, using his Vatican connections to the Red Cross and other international organizations, arranged for the flight to South America of Ustasha Fascists. Among them: Ustasha leader Ante Pavelić, who arrived in Rome in early 1946 with large amounts of stolen assets in his control, and subsequently fled to Argentina.[10]

Other intelligence reports discovered in the National Archives indicate that the Vatican's financial agencies illegally dealt with German banks toward the end of the war. The Institute for Religious Works," says the World Jewish Congress's Aryeh Doobov, "was found to have conducted transactions—often via Switzerland—with the German Reichsbank as late as 1944 and 1945."

The reports cite wires sent by the Vatican's financial agencies to the Reichsbank through Crédit Suisse, and to the blacklisted Swiss-Italian Bank at Lugano via Union Bank. "Three reports cite instructions wired between banks which were intercepted by field officers"—a reality that Doobov insists makes the reports "not informed assessments but documented facts."

Equally documented in a 1956 U.S. Federal Reserve Bank memorandum is the Vatican's ties to 2,500 suspect gold bars in the American bank that were discovered to have been minted by the Germans during the war with false prewar dates stamped on them

---

[10] According to the Eizenstat Report issued by the State Department in June 1998, the pontifical college of San Girolamo "also cooperated with the 'Ratline' created by the U.S. Army's Counterintelligence Corps to smuggle such infamous war criminals—but anti-Communists—as Klaus Barbie to South America."

to hide their true origins. Most of the bars were the property of Swiss banks, who traded them for a variety of third parties—including the Vatican.

When representatives of over forty countries gathered in December 1997 for the London Conference on Nazi Gold, an appeal was made to the Vatican—which refused to participate in the conference but sent two observers—to open its archives to independent researchers so that these and other questions could be answered. Unfortunately, says Lord James Mackay of Clashfern, who chaired the London conference, "the Holy See delegation . . . did not respond."

10

Restitution

Righting Wrongs

This is the last chapter of the Holocaust, and it must be written correctly.
— EDGAR BRONFMAN, president, World Jewish Congress

Every day some more of us die. We are old. We need the help now, not ten years from now.
— MAGDA GOLDSTEIN, Hungarian Holocaust survivor, age eighty-two

The murder and pillage had taken place far from the safety of the New World. But like so many American Jews of their generation, Edgar Bronfman, Israel Singer, and Elan Steinberg grew up haunted by the shadows and ghosts of Europe's war on the Jews. The three would eventually join forces as the president, secretary-general, and executive director of the World Jewish Congress, the unofficial "foreign ministry" that serves as the umbrella representative of Jewish organizations in more than eighty countries. It also became the most determined, and in some minds overly aggressive, force in the current battle for restitution. But as always, the mindset that drove these three was formed in their earliest years.

Bronfman—who became one of North America's wealthiest men when he inherited the $22 billion Seagram Company from its founder, his Russian-born father, Samuel—remembers whispered wartime discussions in the family's redbrick mansion atop Montreal's Westmount. "Maybe I was ten or eleven," he recalls. "But I'd overhear the accented voices of these sad-faced visitors telling my father horrible stories. How people were having everything taken from them, including their lives. How all the Jews in a village would be lined up, made to dig their own graves, and then shot. And this was happening all over Europe. And I thought, if I knew, then others must know, so why wasn't anyone doing anything about it?"

For Singer and Steinberg, both sons of Holocaust survivors, the soul-searing stories they heard as children were even more immediate. As the *New York Times* writer Caryn James puts it, the children of survivors often spend their lives "grappling with a past that is both painfully familiar but forever beyond their reach." Steinberg's Polish-born Jewish parents had lost most of their relatives to the slaughter. With the help of a Polish farm family who hid them in an underground bunker near their home city of Tarnopol, Rose and Max Steinberg survived the war. Then, as did tens of thousands of other desperate survivors, they walked overland and made their way aboard an immigrant ship bound for the newborn state of Israel where Elan Steinberg was born in 1952. Eventually the family came to New York. Yet the stories of how everything in Europe had been destroyed or stolen, and how everyone had been murdered, remained constants.

New York–born Israel Singer's parents fled their Vienna home not long after the Anschluss of 1938. His father, Dr. Konrad Kalman Singer, was a Polish-born economist who had emigrated to

Vienna. One of the city's young Zionist leaders, he had been among the first Jews to be seized and beaten by the Nazis after the Anschluss. "Some of my uncles fared worse," says Singer. "They were sent to Dachau. When their cremated ashes were mailed back in little boxes, my father and mother decided it was time for them to leave."

The Singers first fled to France. After June 1940, when the Nazis arrived, they moved on to Switzerland. But authorities there denied them shelter and "threw them out," says Singer. Forced back across the Franco-Swiss border, Konrad Singer and his wife, Anna, ended up in the brutal internment camp at Gurs under Vichy French guard.

In 1941, the Singers managed to escape to Spain and from there sailed aboard a cattle boat to Cuba. They eventually reached Canada. In 1942, they went to Niagara Falls, walked across the border into the United States, and made their way to Brooklyn, where Anna Singer's parents lived. "They moved into a small apartment with sixteen other refugees," recounts Singer. "My mother was pregnant. After I was born, they were able to become legal American citizens."

It was only after the war that Konrad and Anna Singer learned the fate of the extended family they'd left behind in Poland. "They had been pulled from the synagogue on the festival of Hosana Rabba, dragged away to the pits, and murdered; 113 members of one family. I was only three years old, but I remember my grandmother setting 113 candles on the kitchen table and lighting them in their memory. It's my first real memory."

More than four decades later, Singer had his ancestral memory shaken again. Newly elected as secretary-general of the World Jewish Congress, he had been invited to Vienna together with New York Mayor Edward Koch to speak at the opening of the Austrian capital's new Holocaust-memorial museum. "My father had just died, and I was still wearing my mourning beard. The entrance exhibit was a giant blowup photo of three Viennese Jews being forced to wash the streets in front of St. Stephen's Church the day after the Anschluss. One of the three men was my father. . . . I was speechless, and I had to ask Koch to speak instead of me. I had come face to face with what my father had endured, with what they had all endured, and it was a turning point in my life."

But individual as well as collective memories were not the only turning points that led to the historic struggle to right some of the mountain of injustices perpetrated before, during, and in the aftermath of the Holocaust. A far more immediate turning point came with the fall of the Berlin Wall in November of 1991. "We'd begun tenuous talks with several East European leaders even before the Wall fell," says Bronfman, who became president of the World Jewish Congress in 1978. "Now, with Communism crumbling, we suddenly had open access not only to government officials and remnant Jewish communities that had been off-limits to us for decades but mountains of documents. Fifty years after the war, we could finally try and seek some justice for the Jews of Eastern Europe whose property had been stolen first by the Nazis and then by the Communists."

It was a familiar role for the WJC, historically the central player in seeking indemnification and reparations for Holocaust victims. It was the WJC's charismatic founder, Nahum Goldmann, who had forged the historic reparations agreement with West Germany's Konrad Adenauer in 1953 and then formed the Claims Conference group that administered it. The controversial accord had had vocal opponents in the Jewish community and even triggered bloody riots in Israel, where right-wing groups led by Menachem Begin emotionally likened it to absolving Germany of guilt by accepting "blood money." But the Goldmann-forged agreement ultimately provided more than 11 billion in Deutsche Mark payments to individual survivors as well as mammoth and at the time desperately needed financial infusions for the young, overburdened state of Israel.

With communism on the retreat and the nations of the former

Soviet bloc eager for American trade and aid, a symbiotic relationship was formed between many of them and the World Jewish Congress. Part of it was based on a traditional form of East European anti-Semitic mythology: The Jews controlled everything. "We knew we could help them, and we were certain the Jews could use their enormous influence to help us," privately admitted one Hungarian official. Indeed, Poland, Hungary, Romania, Czechoslovakia, and all the other former Soviet-bloc nations now were not only eager for American and other Western aid but hoped to enter the North Atlantic Treaty Organization. The fact that Bronfman was also one of the world's wealthiest men, and as an American citizen an active and influential Democrat, merely reinforced their opinion that he and the WJC could play a central role. No one from the World Jewish Congress did much to dissuade them.

In 1992, Bronfman and Singer obtained the direct backing for their restitution campaign from Israeli Prime Minister Yitzhak Rabin. "He was not an openly emotional man," recalled Bronfman. "But on this issue Rabin was firm and committed. He saw this as history, as an obligation for justice."

Interim agreements were soon reached for the return of a handful of communal properties in the Slovak Republic and Hungary. And then attention suddenly turned to a long-unanswered question: What happened to all the Jewish assets that had been placed for safekeeping in Switzerland?

"There was no single reason why Switzerland appeared on the horizon," recalls Elan Steinberg. But a confluence of dates, events, and discoveries triggered a chain of investigations and revelations that would shake the world. To mark the fiftieth anniversary of the end of the war in May 1995, Swiss President Kaspar Villiger had for the first time voiced a public government apology for Switzerland's less than welcoming policy toward wartime Jewish refugees. "I want to apologize to those people who suffered, or went to prison, or found their deaths because of us," Villiger declared.

Switzerland and the Jews, a damning book by Swiss-Jewish historian Jacques Picard, detailed much of what Villiger was apologizing for. As an increasing amount of U.S. wartime intelligence material became declassified and available at the National Archives, it suddenly became clear that the Swiss had played dishonest roles both as a "neutral nation" and as caretakers for the savings of tens of thousands of murdered victims of the Nazis.

On September 12, 1995, Bronfman, employing the offices of Rolf Bloch, head of the Swiss-Jewish community, arranged for an initial meeting in Bern with the Swiss President and leading members of the Swiss Bankers Association. The latter made two mistakes. They kept the American megabillionaire standing at the meeting while banker Georg F. Krayer, then chairman of the SBA, read a typewritten statement. "They didn't even offer a chair," Bronfman remembers with some anger, "and they tried to buy us off with a fast offer of $32 million"—the amount that Krayer told Bronfman was the maximum that Swiss banks might still have in assets from dormant World War II accounts.

"They were more than rude," recalls Bronfman, who usually leaves loudness to his choice of ties. "So I told them that I hadn't come to discuss money; I came to discuss process." When Swiss journalists later asked him how much he actually had in mind, Bronfman replied, "Somewhere between $50 million and $50 billion."

Nonetheless, the Swiss bankers had agreed to the concept of an independent audit—and to setting up an investigating commission. But in the months that followed, the Swiss sent a steady flow of signals that their positions were hardening. A Swiss ombudsman, appointed to handle claims from Holocaust survivors and their heirs, indicated little was being found. Then, in a February 1996 press conference, Robert Studer, the chief executive of the powerful Union Bank of Switzerland (UBS), haughtily announced that his bank's internal audit had produced evidence of only about

$8.9 million in possible Holocaust-victim dormant accounts: "I think that I can say that in this case the original amounts were peanuts."

The churlish talk—and Studer's refusal to indicate how he had conducted the audit—angered Bronfman and his staff. "That's just about when I called Al D'Amato," the tough former New York Republican senator, then chairman of the Senate's powerful Banking Committee, and the driving force behind the Whitewater investigation that had rocked the Clinton administration to its foundations.

Convinced it was a good cause—not to mention a possible major boost to his sagging popularity among New York's large Jewish electorate—D'Amato quickly announced plans for major hearings in the Senate. As one of D'Amato's aides described it, "We agreed to put Switzerland and its banks on trial."

At the same time, Bronfman successfully enlisted the support of two other powerful American political figures who were clearly no great fans of D'Amato: President Bill Clinton and First Lady Hillary Rodham Clinton. Mrs. Clinton was visiting Bronfman's Fifth Avenue home for a Democratic Party fundraiser when the WJC president first raised the Holocaust-restitution issue with her. She in turn briefed the President, who soon thereafter met privately with Bronfman at the White House, pledged American support for an investigation, and announced he was naming then Undersecretary of Commerce Stuart Eizenstat as the administration's point man for this issue.

Clinton also ordered the declassification of a massive trove of invaluable documents in the National Archives. Among them: the full archives of Operation Safehaven, the U.S. wartime-intelligence team that had tracked the flow of Nazi money on three continents. "Here were most, if not all, the answers we were looking for, all the smoking guns," says Steinberg. "The problem was that there were six enormous crates of papers that had to be sifted through, one by one."

To carry out the painstaking job, Bronfman, who personally bankrolls "an important part" of the WJC's operations, now agreed to fund the formation of a research strike force of young Holocaust scholars and historians. Working in shifts at the National Archives in Washington, the researchers—who soon found themselves in good-natured competition with research teams sent in by corporate lawyers and the Swiss Bankers Association—pored through the newly declassified Safehaven papers. They quickly discovered leads not only on Swiss-Nazi gold trading but on Nazi deposits into Swiss bank accounts.

Among the first discoveries: a 1944 report indicating that Adolf Hitler himself had maintained his own personal Swiss bank account. Opened at the Bern branch of the Union Bank, it was managed by the Führer's longtime friend Max Ammann, chief of the Nazi publishing empire, and it was apparently used to bank royalties from the international sale of Hitler's ideological blueprint, *Mein Kampf*.[1]

Even more stunning were details of a wartime fund maintained at Zurich's once highly respected Johann Wehrli & Company Bank. Opened in the name of the Wilhelm Gustloff Foundation, named for the murdered head of the Swiss Nazi Party, this special account was actually controlled by senior officers of the SS who used it, according to a June 1945 Safehaven memo, as the primary repository for "the assets and titles of property taken by the Nazis from Jewish businessmen in Germany and the occupied countries."

The Gustloff fund disappeared with other German accounts when the Wehrli family, who had transferred much of their banking to South America, liquidated their bank at the end of the war. But there was evidence that other Nazi accounts containing confis-

---

[1] The World Jewish Congress leaked news of the find to the press, some of whom contacted the Union Bank for confirmation. The bank's spokesman refused comment, invoking banking-secrecy laws.

cated Jewish assets had remained in Swiss banks and been drawn upon in the years that followed the war.

More damning was evidence that for all their denials, there was indeed a flood of valid survivor claims on dormant Swiss accounts. At hearings held in Washington and New York, the Senate Banking Committee, chaired by Senator D'Amato, and its House of Representatives counterpart, chaired by Iowa Congressman Jim Leach, heard emotional testimony from a steady stream of Holocaust survivors. "I come before this committee to denounce the Swiss banks," Hungarian-born survivor Alice Fischer told the Leach Committee. "I want this committee to know that I am not doing this out of greed. I did not want blood money. But this is my money, and the Swiss banks have no right to hold it from me!"

There was also initial talk of American boycotts and government sanctions against Swiss banks. The floodgates had been opened. Faced with the inability to continue their total stonewall, the panicked Swiss Bankers Association reluctantly agreed to finance the establishment of The Independent Committee of Eminent Persons, an investigative body to be headed by no less than Paul Volcker, the former Federal Reserve Chairman. In an unprecedented move, they also agreed to lift that holy of holies, Swiss banking secrecy, so that the three international accounting firms Volcker retained could carry out a painstaking "criminal audit," as the tall and taciturn Volcker put it to a closed-door meeting of World Jewish Congress delegates in Oslo.

As if this were not bad enough, the Swiss suddenly found themselves confronted with a series of class-action suits by individual Holocaust survivors and claimants, all of whom retained high-profile American firms to fight their battles. Some worked pro bono; others took the cases on contingency.

The first suit, for $20 billion, was filed against Swiss Bank Corporation and the Union Bank in the U.S. District Court in Brooklyn, New York, on October 1, 1996, by Auschwitz survivor Gizella Weisshaus. Very quickly the Swiss found themselves facing claims from more than 10,000 aging survivors or their heirs. (U.S. District Court Judge Edward Korman eventually combined the three class-action suits into one.)

The Swiss public responded with mixed feelings. While many resented the ugly charges being leveled against them—and particularly what they considered the "bellicose tones" from Senator D'Amato and the World Jewish Congress—there were others, especially from Switzerland's younger generation, whose consciences had been jolted by the revelations. "We grew up with certain myths about our World War II bravery," explained eighteen-year-old student Margetta Terli. "Now we want to know just what our parents and grandparents did or didn't do."

They found a spokesperson in parliamentarian Verena Grendelmeier. "We have been morally guilty in this whole question, and we have to accept responsibility," the once popular Swiss stage actress declared. "This is a question of our history, of our generation . . . and if we throw a rock and it brings down the mountain, then that is what we must do."

At Grendelmeier's urging and that of other determined Swiss political and cultural figures, the Swiss parliament agreed in December 1966 to establish an Independent Commission of Experts from around the world, to be headed by respected Swiss historian Jean-François Bergier. In its first report, issued less than two years later, the historical commission revealed that private Swiss banks had received three times more Nazi gold than previously reported—some $61 million at wartime values, close to $610 million today. About one-sixth of the total Nazi gold, the commission said, was likely "victim gold"—gold stolen from concentration-camp prisoners and other victims—a total of $146 million at 1945 prices, roughly $1.5 billion today.

The chance discovery of another document indicated that while most of the 377 tons of gold the Allies' Tripartite Gold Commission had taken control of in 1946 had been distributed to the nations from whom it had been looted, some 5.5 tons were still extant. (And simply by asking British authorities, former Labour MP Greville Janner, head of the British branch of the WJC, discovered that 3 tons were in the vaults of the Bank of England and 2.5 were in the basement of the Federal Reserve Bank in New York.[2]

The long-overdue campaign for belated restitution also triggered an embarrassing and potentially destructive scramble among the multitude of American-Jewish organizations. "As Jimmy Durante used to say," the WJC's Steinberg notes, " 'Everyone wants to get in on the act.' " With the number of headlines and revelations in the press increasing each day, many of the groups began to compete openly for position. The Anti-Defamation League, the American Jewish Committee, and the Simon Wiesenthal Center each sent its own delegation to meet with Swiss banking officials and began issuing reports. Several ultra-Orthodox groups warned that they would accept no judgments that did not place them in the highest-priority bracket of beneficiaries. Survivor groups demanded determining roles in any negotiation. Israel's Jewish Agency, the country's central nongovernmental Zionist body, saw itself—and the Jewish state—no less central in the restitution issue.

The World Jewish Congress urged its colleagues in the labyrinth of Jewish organizations to back off. "This campaign," said Steinberg, "cannot be effectively waged by a dozen different organizations all working in dozen different directions." The WJC had already established a Jerusalem-based super-umbrella organization called the World Jewish Restitution Organization, in which all the major survivor groups and the Jewish Agency were represented.

Bronfman, who had already received the endorsement of Israeli Premier Yitzhak Rabin, now sought new affirmation of his role from Rabin's successors, Shimon Peres and later Benjamin Netanyahu. He received it in the form of an official letter confirm-

---

[2] Negotiations are now under way to have the balance of the gold declared that symbolic portion of the recouped gold that represents "victim gold," the fillings, rings, and personal belongings that were stolen from Holocaust victims and melted down. The gold would then be turned over to restitution funds.

ing his and the WJC's prime role, not just in recouping communal and private Jewish property in newly free Eastern Europe but in looking into all aspects of unrequited restitution. He became the subject of a March 1997 *Vanity Fair* profile, which described him as "an avenging angel seeking comfort for the ghosts of his slaughtered brethren."

Panicked, but still grasping neither the historic, moral, or even pragmatic public-relations significance of what was coming to light, the Swiss remained in denial. They also decided that one of the more effective ways of combating the growing surge of worldwide anti-Swiss public opinion was to place Jews in the forefront of their public defense. Hans Bär, the former chairman of Zurich's Bank Julius Bär, became the first spokesman of the Swiss Bankers Association. The SBA acquired the services of several Jewish lawyers to represent it in legal proceedings as well as in televised news debates and eventually hired an American-Jewish-owned New York public-relations firm to try to explain away all the bad headlines and enhance its rapidly tarnishing image.

In a direct attempt to reach out to the press—especially the American-Jewish and Israeli press—the Swiss even arranged all-expenses-paid journalist junkets to Zurich. "They wanted to give us their point of view," explains Marilyn Henry, the New York correspondent of the *Jerusalem Post* and one of a number of Jewish journalists to accept the Swiss invitation. Indeed, insists Henry, many of the discussions during the Swiss-government-sponsored trip were "surprisingly open."

But for all their attempts at explaining away the scandals now haunting them, the Swiss continued to build an Alpine-size mountain of public-relations gaffes. In a 1997 New Year's address to his nation, outgoing Swiss President Jean-Pascal Delamuraz made his now famous "Auschwitz was not here" remark and complained that Switzerland was being subjected to "extortion and blackmail" by world Jewry. The storm his anti-Semitic comments caused led him to apologize publicly soon after. But the following month,

Swiss ambassador to the United States, Carlo Jagmetti, was forced to resign after a secret memo was leaked in which the diplomat had undiplomatically described the efforts he felt Switzerland had to exert to quash the uproar over the discovery of Nazi gold in Swiss banks as nothing less than "waging a war."

Still, for Swiss clumsiness, nothing surpassed the disclosure that the Union Bank had been caught brazenly shredding and burning wartime documents—and that despite a recent strict Swiss prohibition forbidding the destruction of any period records before both the Volcker and Bergier committees could review them. The whistle-blower, a conscience-stricken bank guard, Christopher Meili, managed to save some records that dealt with the forced sale of German-Jewish properties by a German bank that had later been absorbed by UBS. Stuffing the documents under his shirt, Meili soon handed them over to a clerk at the Zurich Jewish Community; officials there quickly turned over the fiscal hot potatoes to the police.

The immediate result was a threat to arrest Meili for breaking bank-secrecy rules. Rather than apologize for the incident, UBS president Robert Studer questioned the bank guard's motives, implying in the minds of many that Meili, a born-again Christian, was a villain in the pay of the Jews.[3]

The swirling controversies also unleashed a disturbing new outbreak of Swiss anti-Semitism. Some Swiss extremists depicted the World Jewish Congress as a large, powerful, high-tech, latter-day version of the mythical Elders of Zion. (In point of fact, the organization operates with only six full-time staffers at its Madison Avenue, New York, headquarters, where most of the more sensational documents researchers found were "informally" filed in cardboard boxes kept in a closet.) Swiss-Jewish leaders were en-

---

[3] No charges were ever filed against Meili or the UBS, but the bank guard was fired, received threats against his and his family's lives, and eventually fled to the United States, where Senator D'Amato arranged for him to receive political asylum—and where the Jewish community hailed him as a hero.

gulfed with hate mail, and several synagogues received threats. The nationalist Swiss press sprang to the country's defense. Letters to the editor charged that "the Jews are interested only in money, money, money." One newspaper ran a cartoon depicting people praying at a Wailing Wall of gold bricks. "I don't recall anything like it," fretted Jewish-community leader Rolf Bloch.

With the world press screaming such headlines as WE WERE HITLER'S BANKERS!, the Swiss began pinning any hopes they had of saving their international reputation on Thomas Borer, the boyishly charming thirty-nine-year-old career diplomat whom the Swiss appointed head of the Swiss Government Task Force on the Assets of Nazi Victims. Charged with coordinating all federal Swiss involvement in the review of the Nazi and postwar periods, Borer had the task of ensuring that all concerned was doing their jobs and cooperating: the Swiss National Archives, the ministries of Justice and Finance, the Swiss National Bank, and even the Swiss Bankers Association.

It also became Borer's thankless task to officially represent the Swiss government in appearances before the D'Amato and Leach hearings. He was the perfect choice. Conciliatory and charming, he was the face of the young new Europe, not World War II's coldhearted Swiss official. But even Borer slipped in the mud. When it was revealed that Switzerland had knowingly accepted looted Nazi gold, Borer told a press conference that "after all, under international law at the time, it was not illegal."

The first major melt of Switzerland's glacial denial came in February 1997: a goodwill offer brokered by the Crédit Suisse bank to establish a $71-million "Humanitarian Fund" to benefit Holocaust victims and their descendants. Jointly financed by Crédit Suisse as well as the UBS and other major Swiss banks and businesses, it ultimately totaled $185 million and began its grant distributions the following year with $400 payments to a handful of Latvian-Jewish slave-camp survivors.

The Swiss government also made its own conciliatory moves

and proposed establishing a multimillion-franc Swiss Solidarity Foundation to benefit people around the world "confronted with poverty, suffering or persecution." That, explained the Swiss Foreign Ministry, "could include" Holocaust survivors.

More to the point, Swiss banking officials finally broke their traditions of secrecy and published the first of a series of long-awaited lists of dormant World War II accounts. Posted on the Internet and in major newspapers around the world, and comprising some 2,000 names, the initial list was a varied one that included to the shock of many, not only Holocaust victims but a number of Nazi officials and personalities, and the German-Jewish mother of the American ambassador to Switzerland.

While welcomed as meaningful gestures, the moves did not diminish increasing pressures on the Swiss. In May 1997, U.S. Undersecretary of State Stuart Eizenstat released a lengthy and much anticipated intergovernmental study of U.S. and Allied efforts to recover and restore gold and other assets stolen by the Nazis. The 207-page report was prepared with the help of State Department historian William Slany and teams from the Central Intelligence Agency, the departments of Commerce, Defense, Justice, State, and the Treasury, as well as the Federal Bureau of Investigation, Federal Reserve Board, National Archives, National Security Agency, and the U.S. Holocaust Memorial Museum. It included damning new evidence of Swiss financial collusion with the Nazis, not to mention a fifty-year Swiss pattern of concealment and obscuration. It also included the damning indictment that "Swiss economic cooperation with Germany had possibly extended World War II by as much as two years."

Adding to the assault were highly publicized decisions by New York State Comptroller Alan Hevesi, California State Treasurer Matt Fong, and municipal and state officials in Illinois and California to consider or approve economic sanctions against Swiss banks—a move that threatened not only multimillion-dollar deposits from various American pension funds but pending mergers of several Swiss banks with American ones. In one of the first moves, New York City barred Union Bank from a $1-billion city bond offering.

The boycott threats were not welcomed by the State Department, which denounced them as "counterproductive." But the Swiss finally got the message. By the end of 1997, heavy negotiations were under way between the Swiss banks, the lawyers for the class-action plaintiffs, and representatives of the World Jewish Congress. An initial settlement offer of $600 million from the Crédit Suisse, Swiss Bank Corporation, and Union Bank was rejected as quickly as it was made in June 1998. "We are not about to settle history's accounts for fifty cents on the dollar," Bronfman declared.

Finally Federal Judge Korman called all parties to a private dinner at the venerable Brooklyn Steak House "Gage and Tollner." One of the participants recalls the evening: "The judge basically told us—and he was only half joking—that no one would leave the room until there was a deal."

By the time coffee was served, the deal had been struck. On August 12, 1998, representatives of the Swiss banks, the Holocaust survivors, and the U.S. government announced an overall $1.25-billion settlement of all claims as reparations to victims of the Holocaust. Among those on hand to watch the ceremonial announcement outside Brooklyn's Federal District Courthouse: seventy-three-year-old Estelle Sapir,[4] one of the first claimants, and Christopher Meili, the Swiss bank clerk who saved documents from the Union Bank's shredder.

The tossed rock that Swiss parliamentarian Verena Grendelmeier had once spoken of had begun to bring down more than just Alpine mountains. In addition to Switzerland and France, Spain, Portugal, Argentina, Sweden, Norway, Brazil, Canada, the Nether-

---

[4] Sapir received her own settlement from Crédit Suisse of a reported $500,000. Several months later, she died.

lands, Uruguay, and the United States announced national commissions to investigate the fate and whereabouts of stolen Nazi booty. Norway, which also brokered the first fragile steps toward a Mideast peace settlement, became the first nation in the world to offer serious compensation to its Jews for the crimes of the Nazi period. Major international conferences on missing Holocaust assets—gold, cash, and art—took place in both London and Washington. And the international success of Hector Feliciano's *The Lost Museum* triggered new interest in the true provenance of thousands of works of art hanging in private and museum collections on four continents. Both the World Jewish Congress and the B'nai B'rith formed their own art-search foundations. And just as significantly, the American Organization of Museum Curators agreed to establish new rules and criteria for determining the true origin of suspect art—and for pinpointing items looted during the Nazi period.

Emboldened by the attempts of so many nations to come to terms with their World War II records—not to mention by the hefty Swiss-bank claim settlement—other groups of survivors who felt they'd been denied their rights began pressing for belated justice. In April of 1997, a group of death-camp survivors filed three separate multibillion-dollar class-action suits against some of the world's largest and most prestigious insurance companies, charging that either their policies had been stolen from them and illegally cashed by the insurance companies or they had been wrongfully denied claims. And indeed some had.

While some German-Jewish survivors of Nazi persecution had eventually received at least partial postwar restitution for policies they had been forced to surrender before leaving the Reich, most other European Jews and their heirs had received nothing for policies plundered from them by the Nazis and their helpers—or, in several cases, even for policies with which they'd managed to escape.

The number of people affected was even greater than that

touched by the Swiss-bank scandal. "Insurance in prewar Europe was not just for rich men," says Dutch historian Isaac Lipchits. "Almost every poor Jew in Europe managed to put aside a few insurance pennies—either to provide a dowry for his daughters or to help his family if he died. My father was a banana peddler in the Hague marketplace, but he never missed payment on his insurance policy."

The sum total of all these penny-and-dime policies—as well as many larger ones—was enormous. World Jewish Congress researchers estimate that the 1940 value of only prewar life-insurance policies owned by European Jews was approximately $250 million—about $2.5 billion in today's values. Yet few survivors or heirs of victims were ever able to receive any postwar payments from insurance companies—not for life insurance, nor for property and casualty claims. Like Swiss bankers and European government officials, insurance companies demanded unproducible death certificates or simply claimed that company records "had been lost during the war" or that the issuing branch was no longer under their control.

Insurance companies named in the class-action lawsuit included:

AUSTRIA:	Wiener Alliance Versicherungs Aktiengesellschaft
	Der Anker Allgemeine Versicherungs-AG
FRANCE:	Union des Assurances de Paris
GERMANY:	Allianz Group of Munich
	Victoria Lebensversicherung-AG
	Gerling Konzern Lebensversicherungs-AG
	Zurich Nordstern Lebensversicherungs-AG
	Vereinte Versicherung-AG
	Mannheimer Lebensversicherung-AG
ITALY:	Adriatica SpA
	Assicurazioni Generali SpA
	Riunione Adriatica di Sicurtà SpA

SWITZERLAND: Basler Lebens-Versicherungs Gesellschaft
Lebensversicherungs Gesellschaft
Winterthur Lebensversicherungs Gesellschaft

The class-action plaintiffs found sympathetic ears in the National Association of Insurance Commissioners, the organization of officials who control every aspect of the vast American insurance industry. NAIC-sponsored hearings began in Philadelphia in April 1998 and continued in New York. Testimony proved as moving to the public—and as embarrassing to the insurance companies—as testimony before the D'Amato and Leach committees had been to the Swiss banks.

Holocaust survivor Rudy Rosenberg, who grew up in the Belgian capital of Brussels, told how he distinctly remembered agents from the Winterthur Insurance Company visiting his parents' home to sell his father a life-insurance policy that he paid in full before the war. The elder Rosenberg died; Rudy survived twenty-seven months in hiding. When the war ended, Winterthur refused to pay on his father's policy, saying the claim was invalid.

Czech-born Mattel Zaks, whose mother had purchased a dowry-insurance policy for her just before the war, related how she took all her policy documents and receipts at the end of the war to the issuing Vienna-based bank—which turned her away. There were dozens of similar stories.

"The European insurance community systematically failed to honor insurance contracts written on the lives of European Jews and their property," concluded New York State Insurance Comptroller Neal Levin.

Many of the castigated insurance firms invoked the postwar closing of the Iron Curtain as their justification for nonpayment. It was an excuse heard often by Holocaust survivors. Samuel Hirsley of New York was sole beneficiary of a $2,000 life-insurance policy purchased in 1935 by his father in Kraków, Poland. When Hirsley contacted the New York offices of Italy's giant Assicurazioni

Generali in 1951, a clerk there told him to make his claim with the Communist government of Poland.

The European insurers moved quickly to try to deflect criticism. Like many of the others, Trieste-based Generali consistently maintained that it had no legal or moral obligation to pay on any policy written by its branches in Eastern and Central Europe. Those policies, Generali said, not only had been subject to local laws but had been secured by assets that were held locally. When Generali's assets and insurance offices were seized by postwar Communist governments, the company pleaded, Generali had received no compensation, and the governments involved therefore assumed the insurance liabilities. Swiss banks had retained deposits made in banks there; the insurance companies, went the explanation, had lost their assets.

Advocates for Holocaust survivors claimed that the arguments were overly legalistic. But in point of fact, the nationalizations and expropriations in Eastern and Central Europe had dealt some of the European insurance companies crippling blows. This was especially true of Generali, which claimed that over one-third of its entire balance sheet had been lost.

The insurers also protested that accusations against them were often "malicious distortions." To which Holocaust survivor Gidon Harel replied, "That's what the Swiss said."

But Generali, in particular, stood firm. "Generali never refused to pay valid claims," says Guido Pastori, the company's general counsel and deputy director. "But we could not pay on policies . . . where Communist governments had nationalized branches— or in Egypt, where British authorities had confiscated Generali offices during World War II and never returned them."

Moreover, Pastori insists, "policies on those countries weren't paid to anyone—Jew or gentile."

Generali was especially outraged over charges that it had acted anti-Semitically. Far from being anti-Semitic, said Pastori, the Jewish-founded company (whose current chairman, Antoine Bernheim, is himself an Auschwitz survivor) had paid many claims between 1946 and 1948 in which the cause of death was given as "died in a concentration camp"—and certainly if the policy had been written by a still-existent Generali office, such as in Italy or elsewhere in Western Europe.

Other European insurance companies had less noble records. According to U.S. government reports, the German Allianz Group had worked hand in glove with the Nazi regime, helping to facilitate the confiscation of Jewish-owned policies and receiving large government policies in return (it was Allianz that insured the construction work at Auschwitz). Italy's Riunione Adriatica had also been among those that had worked closely with Allianz to confiscate policies in Nazi-occupied countries. As for the Swiss insurance companies, most had shown the same lack of compunction as the Swiss banking and industrial industry banks in exploiting the Nazi war effort for profit. According to an interim report issued in 1998 by the Swiss government's own Bergier Historic Commission, no fewer than sixteen Swiss insurance companies were still operating in Germany at the end of the war, earning a full two-thirds of all their foreign premiums there. By 1944, Swiss insurance companies already had nearly SFr1 billion (about $200 million at the time) invested in the Reich. Worse yet, as the war drew to a close, the Swiss insurance companies desperately sought to be paid what they were owed in Nazi gold, despite the almost indisputable evidence that the gold they were accepting from the Germans had been looted from war victims.

Spokesmen for the insurance companies were quick to deny evil intent. At an emotionally charged hearing in New York, James David, an attorney representing Switzerland's Basler Company, testily told the commissioners, "I am not morally bankrupt. I represent a good and decent Swiss insurance company, and I am proud to be acting in that role."

David rejected allegations from the complainants "that European insurers were accomplices, effectively at least, of the Third

Reich. In a world where the Holocaust will always set the standard for human depravity, I'm here to say the accusation is not true."

Then, after acknowledging their "pain and suffering," he went on to promise the survivors at the hearing that Basler and other insurance companies would do "everything we can to deal with your claims."

What they were already doing was launching negotiations to work out mutually acceptable settlements with lawyers representing the plaintiff survivors as well as with the World Jewish Restitution Organization, which consulted closely with American-Jewish activist Neal Sher on the insurance portfolio. A lawyer by training, Sher had served as director of the U.S. Justice Department's Office of Special Investigations, the government bureau charged with tracking down and prosecuting war criminals.[5]

Most of the insurance companies also began to make compensatory moves. Allianz hired auditors to sift through 800,000 policy files from the Nazi era. Zurich followed soon thereafter. Also, faced with a threat to block their bid to take over Israel's large Migdal Insurance Company, Generali announced plans for a $12-million discretionary fund for relatives of the defunct policyholders murdered by the Nazis and also provided a computerized list of over 300,000 names of insured clients between 1920 and 1945—many of them Holocaust victims—and promised to pay out on any claims against policies that were written by company branches still in existence.

"I'm the last person not to want justice for Holocaust victims," says Generali's Israeli lawyer Amihud Ben-Porat. "But there were many groundless, vicious accusations made against Generali in Israel by persons who didn't always verify the facts." Another Israeli lawyer connected to the insurance-agency side of the case bit-

---

[5] As such, Sher had also played a central role in tracking down the records that finally proved the WJC accusations that former UN Secretary-General and Austrian President Kurt Waldheim had hidden details of his Nazi criminal past.

terly likened the atmosphere "to being in a pogrom perpetrated by Jews."

Ultimately, adds Guido Pastori, "we all had to bend a bit under the pressures of any more public charges, unfounded as they might be." And, as in the case of the threatened sanctions and court proceedings against the Swiss banks, most of the insurance companies agreed to negotiate, out of fear that they too would be blocked from expanding their American markets and forming major new conglomerations.

The torrent of accusations, demands, and deals also produced an inevitable negative reaction. In a *U.S. News & World Report* essay of December 12, 1997, John Marks, the magazine's former Berlin bureau chief, wrote that the hunt for stolen assets hoarded by the Swiss and other European nations was in danger not only of overshadowing the historic memory of the war period but of helping diminish the guilt of the primary villain of the Holocaust—German Nazism. "No one would argue that German evil absolves Swiss cupidity or French collaboration," Marks declared. "But it would be a very odd paradox indeed if the partial eclipse of German culpability became a permanent historical fixture."

In fact, it has not. The long-delayed reckoning of how other nations and peoples exploited Nazi evil might have beamed history's embarrassing spotlight directly on them, but ultimate German guilt for the Holocaust has remained a constant in this drama, if not always at center stage, than as a heavy, overbearing backdrop. If anything, the current process has served to sharply underscore German guilt. In fact, it has led modern Germany finally to accept responsibilities it had conveniently forgotten. For the first time since the Reich fell, a democratic and unified Germany has agreed to begin sending compensation payments to Holocaust survivors living in former Soviet-bloc nations. And for the first time since Allied troops liberated the human skeletons who'd survived the Nazi hell camps, wealthy German industry—from electronic companies like Siemens to auto manufacturers like Volkswagen—

has begun to face up to the fact that it was manned and enriched throughout the war by a vast wartime prisoner army of forced foreign labor, part of it Jewish. Even the giant Deutsche Bank has finally been forced to admit that it helped finance the construction of the most notorious of all the death camps—Auschwitz.

Equally answerable is the growing revisionist backlash, which charges that the emphasis on hunting for Holocaust money, gold, and property merely besmirches its victims. The restitution battle, declared the Anti-Defamation League's Abe Foxman, himself a survivor, is "desecrating the memory of the Holocaust."

Foxman, who once led his own ADL delegation to negotiate with Swiss bankers, now feels that "it would be tragic if the lasting remembrance of this tragic period were of money and gold bars." And French author Marek Halter, calling for a rapid close of the entangled court processes he called "a macabre dance," recently reminded readers of the French newspaper *Le Monde* that the Jews were not killed for their money, they were killed because they were Jews. "Enough of bargaining about their money," said Halter, who urged funds for battling anti-Semitism, preserving Yiddish culture, and Holocaust education.

Other usually crystal-clear writers have weighed in with far murkier criticisms. Jonathan Tobin, one of the brighter voices in American-Jewish letters, has worried in print that the rash of "grandstanding" on Swiss loot, Nazi gold, and stolen art by Jewish organizations is "distorting our view of the Holocaust." And syndicated columnist Charles Krauthammer, in one of the more extreme pieces, emotionally attacked what he called "the grotesque scramble for money" that would, he cautioned, revive "Shylockian stereotypes."

It is this that is the weakest—and in many ways most dangerous—of these neo-revisionist arguments: that struggling for truth and justice will somehow conjure up new anti-Semitism. As former Nazi slave laborer Rudy Kennedy puts it, "Anti-Semitism is not created by Jews, it is created by non-Jews."

If one follows the skewed logic of the critics, rather than risk giving the world's anti-Semites a self-fulfilling view of Jews as gold grubbers, it would be better that the monies being sought remain with the Swiss bankers who have hoarded them for fifty years, or that the French and Austrians retain the looted art and precious books they have ferreted away, that wealthy German industry not compensate its surviving slave laborers, that the United States and Britain not live up to their sins of omission, or that the Norwegians, Dutch, Croatians, Poles, Czechs, Slovaks, Swedes, Hungarians, Romanians, and others who profited from the Holocaust retain the plundered profit they continue to hold. As for the aging survivors and their heirs, giving up their quest for restitution might deprive them of some degree of financial comfort and dignity in their final years, but it would provide them instead with a sense of moral superiority, allowing them to be happy in the knowledge that they have relieved their critics' discomfort.

Ultimately the real question may be how best and most efficiently to distribute these long-overdue compensation funds, how to avoid the bureaucratic delays and disappointments that have marked previous Holocaust restitutions—notably the Claims Conference. More than $22 million have already been dispensed to some of the neediest of the Holocaust survivors, those in Eastern Europe. An additional $32 million have been distributed to needy Holocaust survivors in the United States. During 1999, another $100 million will be distributed throughout sixty-four countries. But if the victims are to be the primary beneficiaries, then it is imperative that the distribution system be streamlined. The average age of the remaining Holocaust victims is already eighty. Within ten or twenty years, few will remain.

"The scales of justice must be balanced soon," warns David Altshuler, director of New York's Museum of Jewish Heritage. "Otherwise history will not only record the atrocities of the Holocaust but the inequities and immoralities of its aftermath."

And what will become of the hundreds of millions of dollars

that will remain or are yet to be released in restitution funds? Holocaust-survivor organizations are pressing for funds to be distributed first to their membership, then to the individual heirs and those of other Holocaust victims. Israel, which gave new life to hundreds of thousands of Holocaust survivors and more than two million other Jews in need, views itself as the natural postwar center of Jewish life and creativity, the national heir of the 6 million victims. Europe's surviving Jewish communities, both those that thrive in the West and those newly renascent in Eastern Europe, believe that they and their institutions are worthy of support. Others, such as the French-Jewish community, want to see the establishment of a Holocaust-education fund.

Many Jewish leaders fear that once the battles for restitution are won, an ugly "War of the Jews" will develop as organizations tussle over control of the funds. "I'm ashamed to admit that it has already begun," says retired Israeli Supreme Court Justice Moshe Bejski, who as a young man was one of the 1,868 Polish Jews saved in the Kraków Ghetto by the legendary Oskar Schindler. "There are twenty organizations pulling in different directions," says Bejski, a major witness at the 1962 trial in Jerusalem of Adolf Eichmann. "We have to establish criteria before matters degenerate further."

Edgar Bronfman and the World Jewish Congress believe that Jewish squabbling over the restitution funds can best be avoided— and the goals of the restitution battle most equitably met—by establishing a three-level system for dispensing of funds. "First and foremost, we must provide for those survivors with legitimate claims and those in need," says Bronfman. "The next level should provide compensation for victims' heirs."

The third "slice," says Bronfman, should go into the creation of an international foundation that would benefit both Israel and the rest of the world Jewish community with massive amounts of money for Jewish education and communal continuity.

The idea has already met with some powerful opposition.

"The new generation of Jews can and should take care of educating its young," says Bejski. "The people who must be the beneficiaries are survivors and their heirs."

Whether the Jewish-communal world can overcome its unfortunate, sometimes tragic propensity for internecine, self-defeating disagreement remains to be seen. The shameful turf battles between organizations, and between some national communities and the World Jewish Congress, could grow worse.

There is no question that Holocaust survivors and their legitimate heirs must be the primary and first-line beneficiaries of this historic restitution process. But major portions of the pool of restitution funds should also be provided for cultural and educational funds, both in Israel and throughout the worldwide Jewish diaspora.

Holocaust chronicler Elie Wiesel has said, "No amount of money will return the six million Jews slaughtered, no amount of gold can compensate for the more than one million children murdered."

But what better memorial to this multitude of innocent victims can there be than to guarantee the future of Jewish life? And what better response to Hitler, his scheme to obliterate the Jewish people, and to all those who participated in his evil frenzy of murder or joined forces with his insatiable pack of thieves than Jewish survival.

JEWISH ASSETS SEIZED 1934–1945*

	Population in Thousands	Minimal Estimate Per Capita Dollars	Minimal Estimate Value (in Millions of Dollars)	Maximum Estimate Per Capita Dollars	Maximum Estimate Value (in Millions of Dollars)
Germany	575	3,500	2,000	5,200	3,000
Hungary	500	1,600	800	3,200	1,600
Czechoslovakia	360	1,700	600	2,800	1,000
CZECH REPUBLIC	[120]	[3,500]	[420]	[5,800]	[700]
SLOVAKIA	[130]	[1,300]	[160]	[1,700]	[200]
SUB-CARPATHIA	[110]	[500]	[50]	[700]	[75]
Austria	185	2,200	400	3,300	600
Netherlands	130	2,300	300	3,900	510
France	270	1,500	400	3,000	800
Belgium	65	2,100	140	3,000	100
Italy	30***	1,500	50	3,000	100
Romania	850	700	600	1,100	900
Yugoslavia	80	1,200	100	1,500	160
Greece	75	600	40	800	60
Bulgaria	50	700	30	900	50
Poland	3,300	700	2,000	900	3,000
West. U.S.S.R.	2,000	200	400	300	600
Lithuania	145	700	100	900	130
Latvia	90	700	70	900	90
Other**	18	3,000	50	3,000	50
TOTAL	8,700		8,080		12,850

* This chart of carefully estimated figures was prepared for the World Jewish Restitution Organization by historian Sidney Zabludoff. Some of the total figures may be somewhat lower or higher than those in my text (e.g., Netherlands) because of differences in available research and source material as well as in exchange rates used.

** Denmark, Estonia, Luxembourg, and Norway

*** In Nazi-occupied Italy as of July 1943

NOTE: All countries and regions calculated within their 1937 borders.

Afterword

Because of the monumental scope of the restitution struggle, there are almost daily developments and discoveries. Here is a brief attempt to bring the issues up to date as of July 15, 1999.

GERMANY

After more than half a century of systematically avoiding major responsibility for compensating the millions of people—Jews and non-Jews—who were compelled into slave and forced labor by the Nazis, the German government has finally agreed to facilitate the indemnification of survivors and their heirs. A government-established foundation, to be funded by leading German corporations and banks, will address all slave and forced labor claims, as well as any other claims remaining from Nazi "Aryanization" of Jewish property. German and Jewish officials say they hoped to have the multi-billion-dollar fund in place and in operation by September 1, 1999—the sixtieth anniversary of the outbreak of World War II, but it will clearly take longer.

The Germans have also agreed to reverse their Cold War period decision to refuse to compensate Holocaust survivors in Eastern Europe. During 1999, aged Holocaust survivors in the former Soviet bloc began to receive monthly pensions of about $250 per month. Some eighteen thousand individuals have already received assistance; that number is expected to grow to forty thousand in the year 2000.

Less certain is the fate of confiscated properties in the former East Germany that are now in the hands of the Conference on Jewish Material Claims Against Germany. Under the terms of the restitution agreement, the Claims Conference was granted the right to take possession of unclaimed Jewish properties in Germany—which now total more than forty-nine thousand. Most have never been identified with specific owners. And under German government rules, any survivors and heirs who could lay claim to properties in East Germany had until 1992 to file them. Failure to do so resulted in a loss of claim or a sharply reduced payment for the property's worth. Many heirs are now seeking a change in that policy.

AUSTRIA

A New York court voided District Attorney Morgenthau's confiscation of two Egon Schiele paintings allegedly looted during the Holocaust and lent by an Austrian foundation to the Museum of Modern Art. Over the strenuous objections of MOMA Chairman Ronald Lauder and others, a higher court reversed the ruling. No final judgment has been made as of mid-July 1999.

For their part, the Austrians have begun to return works of art stolen from Austrian Jews. Witness the recent $90 million record-breaking auction in London of a trove of art treasures looted from and finally returned to the Austrian branch of the Rothschild family.

Austrian banks have not yet agreed to settle additional claims against "Aryanization" of Jewish property.

CZECH REPUBLIC

The restitution record of Eastern Europe's most democratic state remains almost as poor as it was. Requests for both records and compensation continue to be summarily rejected or countermanded by the invocation of complex laws. Now aged more than ninety, Eliska Fabry, for example, still awaits the return of even a portion of her family's once large estate. Nonetheless, there have been some signs of change: At the urging of President Havel, the Czech government has finally agreed to open a dialogue with the World Jewish Restitution Organization.

SLOVAKIA

Though far from perfect, Slovakia has continued to return some Jewish properties to the World Jewish Restitution Organization as well as to the tiny local Jewish community. Private claims continue to have mixed results.

NETHERLANDS

The Netherlands' five investigatory commissions have yet to complete all their work, but initial reports have been subject to sharp criticism and accusations of whitewash—especially the principal commission on securities and banking headed by Willem Scholten.

On the positive side, the Dutch government has agreed to contribute some $10 million of its gold holdings into a fund to be administered by the Dutch Jewish community.

Officials of the World Jewish Congress insist that the Netherlands will ultimately be one of the major claims to be resolved. After a period of deadlock and disagreement with the Dutch Jewish community, there have been new and more cooperative contacts.

NORWAY

Here is the model of how a European nation can admirably come to terms with its Holocaust record. A parliamentary commission established in 1996 completed its work in 1998 with two reports: a majority one and a minority one. The former followed a narrowly legalistic route and basically absolved the postwar Norwegian governments of any legal or moral responsibility for the actions of the Quisling collaborationist government. In the end, it provided only for parsimonious restitution to some Norwegian Holocaust survivors. The minority report took a broader historic and ethical view of Norway's wartime mistreatment of its tiny Jewish community. It called for broader restitution and a declaration of national responsibility for the events of World War II.

To its great credit, the Norwegian government—which also played a central role in the efforts to launch Israeli-Palestinian peace negotiations—accepted the minority view and provided moral and material restitution totaling some $60 million. The funds will be distributed among individual survivors and claimants, the balance to be used for education and Holocaust memorial purposes in Norway, as well as through an international Holocaust memorial foundation headed by Nobel Prize laureate Elie Wiesel.

FRANCE

The French have yet to come to full grips with the ignobility of their Vichy history. They did establish the Matteoli Commission to investigate the theft of Jewish property. But the process has not proved fully accountable.

Among the specific anomalies: Although 70 percent of France's Holocaust victims were non-French Jews, to whom the Vichy regime refused all protection, the French government and its commission still insist that restitution questions are strictly a French Jewish issue. The government has even gone so far as to instruct French banks and others not to deal with "representatives of foreign Jews."[1] The result has been an increasingly ugly public dispute over jurisdiction between the World Jewish Congress and the CRIF, the representative body of French Jews. "How does a

---

[1] Letter from Natexes Bank, Paris to Hon. Alan Hevesi, Comptroller of the City of New York, April 23, 1999.

Polish Jew, plundered in France and now living in New York," asks the WJC's Elan Steinberg, "expect the CRIF to represent his or her interests when some of the CRIF's own leaders represent the French banks now under scrutiny?"

Simultaneously, there has been a rash of new and embarrassing discoveries. Among them: evidence that SACEM, the French body that coordinates royalty payments to artists, writers, and musicians, not only withheld royalties from Jewish members during the Vichy period, but that they did not turn them over to their families after the war.

Yet another recent discovery indicates the degree to which the postwar French government was prepared to lie to hide Jewish assets under its control. In a letter to the State Department dated May 4, 1948, by which the French had already designated thousands of art objects as "unclaimed loot"—not to mention amounts in banks and state vaults—the Quai d'Orsay wrote the following: "no heirless estates belonging to vitims of nazi [sic] action have been found in France."[2]

EASTERN EUROPE

POLAND

There have been mixed results. Though the Polish government has agreed to restitute much of the communal property of what was once Europe's largest Jewish community, the World Jewish Restitution Organization is still at jurisdictional loggerheads with today's tiny Polish Jewish community. Despite a series of cooperative agreements signed with the WJRO, the community, clearly encouraged by the Polish government, continues to insist that it alone has primary rights to restitution—an argument that ignores the enor-

[2] RG 59 Box 4245, U.S. National Archives, Letter of Quai d'Orsay to U.S. Embassy, Paris, May 4, 1948.

mous Polish Jewish diaspora and would mean that some thirty-five hundred souls are the heirs of almost 3.5 million Jews.

HUNGARY

Developments in Hungary are far more positive—though not totally. Pensions and the individual restitution of properties have been forthcoming and some communal properties have been returned. To compensate for those many others that have not been returned, the Hungarian government has established a foundation that pays local currency into a pension fund for Holocaust victims and their heirs. However, recent Hungarian government decisions have placed survivors and their heirs at a disadvantage: Victims of Nazi persecution are now being paid only $1/10$ of the amount being given to victims of Communist persecution.

ROMANIA

Romania is another example of progress. Possibly because of their eagerness to join NATO, the Romanian government has initiated steps to return Jewish communal property that was confiscated by Romania's Fascist and Communist governments. A task force of young Romanian Jewish volunteers led by Tovah Ben Nun, a Jewish agency emissary from Israel, has been roaming the country, scouring records in an attempt to compile a comprehensive list of the thousands of properties that once belonged to Romania's Jews. There is "good coordination" between the remaining community and the World Jewish Restitution Organization.

SWITZERLAND

The $1.4 billion global settlement of claims agreed to by the major Swiss banks is soon to be distributed. The Swiss government's Humanitarian Fund of some $200 million raised by major banks, the

Swiss National Bank, and Swiss industry has already benefitted 120,000 Holocaust survivors. By the end of 1999, a total of 200,000 survivors will have received settlement purses of up to $1,200.

The plan for a so-called "Solidarity Fund" of the Swiss government is still floating around and has never been confirmed.

On the moral front, the Swiss government's Bergier Commission has already issued its devastating report on gold which demonstrated that 80 percent of looted Nazi bullion was laundered by Switzerland. In November, the Commission will release its report on how Switzerland dealt with and largely rejected Jewish refugees.

THE OTHER NEUTRALS

Spain is contributing a million dollars to promote Sephardi Jewish culture as an expression of its regrets for the role the Franco government played in the laundering of looted Jewish assets.

Neighboring Portugal is less contrite. A long-awaited Bank of Portugal report on Portuguese gold laundering during World War II has been roundly criticized as a blatant whitewash.

Also released recently are a number of postwar allied documents. One, a declassified British government report from 1946, says that the postwar Portuguese government lied about having any looted Nazi gold—most of which had been smelted into new bars by the Nazis and given counterfeit markings. Lisbon was finally forced to confess, says the document, when it was discovered that four tons of the gold it willingly laundered for the Nazis was still in its original Dutch treasury wrappings.[3]

Sweden, which is still examining what financial restitution it will make, is sponsoring a major international conference on Holocaust education in the year 2000.

[3] Note Verbale of the British Embassy, Lisbon, to the Portuguese Foreign Ministry, February 2, 1949.

Argentina's commission on Nazi looted assets continues to make headway. Commission documents already make it clear that the regime of Juan and Evita Perón actively recruited Nazi war criminals in exchange for transfers of gold, jewels, and cash. Equally hard-hitting reports have been issued in Brazil.

The Vatican still refuses to cooperate with outside attempts to investigate its wartime and postwar role in the cloaking and smuggling of Nazi loot. It has also continued to turn down all requests to open its period archives and even the U.S. State Department has expressed its "disappointment" at Papal stonewalling.

Still, newly declassified Allied documents continue to reveal hitherto unknown details regarding wartime Vatican activities. A 1944 U.S. document reports evidence that Nazi convoys were using Vatican convoys as cover from Allied bombings. The document reveals that the Allies seriously considered—but did not—bombing the Vatican convoys in such cases.[4]

THE ALLIES

Europe's liberators continue their own record and soul search. Britain has finally agreed to accept claims from Jews and other victims of Nazism whose British bank assets were confiscated by His Majesty's Government during the war because they were "enemy aliens." It is also examining paintings of questionable origin in its national galleries.

The British government also sponsored the 1997 London Gold Conference where the representatives of many countries agreed that the six remaining tons of looted gold repossessed after the war by the Allied Gold Commission would be dedicated to Holocaust victim relief. Monies have already been distributed for health care among aging survivors in the former Eastern bloc.

[4] Secret internal State Department memo to the Secretary of State, May 13, 1944.

THE UNITED STATES

No nation has provided more force to the belated search for truth than the United States. America, which in the wake of World War II was part of the problem that led to Holocaust survivors being denied their rightful assets, is now a major part of the solution. "Without U.S. moral and political clout," says WJC President Edgar Bronfman, "we wouldn't have gotten as far as we have."

To further that search, President Bill Clinton has established a special Presidential Advisory Commission on Holocaust Assets in the United States. Chaired by Bronfman, it includes several leading congressman and senators. Its report is scheduled for the end of 2001. But there have already been extraordinary preliminary findings, among them the discovery of twenty-four thousand rare works of Judaica looted by the Nazis, liberated by the U.S. Army, and held without public acknowledgment in the Library of Congress since 1946.

Other discoveries include 1948 State Department reports suggesting that part of the loot from the Hungarian Gold Train, the 1945 transport that carried retreating Nazis, Hungarian sympathizers, and large quantities of gold, jewels, cash, and art objects plundered from Budapest's Jews, may have been shipped by the American occupation authorities to the United States from Germany after the war. Among them: quantities of "melted down gold fillings."[5]

There is also mounting evidence that the number of securities sent by European Jews to the United States for safekeeping just before and in the early years of the war, and never claimed after the war, was larger than believed previously.

Another potential bombshell: indications that the inventories of many major American museums, including the National Gallery in Washington, may contain some art stolen during the Holocaust.

[5] Secret Document #7, Letter of Robert Murphy, U.S. Political Advisor for Germany to the Secretary of State, Washington, January 5, 1948.

ART

Revelations about stolen art are already causing a revolution in the art world where until recently one could acquire almost anything without even the type of title search needed to buy a piece a property in the poorest section of any city in America.

Recent guidelines established by American museums now insist that curators have responsibility to examine their inventories and never to deal in works of art of "dubious pedigree."

The result has been an increasing return of art looted during the Holocaust to its original owners or their heirs: e.g. a Monet recently returned to the descendants of French collector/dealer Paul Rosenberg; and a portrait of a seamstress by Lesser Ury returned by the Austrian city of Linz to the grandson of the Berlin Jew whom the Nazis forced to sell it—before executing him in the death camps.

LIFE INSURANCE

Most of the multi-billion-dollar policy claims are still not settled. But agreement on what were for many Europe's poor Jews their equivalent of a bank account could prove the most far-reaching of the restitution agreements.

There has been at least a conceptual breakthrough in negotiations with European insurance companies, most of whom have finally agreed that they must redeem Holocaust era policies. Moreover, former U.S. Secretary of State Lawrence Eagleburger, who leads the international commission on Holocaust insurance claims, is determined that the companies will pay in current "real values"—including fifty years of devaluations and inflations.

ISRAEL

Even the Jewish state is trying to set its records straight on Holocaust assets. While deeply involved in the quest for global restitution, Israeli authorities are also investigating the fate of lands that were acquired in prewar Palestine through the Jewish National Fund by individual European Jews as well as European Jewish communities—properties which became state property in the aftermath of the Holocaust and the creation of the State of Israel.

PEOPLE

Changes have also come to the lives of many of the prime players in this drama—especially those involved in the battle with the Swiss. After eighteen years in the United States Senate—and despite his successful campaign for restitution for Holocaust victims—New York Republican Alphonse D'Amato was defeated in the 1998 congressional elections and was replaced by his Democratic opponent, Charles Schumer. Nonetheless, D'Amato's role in restitution efforts has not ended; in 1998 he was appointed a "Special Master" by a U.S. federal court and now acts as an arbiter in class actions by Holocaust victims against Austrian banks and German financial institutions.

Estelle Sapir, who had struggled unsuccessfully for forty years to retrieve monies her Polish banker father had deposited in Switzerland before the war and then became one of the first and most effective of the witnesses at D'Amato's Senate hearings, finally received a settlement of her claims againt Credit Suisse that is believed to have been more than $500,000. She died less than a year later.

Gone too is the late Swiss President Jean-Pascal Delamuraz, whose anti-Semitic ramblings embarrassed many of his countrymen.

Swiss bank guard Christoph Meili, who blew the whistle on

Union Bank's destruction of Holocaust period records, was hounded from his Swiss home and finally settled with his wife and children in the United States, where he now works as a secruity guard. Union Bank President Robert Studer was edged out of his post. Swiss officials eventually disbanded their Task Force on the Assets of Nazi Victims. Thomas Borer, the hapless Swiss diplomat who once headed it, married a Texas socialite, added her name to his, and was rewarded for his defense of his nation's reputation by being named Switzerland's Ambassador to Germany.

World Jewish Congress President Edgar Bronfman is busy as chairman of the newly formed Presidential Advisory Commission on Holocaust Assets investigating any and all Holocaust assets that may be in the United States.

The WJC's Israel Singer and Elan Steinberg continue their efforts on behalf of restitution for Holocaust victims. They have also recently launched research into the fate of the multi-millions of dollars in assets that were confiscated from the more than 600,000 Jews forced to flee their native Arab lands—especially Egypt and Iraq—in the wake of the creation of the State of Israel.

Yet perhaps the most astounding human development regards the dead, not the living. In the frenzy of their campaign to exterminate Europe's Jews, the Nazis and their helpers sent millions to their deaths without even registering their victims' names. Now, as a result of the flood of new documentation that has come to light and by cross-checking the massive files that have been uncovered or declassified during the search for the Holocaust assets, archivists at Jerusalem's Yad Vashem, Israel's central Holocaust memorial, have been able to compile a new digitized master list of the names of Holocaust victims. Using an especially developed software for the project, Yad Vashem—which previously had the names of only 1.5 million out of the estimated 6 million Holocaust victims—has already been able to identify more than 3 million men, women, and children who fell victim to hatred and avarice and who for more than half a century remained nameless and faceless. By next year, it is hoped the lists will reach 4.5 to 5 million names.

A final note. Michael Blumenthal, the young blond-haired Jewish boy who dared to venture out onto the streets of Berlin in November 1938 to witness the results of Kristallnacht, then escaped to China and eventually to the United States, where he later became Secretary of the Treasury, has finally returned to Germany. Semi-retired, Blumenthal spends part of each year back in Berlin, where he serves as chairman of that reunited city's new Jewish Museum.

Notes

These notes indicate primary interview sources and texts used in the preparation of this book. For the sake of brevity, I have not detailed the countless newspaper and magazine articles referred to. Full details of the texts appear in the bibliography on page 307.

CHAPTER 1: GERMANY

PRIMARY INTERVIEWS
Maria W. Bamberger, New York
Judge Moshe Bejski, Tel Aviv
Secretary W. Michael Blumenthal, Princeton
Stefanie Blumenthal-Derives, California
Saul Friedlander, Los Angeles
Daniel Goldhagen, New Haven
Rabbi Alexander Schindler, Wesport
Israel Singer, New York
Elie Wiesel, New York

PRIMARY TEXTS
Adolf Hitler, John Toland
As I Recall, Edward M. M. Warburg
Ben-Gurion and the Holocaust, Shabtai Teveth
Explaining Hitler, Ron Rosenbaum
Germany, Israel Gutman (in *Encyclopedia of the Holocaust*)
Hitler's Willing Executioners, Daniel J. Goldhagen
The Invisible Wall, W. Michael Blumenthal
Nazi Germany and the Jews, Saul Friedlander
The Seventh Million, Tom Segev
Soaring Underground, Larry Orbach and Vivien Orbach-Smith
Times and Tides, Eric M. Warburg

Notes

CHAPTER 2: AUSTRIA

PRIMARY INTERVIEWS
Avi Beker, Jerusalem
Marion Granger, Norwalk, Connecticut
Frank Klepner, Melbourne
Ronald Lauder, New York
Henny Lowy King, Dundee, Scotland
District Attorney, Robert Morgenthau, New York City
Ulf Pacher, Washington, D.C.
Hella Pick, London
Shimon Samuels, Paris
Israel Singer, New York
Elan Steinberg, New York

PRIMARY TEXTS
Austria, Israel Gutman (in *Encyclopedia of the Holocaust*)
Dr. Freud: A Life, Paul Ferris
The Fate of Stolen Jewish Properties, Itamar Levine
Jews for Sale? Nazi-Jewish Negotiations, 1933–1945, Yehuda Bauer
Simon Wiesenthal, Hella Pick
Vienna and Its Jews, George Berkley

CHAPTER 3: CZECHOSLOVAKIA

PRIMARY INTERVIEWS
CZECH REPUBLIC
Deputy Mayor Jaromir Cabela, Kolin
Deputy Prime Minister Viktor Doubal, Prague
Eliska Fishman Fabry, Prague
Peter Glaser, Massachusetts
Tomás Kraus, Prague
Fred and Kitty Liebrich, Prague/London
Lisa Lichtenstern Mikova, Prague
Under Secretary James Rubin, Washington, D.C.
Peter Van Witt, Westport, Connecticut
Helga Weissova-Hoskova, Prague
Michael Zantovsky, Prague

SLOVAK REPUBLIC[1]

Fero Alexander, Bratislava
Valentin Bystricky, Bratislava
Pavel Frankl, Zilinia
Peter S. Green, Prague
Tomás Lang, Nove Zamky

PRIMARY TEXTS
And It All Disappeared, Sidney Zabludoff
The Fate of Jewish Prague, Jiri Kudela and Jiri Vsetecka
The War Against the Jews, Lucy Dawidowicz
Where She Came From—A Daughter's Search for Her Mother's History, Helen Epstein

CHAPTER 4: NETHERLANDS

PRIMARY INTERVIEWS
Gerard Aalders, Amsterdam
Judith C. E. Belinfante, Amsterdam
Henriette Boas, Amsterdam
Joeri Boom, Amsterdam
Fina and Shimon Cohen, Houston
Hector Feliciano, Paris
Jutka Halberstadt, Amsterdam
Victor Halberstadt, Amsterdam and Paris
Isaac Lipchits, Amsterdam
Henri Markens, Amsterdam
Sander Pleij, Amsterdam
Willem Scholten, The Hague
Thomas de Swaan, Amsterdam
Richard Vos, Amsterdam
Jacob van Hasselt, Amsterdam (deceased)

PRIMARY TEXTS
The Destruction of the Dutch Jews, Jacob Presser
The Destruction of European Jews, Raul Hilberg
Documents of the Persecution of the Dutch Jewry, 1940–1945,
   L. Polak

[1] Interviews conducted by Peter S. Green.

Dutch Jewish History, Jozeph Michman
The Fate of Stolen Jewish Properties, Itamar Levine
Het Koninkrijk der Nederlanden in de Tweede Wereldoorlog,
    L. de Jong
Jewish Historical Museum, Judith C. E. Belinfante
Restitution of Economic Rights After 1945, A. J. Van Schie

CHAPTER 5: NORWAY

PRIMARY INTERVIEWS
Bjarte Bruland, Oslo
Rabbi Michael Melchior, Oslo
Julius Paltiel, Trondheim
Berit Reisel, Oslo
Arne Ruth, Stockholm
Bjørn Westlie, Oslo

PRIMARY TEXTS
Coming to Terms with the Past, Bjørn Westlie
Report on the Confiscation of Jewish Property, Government of Norway
På tross av alt, Vera Komissar

CHAPTER 6: FRANCE

PRIMARY INTERVIEWS
Claudia Ann Carlin, New York
Serge Cwajgenbaum, Paris
David Douvette, Paris
Jacky Fredj, Paris
Ambassador Patrick Gautras, New York
Henri Hejdenberg, Oslo
Marek Halter, Paris
Serge Klarsfeld, Paris
Samuel Pisar, New York
Robert Rothschild, Paris
Rabbi René Sirat, Auschwitz
André Wormser, Paris

PRIMARY TEXTS
Être Juif dans la société Française, Béatrice Philippe
Français Israélites, Georges Wormser

French Children of the Holocaust, Serge Klarsfeld
Il y a 50 Ans: Le Statut des Juifs de Vichy, Serge Klarsfeld, editor
The Italians and the Holocaust, Susan Zuccotti
La France et la Question Juive, André Kaspi, Serge Klarsfeld, and
   Georges Weller, eds.
Le Commissariat Général aux Questions Juives, Joseph Billig
Le "Fichier Juif," René Rémond
Not the Germans Alone, Isaac Levendal and Robert O. Paxton
The Lost Museum, Hector Feliciano
Pétain's Crime, Paul Webster
The Rape of Europa, Lynn H. Nicholas
Sonderstab Musik, Willem De Vries
Uzès, Gaston Chauvet
Vichy France and the Jews, Michael Marrus and Robert Paxton
Vichy Law, Richard Weisberg

CHAPTER 7: EASTERN EUROPE

PRIMARY INTERVIEWS
Avi Beker, Jerusalem
Tova Bin Nun, Bucharest
Naphtali Lavie, Jerusalem

POLAND:

Eleanora Bergman, Warsaw
Yaffa Eliach, Eishyshok
Marek Halter, Paris
Zvi Michaeli, New York
Grażyna Pawlak, Warsaw
Lea and Efrayim Paz, Ramat Chen
Aron Semel, Los Angeles
Krzystzof Śliwiński, Warsaw
Lawrence Weinbaum, Jerusalem
Pawel Wildstein, Warsaw

PRIMARY TEXTS
The Destruction of European Jews, Raul Hilberg
Hitler's Willing Executioners, Daniel J. Goldhagen
The Holocaust: The Fate of European Jewry, Leni Yahil
The Path of the Righteous, Mordechai Paldiel

Poland's Jews, Israel Gutman (in *Encyclopedia of the Holocaust*)
There Once Was a World, Yaffa Eliach
The War Against the Jews, Lucy Dawidowicz

HUNGARY

PRIMARY INTERVIEWS

László Akar, Budapest
Hilda Barinkai, Budapest
Ambassador Douglas Blinken, Budapest
Charles Fenyvesi, Washington, D.C.
Éva Kahn, Budapest
Robert Lándori-Hoffmann, Budapest
Lilly Levinson, New York
Susan Mesinai, New York and Moscow
Victoria Pope, Washington
Gustáv Zoltai, Budapest

PRIMARY TEXTS

Desperate Mission, Alex Weissberg
Hungary's Jews, F. Brauder (in *Encyclopedia of the Holocaust*)
My Story, Gemma La Guardia Gluck
Righting an Historic Wrong, Lawrence Weinbaum
Tzedek—The Righteous (film script), Marek Halter
When the World Was Whole, Charles Fenyvesi
With Raoul Wallenberg in Budapest, Per Anger

CHAPTER 8: SWITZERLAND

PRIMARY INTERVIEWS

Hans Bär, Zurich
Rolf Bloch, Zurich
Thomas Borer, New York
Edgar Bronfman, New York
Steven Crisman, Zurich
Senator Alphonse D'Amato, New York
M.P. Verena Grendelmeier, Zurich
Heinrich Huber, Lausanne
Kitty La Perrière, New York
Lisa Mikova, Prague
District Attorney Robert Morgenthau, New York City
Ada Nicolescu, New York

Lea Paz, Ramat Chen
Jacques Picard, Bern
Marc Richter, Zurich
Gerhart M. Riegner, Geneva
Gaylen Ross, New York
Estelle Sapir, New York (deceased)
Israel Singer, New York
Elan Steinberg, New York
Robert Studer, Zurich
Herbert Winter, Zurich

PRIMARY TEXTS
All Rivers Run to the Sea, Elie Wiesel
Blood Money (film script), Gaylen Ross and John Broder
Guide de la Banque Suisse et de ses Secrets, Edouard Chambost
Hitler's Secret Bankers, Adam LeBor
Movements of Nazi Gold, Sidney Zabludoff
Die Schweiz und die Juden, Jacques Picard
The Swiss, the Gold, and the Dead, Jean Ziegler
Trading with the Enemy, Charles Higham

CHAPTER 9: THE OTHER NEUTRALS

PRIMARY INTERVIEWS
Gerard Aalders, Amsterdam
Rubén Beraja, Buenos Aires
Edgar Bronfman, New York
Under-Secretary Stuart Eizenstat, Washington
Nina Ersman, Swedish Embassy, Washington
District Attorney Robert Morgenthau, New York City
Eli Rosenbaum, Washington
Arne Ruth, Stockholm
Israel Singer, New York
Elan Steinberg, New York
Cees Wiebes, Amsterdam

PRIMARY TEXTS
The Art of Cloaking: The Case of Sweden, Gerard Aalders and Cees
    Wiebes
Clandestine German Naval Activities in Argentine Waters, Ronald C.
    Newton

Hitler and His Secret Partners, James Pool
Hitler's Silent Partners, Isabel Vincent
Perón and the Enigmas of Argentina, Robert Crassweller
Preliminary Study on U.S. and Allied Efforts to Recover Assets, U.S.
  Department of State
Spain Under Franco, Max Gallo
Sweden and the Shoah. Sven Fredrik Hedin, Goran Elgemyr
Trading with the Enemy, Charles Higham
The Vatican in the Age of the Dictators, Anthony Rhodes

CHAPTER 10: RESTITUTION

PRIMARY INTERVIEWS
Amihud Ben Porat, Tel Aviv
Thomas Borer, New York
Edgar Bronfman, New York
Alphonse D'Amato, New York
Stuart Eizenstat, New York
Verena Grendelmeier, Zurich
Ronald Lauder, New York
Guido Pastori, New York
Ulrich Richard, Zurich
Estelle Sapir, New York
Israel Singer, New York
Elan Steinberg, New York

Bibliography

Aalders, Gerard, and Cees Wiebes. *The Art of Cloaking Ownership: The Case of Sweden.* Amsterdam University Press, Amsterdam, 1996.

Anger, Per. *With Raoul Wallenberg in Budapest.* Holocaust Library, New York, 1981.

Ausubel, Nathan. *Pictoral History of the Jewish People.* Crown Publishers, Inc., New York, 1953.

Bauer, Yehuda. *Jews for Sale? Nazi-Jewish Negotiations, 1933–1945.* Yale University Press, New Haven, 1994.

Beker, Avi. *Unmasking National Myths.* Institute of the World Jewish Congress, Jerusalem, 1997.

Belinfante, Judith C. E. *Jewish Historical Museum.* Joh. Enschede en Zonen Grafische Inrichting B.V., Haarlem, The Netherlands, 1978.

Benjamin, Lya, ed. *The Jews in Romania Between 1940–1944.* Editura Hasefer, Bucharest, 1993.

Berkley, George E. *Vienna and Its Jews: The Tragedy of Success, 1880–1980s.* Abt Books, Cambridge, and Madison Books, Lanham, Maryland, 1988.

Bieri, Ernst, Peter Holenstein, and Karl Volk. *A Bank and Its Family.* Bank Julius Bär, Zurich, 1990.

Billig, Joseph. *Le Commissariat Général aux Questions Juives (1941–1944).* Editions du Centre CDJC, Paris, 1960.

Blumenthal, W. Michael. *The Invisible Wall.* Counterpoint, Washington, D.C., 1998.

Bower, Tom. *Klaus Barbie: Butcher of Lyons.* Transworld Publishers Ltd., London, 1984.

Bronfman, Edgar M. *The Making of a Jew.* G. P. Putnam's Sons, New York, 1996.

Brustein, William. *The Logic of Evil: The Social Origins of the Nazi Party, 1925–1933.* Yale University Press, New Haven, Connecticut, 1995.

Burrin, Philippe. *France Under the Germans.* The New Press, New York, 1996.

Chambost, Edouard. *Guide de la Banque Suisse et de ses Secrets.* Balland, Paris, 1997.

Chauvet, Gaston. *Uzès.* Atelier H. Peladan, Uzès, 1964.

Crassweller, Robert. *Perón & the Enigmas of Argentina.* W. W. Norton & Co., New York, 1987.

Dawidowicz, Lucy. *The War Against the Jews 1933–1945.* Holt, Rinehart & Winston, New York, 1975.

De Vries, Willem. *Sonderstab Musik: Music Confiscations by the Einsatzstab Reichsleiter Rosenberg Under the Nazi Occupation of Western Europe.* Amsterdam University Press, Amsterdam, 1996.

Dippel, John V. H. *Bound Upon a Wheel of Fire: Why So Many German Jews Made the Tragic Decision to Remain in Nazi Germany.* HarperCollins Publishers, Inc., New York, 1996.

Edelheit, Abraham J., and Hershel Edelheit. *History of the Holocaust: A Handbook and Dictionary.* Westview Press, Boulder, Colorado, and Oxford, U.K., 1994.

Eliach, Yaffa. *Hasidic Tales of the Holocaust.* Oxford University Press, New York, 1982.

Eliach, Yaffa. *There Once Was a World.* Little, Brown & Co., Boston, 1998.

Epstein, Helen. *Where She Came From—A Daughter's Search for Her Mother's History.* Little, Brown & Company, Boston, 1997.

Feliciano, Hector. *The Lost Museum: The Nazi Conspiracy to Steal the World's Greatest Works of Art.* Basic Books, New York, 1997.

Fenyvesi, Charles. *When the World Was Whole.* Viking, New York, 1990.

Ferris, Paul. *Dr. Freud: A Life.* Random House, Inc., London, 1997.

Friedlander, Saul. *Nazi Germany and the Jews, Volume I: The Years of Persecution, 1933–1939.* HarperCollins Publishers, Inc., New York, 1997.

Gallo, Max. *Spain Under Franco.* E. P. Dutton & Co., New York, 1974.

Gluck, Gemma La Guardia. *My Story.* David McKay Company, Inc., New York, 1961.

Goldhagen, Daniel J. *Hitler's Willing Executioners: Ordinary Germans and the Holocaust.* Da Capo Press, New York, 1996.

Gordon, Sarah. *Hitler, Germans, and the "Jewish Question."* Princeton University Press, Princeton, 1984.

Greenfield, Hana. *Fragments of Memory: From Kolin to Jerusalem.* Gefen Books, New York, 1992.

Grunberger, Richard. *The 12-Year Reich: A Social History of Nazi Germany 1933–1945.* Da Capo Press, Inc., New York, 1971.

Gutman, Israel, ed. *Encyclopedia of the Holocaust, Volumes I & II*. Macmillan, Inc., New York, 1990.

Hazera, Jean-Claude, and Renaud de Rochebrune. *Les Patrons sous l'Occupation*. Editions Odile Jacob, Paris, 1995.

Hedin, Sven Fredrik, and Göran Elgemyr. *Sweden & the Shoah*. Institute of the World Jewish Congress, Jerusalem, 1997.

Higham, Charles. *Trading with the Enemy: The Nazi-American Money Plot 1933–1949*. Barnes & Noble, Inc., New York, 1995.

Hilberg, Raul. *The Destruction of European Jews*. 2 vols. Holmes & Meir, New York, 1985.

Hondius, Dienke. *Terugkeer: Antisemitisme in Nederland Rond de Bevrijding*. SDU Uitgeverij, Gravenhage, The Netherlands, 1990.

Kaspi, André, Serge Klarsfeld, and Georges Weller, eds. *La France et la Question Juive. 1940/1944*. Editions Sylvie Messinger, Paris, 1981.

Klarsfeld, Serge, ed. *Il y a 50 Ans: Le Statut des Juifs de Vichy*. Editions du C.D.J.C., Paris, 1991.

Klarsfeld, Serge. *1941: Les Juifs en France. Préludes à la Solution Finale*. Les Fils et Filles des Déportés Juifs de France, Paris, 1991.

Klarsfeld, Serge. *French Children of the Holocaust*. New York University Press, New York, 1996.

Komissar, Vera. *På tross av alt*. H. Aschehoug & Co., Oslo, 1995.

Kudela, Jiri, and Jiri Vsetecka. *The Fate of Jewish Prague*. Grafoprint, Neubert, Czechoslovakia, 1993.

Large, David Clay. *Where Ghosts Walked: Munich's Road to the Third Reich*. W. W. Norton & Company, New York, 1997.

LeBor, Adam. *Hitler's Secret Bankers: The Myth of Swiss Neutrality During the Holocaust*. Carol Publishing Group, Secaucus, New Jersey, 1997.

Levendal, Isaac. *Not the Germans Alone*. Northwestern University Press, Chicago, 1999.

Levine, Itamar. *The Fate of Stolen Jewish Properties*. Institute of the World Jewish Congress, Jerusalem, 1997.

Lipstadt, Deborah. *Denying the Holocaust: The Growing Assault on Truth and Memory*. Macmillan, Inc., New York, 1993.

Marrus, Michael R., and Robert O. Paxton. *Vichy France and the Jews*. Schocken Books, New York, 1981.

Nicholas, Lynn H. *The Rape of Europa: The Fate of Europe's Treasures in the Third Reich and the Second World War*. Random House, Inc., New York, 1995.

Orbach, Larry, and Vivien Orbach-Smith. *Soaring Underground: A

Young Fugitive's Life in Nazi Berlin. Howells House, Washington, D.C., 1995.

Paldiel, Mordecai. *The Path of the Righteous.* Ktav, Hoboken, 1993.

Philippe, Béatrice. *Être Juif dans la société Française.* Editions Montalba, Paris, 1979.

Picard, Jacques. *Die Schweiz und dei Juden.* Verlag: Chronos, Zurich, 1994.

Pick, Hella. *Simon Wiesenthal: A Life in Search of Justice.* Northeastern University Press, Boston, 1996.

Polak, L. Ph. *Documents of the Persecution of the Dutch Jewry 1940–1945.* Athenaeum—Polak & Van Gennep, Amsterdam, 1969.

Poliakov, Leon, and Jacques Sabille. *Jews Under Italian Occupation.* Editions du Centre, Paris, 1955.

Pool, James. *Hitler and His Secret Partners: Contributions, Loot and Rewards, 1933–1945.* Simon & Schuster, Inc., New York, 1997.

Powers, Charles T. *In the Memory of the Forest.* Scribner, New York, 1997.

Presser, Jacob. *The Destruction of the Dutch Jews.* E. P. Dutton & Co., New York, 1969.

Redlich, Fritz. *Hitler: Diagnosis of a Destructive Prophet.* Oxford University Press, New York, 1998.

Rémond, René. *Le "Fichier Juif."* Plon, Paris, 1996.

Rhodes, Anthony. *The Vatican in the Age of the Dictators (1922–1945).* Holt, Rinehart and Winston, New York, 1974.

Rosenbaum, Ron. *Explaining Hitler.* Random House, Inc., New York, 1998.

Ross, Gaylen, and John Broder. *Blood Money.* Film script, 1997.

Rymkiewicz, Jaroslaw M. *The Final Station: Umschlagplatz.* Instytut Literacki, Paris, 1988.

Segev, Tom. *The Seventh Million, The Israelis & the Holocaust.* Hill & Wang, New York, 1993.

Sherwin, Byron L. *Sparks Amidst the Ashes: The Spiritual Legacy of Polish Jewry.* Oxford University Press, Inc., New York, 1997.

Simon, Lucien. *Les Juifs à Nîmes et dans le Gard durant la Deuxième Guerre Mondiale de 1939 à 1944.* Editions Lacour, Nîmes, France, 1985.

Steinberg, Maxime. *La Traque des Juifs 1942–1944, Volume 1.* Vie Ouvrière, Bruxxelles, 1986.

Steinlauf, Michael C. *Bondage to the Dead: Poland and the Memory of the Holocaust.* Syracuse University Press, Syracuse, New York, 1997.

Teveth, Shabtai. *Ben-Gurion and the Holocaust.* Harcourt Brace & Company, New York, 1996.

Toland, John. *Adolf Hitler, Volumes I & II.* Doubleday & Company, Inc., Garden City, New York, 1976.

Tory, Avraham. *Surviving the Holocaust: The Kovno Ghetto Diary.* Harvard University Press, Cambridge and London, 1990.

United States Department of State, *Preliminary Study on U.S. and Allied Efforts to Recover Assets,* May 1997.

Vincent, Isabel. *Hitler's Silent Partners: Swiss Banks, Nazi Gold, and the Pursuit of Justice.* William Morrow and Company, Inc., New York, 1997.

Warburg, Edward M. M. *As I Recall.* EMMW, Passaic, New Jersey, 1971.

Warburg, Eric M. *Times and Tides.* Eric M. Warburg, Hamburg, 1983.

Webster, Paul. *Pétain's Crime: The Full Story of French Collaboration in the Holocaust.* Macmillan London Limited, London, 1990.

Weinbaum, Laurence. *Righting an Historic Wrong—Restitution of Jewish Property in Central & East Europe.* Institute of the World Jewish Congress, Jerusalem, 1995.

Weisberg, Richard H. *Vichy Law and the Holocaust in France.* New York University Press, New York, 1996.

Weissberg, Alex. *Desperate Mission, Joel Brand's Story.* Criterion Books, New York, 1958.

Westlie, Bjørn. *Coming to Terms with the Past—The Process of Restitution of Jewish Property in Norway.* Institute of the World Jewish Congress, Jerusalem, 1996.

Wiesel, Elie. *All Rivers Run to the Sea.* Alfred A. Knopf, New York, 1995.

Wistrich, Robert S. *Antisemitism: The Longest Hatred.* Random House, Inc., New York, 1991.

Wormser, Georges. *Français Isráelites.* Editions de Minuit, Paris, 1963.

Yahil, Leni. *The Holocaust: The Fate of European Jewry.* Oxford University Press, New York, 1991.

Zabludoff, Sidney. *And It All Disappeared.* Institute of the World Jewish Congress, Jerusalem, 1998.

Zabludoff, Sidney. *Movements of Nazi Gold.* Institute of the World Jewish Congress, Jerusalem, 1998.

Ziegler, Jean. *The Swiss, the Gold, and the Dead.* Harcourt Brace & Company, New York, 1998.

Zuccotti, Susan. *The Italians and the Holocaust.* University of Nebraska Press, Lincoln, Nebraska, 1996.

Acknowledgments

Most books require encouragement before you begin writing them. Mort Janklow, this world's finest literary agent, was the first to believe that I had a good idea. Arlene Friedman, then president of Doubleday, soon joined in unflagging enthusiasm, as did her successor, Steve Rubin. Both awarded me the double good fortune of Eric Major's support, as well as his extraordinary talents as a patient yet always quality-demanding editor. I am truly grateful.

Pack of Thieves involved four years of research, reporting trips to fourteen countries, and enormous help and assistance from institutional sources who provided mountains of documentation as well as scores of individuals who provided interviews and testimony—often from tortured personal memory. Not all the assistance was willingly given; there were those who predictably resisted my attempts to uncover details of the long-hidden pasts of their lives and of their governments' actions.

Most sources, however, were extremely cooperative. And I would like to acknowledge and thank at least some of the more outstanding ones: first, that determined trio of Edgar Bronfman, Israel Singer, and Elan Steinberg of the World Jewish Congress, whose cooperation was crucial to this book and who not only provided access to incredible file material but permitted me to watch parts of their restitution battle at firsthand. I am also indebted to the formidable Hella Moritz, Carole Shamula, Joyce Goodman, and Sidney Gruber of the WJC's New York staff, as well as to Serge Cwajgenbaum, head of the Paris office, and Avi Beker and Ambassador Naphtali Lavie of the World Jewish Restitution Organization in Jerusalem.

Distinguished Holocaust historian Yaffa Eliach was of particular help and inspiration. I also received invaluable assistance from New York City District Attorney Robert Morgenthau; David Altshuler and Esther Brumberg of the Museum of Jewish Heritage; Elizabeth Fenyvesi at the U.S. Holocaust Memorial Museum; Eli Rosenbaum of the Office of Special Investigations; David Berenbaum of the Shoah Foundation; Rabbi Marvin Hier, Rabbi Abraham Cooper, Avra Shapira, and Shimon Samuels of the Simon Wiesenthal Center; and Mark Madden and his colleagues at the *U.S. News & World Report* library.

That untiring investigative reporter Hector Feliciano collegially shared of his wealth of information, as did filmmakers Gaylen Ross and Steven Crisman. Thank you also to Carmen Zuckerman Robinson, Rabbi Barry Friedman, Charles Fenyvesi, Claudia Carlin, and Maia Wechsler; in London, to Brenda Foguel, Hella Pick and Robin Knight; in Paris, to Clara and Marek Halter, André Wormser, Serge Klarsfeld, Samuel Pisar, and Jacky Fredj and the staff of the Center for Contemporary Jewish Documentation; in Amsterdam, to historian Isaac Lipchits, as well as Victor Halberstadt—who did not always agree with my conclusions; in Oslo, to Berit Reisel; in Zurich, to Rolf Bloch and Jacques and Mark Richter; in Budapest, to Robert Lándori-Hoffmann; in Warsaw, to Helena Bergman, Graziani Pawlak, and Yale Reisner; and in Bucharest, to Tova Ben Nun.

In Prague, I benefited from the cogent reporting of Peter Green, who helped with my section on the Slovak Republic, as well as the knowledge of Tomás Kraus. In Israel, I am, as always, indebted to lifelong friends Lea and Efrayim Paz and Erika and Moshe Bejski.

Thank you also to Anne Sibbald of Janklow & Nesbit; to Barry Tarshis, my unflappable computer mentor and pal, without whom I would have had to revert to pen, ink, and foolscap; to Elizabeth Walter of Doubleday; and to the research assistants who worked with me in various countries: Hana Cermakova, Irit Kisch, Kelsey Libner, Rachel Licht, Susan Mesinai, Judy Schagen, and Ronit Tarshis.

Many friends provided hospitality and help in travels, notable among them Victoria Pope and Douglas Stanglin in Washington, Marc and Clothilde Cohen in Paris and John and Chantal Hunt in Uzès.

—RICHARD Z. CHESNOFF
Westport, Connecticut July 1999

Index

[317]

Index

Index

Index

Index